This pioneering study of Bertrand Russell's social and political thought deals with the years 1896 to 1938, and is the first book to embark on a thorough investigation of the intellectual and cultural context out of which Russell's ideas emerged. Maintaining a sympathetic but critical stance towards Russell's almost innumerable political postures, and focusing in particular on his concern with the intellectual elite, the author renders that thought both plausible and coherent in a detailed examination of its often tortuous development. As well as giving attention to the aspects of Russell's private life which helped determine the direction of his thought, Dr Ironside undertakes an enlightening exploration of the individuals, groups, and beliefs by which he was influenced: Graham Wallas; D.H. Lawrence; Eliot; Keynes; Conrad; Wells; the Cambridge 'Apostles'; the Fabians; Bloomsbury; Imperialism; eugenics; Anarchism; and Socialism. The result is a wide-ranging and highly original view of an important and enduring figure.

IDEAS IN CONTEXT

THE SOCIAL AND POLITICAL THOUGHT OF BERTRAND RUSSELL

IDEAS IN CONTEXT

The books in this series will discuss the emergence of intellectual traditions and of related new disciplines. The procedures, aims and vocabularies that were generated will be set in the context of the alternatives available within the contemporary frameworks of ideas and institutions. Through detailed studies of the evolution of such traditions, and their modification by different audiences, it is hoped that a new picture will form of the development of ideas in their concrete contexts. By this means, artificial distinctions between the history of philosophy, of the various sciences, of society and politics, and of literature may be seen to dissolve.

The series is published with the support of the Exxon Foundation.

A list of books in the series will be found at the end of the volume.

THE SOCIAL AND POLITICAL THOUGHT OF BERTRAND RUSSELL

The development of an aristocratic liberalism

PHILIP IRONSIDE

CAMBRIDGE
UNIVERSITY PRESS

CAMBRIDGE UNIVERSITY PRESS
Cambridge, New York, Melbourne, Madrid, Cape Town, Singapore, São Paulo

Cambridge University Press
The Edinburgh Building, Cambridge CB2 2RU, UK

Published in the United States of America by Cambridge University Press, New York

www.cambridge.org
Information on this title: www.cambridge.org/9780521473835

First published 1996
Hardback version transferred to digital printing 2006
Digitally printed first paperback version 2006

A catalogue record for this publication is available from the British Library

Library of Congress Cataloguing in Publication data

Ironside, Philip.
The social and political thought of Bertrand Russell: the
development of an aristocratic liberalism / Philip Ironside.
p. cm. – (Ideas in context: 37)
Includes bibliographical references and index.
ISBN 0 521 47383 7 (hc)
1. Russell, Bertrand, 1872–1970 – Contributions in political
science. 2. Russell, Bertrand, 1872–1970 – Political and social
views. I. Title. II. Series.
JC257.R85184 1996
192 – dc20 95–11382 CIP

ISBN-13 978-0-521-47383-5 hardback
ISBN-10 0-521-47383-7 hardback

ISBN-13 978-0-521-02476-1 paperback
ISBN-10 0-521-02476-5 paperback

For Jacqueline, Stephanie, and Olivia

Contents

Acknowledgements

I would like to thank Rodney Barker, John Burrow, and Michael Moran for reading and commenting on earlier drafts of this book. I am also grateful for the extremely helpful criticisms made by those who read the manuscript for Cambridge University Press. My main intellectual debt, though, is to Stefan Collini who many years ago suggested I write on Russell, guided the work in its early stages, and has since provided much-needed advice and encouragement at crucial points in its development. For the rest I owe most to my wife Jacqueline without whom the book would never have been written. I would also like to thank Peggy Crossman, Katharine Jeffery, and Patricia Le Bihan for their generous assistance in the typing of the manuscript, and Justin Young for his invaluable help with the word processing.

Introduction

Bertrand Russell was a late-Victorian/Edwardian intellectual whose longevity, productivity, and occasional notoriety have set him apart from even the most durable of his contemporaries. However, while it is perhaps appropriate that someone who first achieved prominence as a mathematician should enjoy a career of such statistical extravagance, it is – given the nature of Russell's philosophical enterprise – somewhat inappropriate (if understandable) that so much of his work has been more often summarised than analysed. Russell's contributions to philosophy are the exception; carefully examined within a limited context – namely that of the history of the subject – they have been (largely in accord with his own wishes) effectively quarantined from his other writing. Most of the non-philosophical output can be incorporated under the heading 'Russell's social and political thought', a term which includes all gradations from political philosophy to popular journalism; yet even the most substantial of these works have not been included in the political philosophy 'canon': students travelling from Rousseau to Rawls rarely encounter Russell. Not thought weighty enough to warrant close analysis, these books are thus excluded from the context of 'subject' and, within the more general context of Russell's own career, are often used merely to signpost seventy years of remorseless productivity.

Aside from all else, Russell's philosophy and his social and political thought differ on one fundamental point, namely, that the former aspired to be 'scientific' whereas the latter was unmistakably ideological. Thus, even though Russell's philosophical pursuit of truth took place within an established intellectual tradition, the substance of this work is largely independent of its wider cultural background. His social and political thought on the other hand, though it has often been read as if it enjoyed a similarly independent existence, appears insubstantial when abstracted from its context.

A book which does make some attempt to set Russell in context is Alan Ryan's *Bertrand Russell: A Political Life.* Yet while this is clearly the most satisfactory treatment to date of the social and political thought, Ryan – though an extremely sympathetic reader – seems hard-pressed to find in Russell's theoretical writing passages of sufficient interest to merit the kind of close attention routinely devoted to – for example – the ostensibly similar work of Mill. Even in the case of *Principles of Social Reconstruction* which he acknowledges to be 'the most sustained and original political writing in all Russell's enormous output',[1] its main points are summed up in half a dozen pages. Part of the reason for this is that Ryan covers the whole career in a little over 200 pages, producing a survey in which – perhaps inevitably – the 'summary' approach still dominates. Russell's resistance to abstraction does, however, play a part, for although Ryan provides in the 'little histories' which begin each of his chapters a background to the successive stages of Russell's political life, there is little indication that he regards the intellectual context as being central to an understanding of the work itself.

To a limited extent, of course, it is not. Russell's ideas are in the main uncomplicated, his prose exceptionally clear, and if we add to this the fact that in his *Autobiography* he supplied an influential commentary on his own career, we have what appears to be a collection of texts which is both self-contained and extremely readable. Yet precisely because Russell's social thought has so often been read as if it were entirely self-contained and self-explanatory, it no longer seems grounded in the experience of a late-Victorian/Edwardian intellectual. As he repeated and revised his ideas from the 1890s to the 1960s the original intellectual influences were gradually sloughed off, if not by Russell himself then by a readership looking for what was relevant or by commentators concerned with what was significant, and we are left with a body of work which has acquired a spurious modernity. In short, though Russell is – unlike most of his contemporaries – still widely read, he is not read as they are when they *are* read, that is, in the context of their own time. Vigorously productive and famous long after most of them were forgotten, he seems no longer part of their world.

The irony here is that in early middle age Russell, rather like his exact contemporary Max Beerbohm, was seen as being prematurely old, slightly archaic in dress and manner, and stranded in the past at precisely the point at which, according to Virginia Woolf, 'human character changed'[2] and the modern world began. Yet while Max Beerbohm was by 1910 safely mothballed in Rapallo, Russell eluded the confines of intellectual periodisation and assumed an air of permanent contemporaneity which has been hard to dispel. It must be stressed, however, that he *was* a late-Victorian/Edwardian figure and as such his social thought issues out of an intellectual and cultural background which is, if not particularly remote, then certainly of an unusual complexity. That Russell's writing on social and cultural matters has become 'distanced' from its origins is in part due to his being the most famous of English philosophers, for these books have retained their interest as his most accessible work and continue to reappear in a fresh guise almost annually. By way of contrast we might consider the fate of the somewhat similar offerings of Graham Wallas which are usually to be found frankly exhibiting their age, their Edwardian aura shabby but intact.

The autobiographical 'screen' Russell erected in the late sixties also had a distancing effect, for though revelatory rather than Millian, the *Autobiography* is nonetheless a notably seductive text which has been allowed to set the boundaries of any investigation of 'background'.[3] While Russell carefully documents his private life and philosophical influences, his social thought tends to receive only casual mention as interesting examples of spontaneous creation. That it is presented as being both ahistorical and marginal can be ascribed to Russell's habit of withdrawing his approval – he was usually ambitious for the work in prospect, but had little time for it in retrospect. His stance was, in essence, defensive – always slightly embarrassed that having been deprived of an academic career he was compelled to write for money, he was prone to dismiss these books as 'pot-boilers'. We should also take into account Russell's sensitivity with regard to his place in history – he had no wish to be remembered for 'Brains Trust' deliberations after the manner of Cyril Joad, and thus sought to isolate his technical philosophy from his 'lesser' creations. Given this concern for his 'professional' reputation, it is not altogether surprising that Russell's social thought should be of uncertain background, widely regarded as an unfavoured, barely acknowledged by-blow or at best the intellectual poor relation of his philosophy – my purpose here, however, is not to make claims on its behalf, but rather to consider the particular circumstances of its conception.

The aim of this book is to restore Bertrand Russell's social and political thought to its intellectual and cultural context, to trace its often complicated development, and at the same time to provide an explanation of just why he came to hold the views he did, particularly those which were seemingly at odds with his ostensible Liberalism. In bare outline, Russell's political development can be seen as one of steady 'progress' from the kind of radicalism which allowed principled support for the Boer War to the kind which provided principled opposition to American intervention in Vietnam. When considered in detail, however, Russell's political 'progress' is shown to be a reluctant and tortuous process which went against the grain of his essentially aristocratic Liberalism.[4] His Liberalism was aristocratic in that he was concerned above all with the role in society of the exceptional individual. For Russell the continued existence of that which he valued in Western civilisation was largely dependent on the ability of exceptional individuals to function as a clerisy – to, in other words, protect, provide, and perpetuate an acceptable culture. He was less interested in questions of material prosperity and economic justice, partly because he had a certain distaste for the kind of abundance which would allow the whims of the ordinary to be indulged, but mainly because he believed the advocates of economic growth to be sufficiently numerous as to make such material abundance inevitable. In Russell's view this inexorable progress towards an achieved 'utopia' would, if over the same period the clerisy culture was extirpated, result in an intellectually stagnant society mired in a complacent and ultimately tedious materialism. The difficult and not entirely selfless task of the intellectual elite, therefore, was to inspire discontent with the mediocre and to promote if not exactly the 'life of the mind' then the notion that those who lived it should be highly valued.

While Russell's Liberalism was aristocratic in content, it was traditional in its intellectual and emotional loyalties and, in the cause of self-preservation, strategically inventive. In politics Russell liked to style himself an English Whig, and it was this Whiggish suspicion of the state which both prevented his endorsement of reforms offered by the Fabians and the New Liberals, and ensured his support for Syndicalist agitation and the weak-state theories of the Guild Socialists. Thus by the time he came to publish *Principles of Social Reconstruction* in 1916 his traditionalism, while unrelinquished, had ceased to be a disagreeable exercise in foot-dragging, allowing instead political alignment with the young radical intelligentsia. Yet whether Russell was busy allying himself with Bloomsbury intellectuals or taking a sympathetic interest in Fabianism, imperialism, eugenics, Guild Socialism, or Wellsian utopianism, his work maintained an underlying consistency of purpose, namely, the preservation of certain Liberal values in what he took to be an inimical political environment.

Though Russell found the political culture of the twentieth century generally unappealing, he nonetheless thought the strictly cultural questions to be of more immediate importance than were the strictly political, largely because the intellectual elite or 'clerisy' appeared more clearly under threat of extinction than was majoritarian government. Always a democrat with elitist preferences, Russell sought ways to ensure that democracy produced a culture of which he could approve. Like Mill, Russell took the view that 'a good society' was one which placed a high value on individuality, encouraged creativity, and tolerated eccentricity. Yet whereas Russell's ideal was probably Elizabethan England minus a few of its more exuberant barbarities, it is difficult to imagine Mill feeling at home in even a sanitised sixteenth century. Thus, while Russell pursues themes in his work which seem unmistakably Millian, his elaboration of such themes is unmistakably Russellian, and it is the analysis of these aristocratic peculiarities which forms the substance of this book. Offered as an essay in intellectual history, it is written in the belief that a clarification of Russell's convictions, influences, and intentions provides the basis for a new interpretation of texts which have too often been read as rather idiosyncratic contributions to political philosophy. When read as the work of an Edwardian literary intellectual, the allusive detail attains a new significance and Russell's thought emerges as being more anachronistic than it has appeared and more interesting than it has seemed when made to do duty as something other than contemporary cultural criticism.

The period examined is that in which he produced his most notable work in this area – a period bounded by *German Social Democracy*, written not long after he graduated from Cambridge, and *Power*, published as he left England to pursue an academic career in the United States at the age of sixty-six. These years saw the completion of his development as a distinctively *English* thinker, a development which can in some respects be characterised as a gradual approach to, then gradual departure from, those ideas contained in *Principles of Social Reconstruction*. His writing is treated chronologically, from his 'Fabian' episode in the 1890s through to the utopian and dystopian work of the 1920s and 1930s. These later texts are seen as being essentially Wellsian and therefore best understood as a product of Edwardian rationalism. Indeed, it is argued that Russell's most significant writing – irrespective of whether it stresses the creative/romantic or the scientific/rational side of his thinking – issues out of an Edwardian matrix.

Most of Russell's themes were established by the 1920s and fully worked through by the end of the 1930s. After this period he took increasingly to the world stage, and as his concerns became 'international' so the 'English context' became less important. From 1938 Russell's thought tends to become detached from its origins, impervious to new ideas, somewhat repetitious, and to my mind distinctly less interesting. It was, therefore, never my intention to produce an 'overview' of Russell's career (something which, in any case, Alan Ryan provides), but rather to bring out by close textual analysis the extent to which his most important work in this area was 'of its time', being a product of the tension between nineteenth-century intellectual traditions and Edwardian preoccupations.

This is of course not to say that the writing and the political activities of the later Russell are without interest, but it must be allowed that the term 'the later Russell' has rather different connotations than has, for example, 'the later Marx' or 'the later Mill'. Indeed, both these writers died at approximately the same age as was Russell when he set out on his 'international' career. Nor is it the case that Russell's preoccupation with the apparently tyrannical ambitions of the majority meant that he was a writer fundamentally and permanently suspicious of democracy.[5] Russell's doubts concerning democracy were genuine and of a piece with his aristocratic Liberalism, but by the time he published *Power* he had come to accept that the tyranny of the majority was much less tangible and hence more bearable than the other forms currently on offer. It is in fact at this point in 1938 that the complex notion of Russell's development begins to coincide with the simplified version and his career attains a kind of retrospective cohesion as being one of consistent radicalism.

I am, however, less interested in the extent to which his political 'development' brought him into line with late-twentieth-century opinion than with the manner in which he elaborated on the central themes in his writing. Moreover, I am not concerned to rid Russell's social thought of inconsistencies, an endeavour which is in any case as regularly unsuccessful as related attempts to attach to him a political label that will stick. For my part I see no need, for example, when considering his interest in eugenics along with his anarchist tendencies, to play down either in an endeavour to provide an acceptable level of intellectual coherence. Indeed, one of the main advantages of approaching Russell as an intellectual historian as against, say, a philosopher or a political scientist, is that there are rather fewer temptations to dismiss his antipathies, prejudices, and enthusiasms as 'aberrations', that is, as regrettable examples of personal excess or unavoidable contagion which have no place in an assessment of his relevance. Bereft of excess and its – often tactical – engagement with a number of currently impermissible beliefs, Russell's cultural criticism would lose much of its vitality and value. By restoring his social thought to its cultural and intellectual context, and analysing it with regard to its development rather than its consistency, I hope to show that its chief interest lies not in the 'contribution' it makes (or fails to make) to political philosophy, but in its energetic continuance of the nineteenth-century tradition of general social criticism. As such, emphasis is placed on Russell's role as a cultural critic, a writer who persisted with the 'idea of the clerisy' well into the twentieth century, an heir to Arnold and Mill and a predecessor of Leavis and Eliot.

Although the English tradition of cultural criticism begins with the middle class disparaging the middle class, after Matthew Arnold the number of influential intellectuals who were at once English, middle class, heterosexual, male, and educated at both public school and Oxbridge is extremely small. To this extent Russell – neither middle class nor educated at public school – was a typical intellectual perched on the fringes of polite society. He was exceptional only in that his authority as an intellectual derived from his being an aristocratic philosopher, a combination altogether more impressive than being, for example, an American poet, an Irish playwright, or a working-class novelist. Though his social and intellectual superiority carried pleasing Platonic overtones and comported well with Coleridgean notions of a 'clerisy', it had its disadvantages, the main one being that Russell's social criticism – unlike that of intellectuals such as Eliot, Leavis, Shaw, Wells, and Orwell – was entirely divorced from the professional work which underpinned its authority.

In many ways, therefore, Russell seemed to have more in common with a nineteenth-century predecessor such as Mill than with the public intellectuals of the twentieth century, many of whom even when they were not directly involved in English studies participated in a literary culture. Like Mill, Russell combined remarkable intellectual breadth with a somewhat restricted capacity for aesthetic enjoyment: his passionate love of beauty, for example, was never translated into a fondness for art, much as his other passions rarely issued in affection for individuals. Yet while both writers tended to be advocates of the strenuous pursuit of the higher pleasures rather than wholehearted pursuers, Russell was not so averse to the lower pleasures as was Mill. Indeed, if there is credit to be had for the elevation of sexual activity into one of the higher pleasures of the twentieth century, then some of it must be Russell's.

Some of it must also belong to those who, in forming the Bloomsbury Group, discarded Victorian middle-class morality; but in neither case did the celebration of the lower self indicate a reversal of values – less chaste than Mill, they were no less conscious of their needs and, as they saw it, their responsibilities as intellectuals. Though on Bloomsbury's terms Russell was hardly an aesthete, he was – despite a taste for pulp fiction – no philistine either, and his intellect, wit, energy, and independence of mind lent an aristocratic edge to his cultural criticism. To what extent this work was compatible with even the most liberal interpretation of Liberalism is another matter. While doubtless aware that the idea of a 'clerisy' was a somewhat elitist notion, Russell, having waived his patrician rights, might be forgiven for expecting some deference in the area where his evident superiority was 'natural' rather than artificial. As an aristocratic member of the intellectual aristocracy he could, however, be seen as being merely twice favoured by birth, for he certainly accepted Galton's 'evidence' to the effect that genius ran in families. His defence of the 'life of the mind' against an encroaching democracy concerned mainly with matters pertaining to the body was thus even more at odds with the Benthamite tradition than Mill's similarly stubborn refusal to give ground to the mediocre. In both cases the preferred individual possessed autonomy but there was a feeling that his choice of values might require guidance, if only by example.

In the pursuit of his aims Russell was unconventionally, and perhaps even unconsciously, eclectic; therefore, in dealing with his social thought, it is necessary to establish an intellectual context rather wider than that normally associated with work of this kind. Particularly in the period up to 1920, Russell was as much influenced by a literary as a political culture. His Liberal inheritance was of course important, as was his involvement with the Guild Socialist movement, but the initial impetus for his most original social analysis derived not only from the Cambridge/Bloomsbury milieu with which he is most often identified, but from writers such as Lawrence, Conrad, and Eliot. What must also be emphasised is the extent to which the psychological difficulties he experienced at the turn of the century went some way towards determining the direction in which his thought developed, and for this reason I have in the early chapters given detailed attention to the 'problems of personality' and the transformation of his 'character'. In general, though, while I think biography in intellectual history is undervalued, my main interest is in tracing the development of his ideas, and, as the central themes become established, his private life is given less attention.

CHAPTER I

A young man of character

Bertrand Russell was born on 18 May 1872 into the Whig aristocracy. His mother was Kate Spencer, the daughter of Lord Stanley of Alderly, his father, Lord Amberley, the son of Lord John Russell. Both grandfathers were Liberal politicians – Stanley only modestly successful, Russell twice Prime Minister and Leader of the Party until shortly before Gladstone formed his first administration in 1868. Russell's parents were Liberal intellectuals, friends and followers of John Stuart Mill, and as a consequence of this relationship he acquired Mill as a godfather. Although Amberley had political ambitions he was only briefly a Member of Parliament, his career being hampered – in his son's opinion – as much by his 'rigid intellectual honesty' as by his Millian views, particularly on birth control and female emancipation.

The listing of Russell's Liberal credentials is both irresistible and somewhat misleading, for, although connected at all points with the complexities of mid-Victorian Liberalism, the direct influence of this tradition was drastically reduced by a rapid sequence of deaths. Mill died in France a few days before his godson's first birthday. Russell's mother and sister died of diphtheria in 1874, his father of bronchitis in 1876. His grandfather, Lord John Russell, had retired to Pembroke Lodge in 1868 to – as one commentator remarks – 'spend his last days in unhinged petulance',[1] and, following the death of their father, Bertrand and his elder brother Frank were placed in the old man's care. Lord John died in 1878 and, with Frank away at school accumulating undesirable habits, Russell was brought up by his grandmother in protective semi-isolation.

Pembroke Lodge, possessing eleven acres of garden and situated in Richmond Park, was in the gift of the sovereign and had been placed at the disposal of Lord and Lady Russell for the duration of their lives. Russell's childhood memories of the house are associated with the beauty of its surroundings, while the record of a doggedly introspective adolescence takes its tone from the somewhat doleful interior. Aside from the servants, Russell shared the house with three adults: his aunt Agatha, his uncle Rollo, and his grandmother, the Countess Russell, a woman whose Liberal convictions were perhaps of greater strength than her Christian beliefs – she eventually became a Unitarian – but whose sense of sin maintained a Gladstonian intensity.

Although Russell had almost no recollection of his parents, he remembered being impressed by the difference between the Stanleys and the Russells. The Stanleys inclined towards boisterousness, the Russells towards solemnity. Frank had inherited the Stanley temperament, while Bertrand's Russellian tendencies were reinforced by the sepulchral atmosphere of Pembroke Lodge. When in his *Autobiography* Russell attempted to characterise his parents, he accorded his mother seven attributes, all positive, his father only five, two of these being negative: 'My mother, as I came to know her later from her diary and from her letters, was vigorous, lively, witty, serious, original, and fearless. Judging by her pictures she must also have been beautiful. My father was philosophical, studious, unworldly, morose, and priggish.'[2] This is, one suspects, intended to serve as modest self-portrait as well as filial tribute, and, if we discount beauty, there is nothing on the combined list to which Russell could not at some time or other have laid claim. However, while Russell was a natural Russell, his Stanley inheritance required first to be valued and then to be cultivated.

The characteristic which perhaps demanded least cultivation by Russell was one his parents shared – namely a preparedness to be unreasonably rational. The most notable example of this was their apparent agreement that Russell's mother should – on purely clinical grounds – have sexual relations with his brother's tubercular tutor. When Russell gained this information he was middle-aged and in the habit of providing theoretical justification for his own sexual practices, therefore it is not surprising that he found the story endearing. Earlier in his life he would not have been much amused by the disclosure. Had he retained his parents Russell would have been raised in a Liberal culture imbued more with the spirit of Mill than the morality of Gladstone. Even as it was, Amberley had made provision for his sons to have men of sound – that is, secularist – views to act as their guardians. Rescued first by misfortune and then by legal means from what the remnants of his family regarded as the excesses of Millian influence, Russell was subsequently given an education which, though both aristocratic and Christian, oddly approximated his godfather's in that, like Mill, he was thoroughly prepared under controlled conditions for a particular role in life.

In George Santayana's view Russell

> had been beautifully educated by private tutors at Pembroke Lodge. After the dreadful experience she had had with her elder grandson, who would throw her letters unread into the fire, Lady Russell dreaded the fatal influence of school: Bertie at least must be preserved, pure, religious, and affectionate; he must be fitted to take his grandfather's place as Prime Minister and continue the sacred work of Reform ... It was perfect princely education, but a little like cultivating tropical flowers under electric light in a steaming green-house. The instruction was well selected, competently given, and absorbed with intense thirst; but it was too good for the outdoor climate.[3]

Santayana's evident intention is to identify a peculiarly aristocratic quality in Russell's education, and his imagery, which is suggestive of a delicate aestheticism, a romantic symbiosis of blue blood and green carnations, is not entirely off the mark despite being at odds with all else he has to say on the matter. Noel Annan is likewise taken with the notion that the raising of Russell had certain affinities with the more exotic areas of horticulture, citing him as 'perhaps the one aristocrat who has successfully transplanted himself to the rock garden of the intelligentsia without a sigh for the more luxuriant flower beds of the nobility'.[4]

In reality Russell's upbringing combined Liberal high politics, low Church piety, a singular education which exceeded Mill's with regard to aesthetic experience, and the conventions of aristocratic life. By turns Gladstonian, Paterian, and proto-Wodehousian, he displayed a versatility which made him hard to place. Yet while the Russell Santayana met in the summer of 1893 had recently adopted the manner favoured by his aesthetically inclined future brother-in-law, Logan Pearsall Smith, this should not obscure the fact that life at home had been more analogous to the rock garden than the flower bed. Indeed, it was characterised by just the kind of high-minded austerity which made Russell's entry into the world of the middle-class intellectual appear natural and in some ways inevitable.

The product of Pembroke Lodge was keen, shy, and priggish, alert to the prevalence of sin and sternly conscious of his duties as a Russell. He was also habitually deceitful, and his apparent docility masked a growing impatience with his grandmother's intellectual limitations. Though a woman of character, believed by Gladstone to have had a marked and pernicious influence on Lord John's decision-making, she was scarcely in James Mill's league when it came to keeping the precocious under the thumb.

For his part Russell decided it was time to put the family values under scrutiny and, neatly combining a tendency to dissemble – in both senses – with a passion for truth, set out in 1888 to 'Look into the very foundations of the religion in which I had been brought up', recording his progress in a diary and using Greek characters to preserve the secrecy of conclusions which would 'shock my people'.[5] His loss of faith was slow and methodical, a logical dismantling of belief remarkable in an adolescent, yet, in a manner characteristic of the late-Victorian, he regarded the uncertainties of theology as an incitement to a more rigorous adherence to Christian morality. Not only did Russell fear that without the constraints of religion the 'masses' might 'relapse into excesses of immorality',[6] he also regarded his own class as being in precarious moral health, and was particularly pained by the example of supposedly Christian youth he encountered at Greens, the army crammer in Southgate where he went to prepare for his Cambridge Entrance:

> Here I am, home again for the first time from Southgate. It seems a pleasant place, but it is sad really to see the kind of boys that are common everywhere. No mind, no independent thought, no love of good books, nor of the higher refinements of morality, it is really sad that the upper classes of a civilized and (supposed to be) moral country can produce nothing better. I am glad I didn't go away from home before, as I should never have come to my present state had I done so, but should have been merely like one of them.[7]

Though by this time engrossed in his own sexuality, Russell recoiled from the vulgar and, despite adopting a sorrowing tone, he evidently found his superiority bearable.

Like Russell, and for much the same reasons, Mill had been spared contact with the common run of boy, but in recalling his education he expressed doubts as to whether this had been wise. Mill complained chiefly of being 'inexpert in anything requiring manual dexterity' and Russell proved similarly inept.[8] Southgate, coming too late to provide the benefits of school, had merely pointed up the deficiencies of the ordinary and Russell derived little from his companions save some potentially useful information on the early symptoms of syphilis. In defence of Southgate, it should be said that Russell was by this time remarkably fastidious, capable of detecting one or two 'slight wants of taste'[9] in the weekly sermon.

In keeping with his religion, Russell's youthful politics tended to be primarily intellectual, and at Southgate this connoisseur of sermons also demonstrated a firm theoretical grasp of his Liberal inheritance when writing essays with such titles as 'Evolution as Affecting Modern Political Science', 'State-Socialism', and 'The Advantages of Party Government'. As a student at a military crammer in the late 1880s, Russell doubtless felt the full weight of Spencer's influence, yet, while convinced that 'Nature, if left to herself, constantly causes a development and differentiation of life, and by a gradual but continual progress produces a higher type from a lower', he was not entirely seduced by the social Darwinist doctrines of the 'vulgar' Spencerians. On the other hand, he was obviously dismayed by the growth in 'Socialistic legislation', which 'of late years ... has become very common, ... the State now recognises in England hardly anything with which it may not interfere'.[10] Although well schooled in a judicious Liberalism, Russell's attempts to occupy the middle ground tend to be somewhat equivocal:

> The mere existence of work-houses is to many a great encouragement to idleness or extravagance, and many labourers who received good wages save nothing for illness or old age but count on ending their days in the work-house or the hospital. So long as work-houses exist it is impossible to make such men thrifty, but to abolish work-houses would seem a step backwards towards barbarism, and few would say that the poor and destitute should in no way be provided for.[11]

Thus, while Russell advocates 'gentler and rapider methods than that of the "Survival of the Fittest"', he believes the 'growing force' of Socialism should be 'fought against by all who wish sturdiness and energy to be maintained, and those forces which have produced our civilization to continue to perfect it'.[12]

There is nothing in these essays to indicate that Russell's politics were other than 'orthodox', nothing likely to displease his family, yet there is nothing, either, to suggest commitment, enthusiasm, or even much in the way of interest – at this stage there are few parallels to be drawn with the young John Stuart Mill. Of course, the writing was done to order, and thus likely to elicit little more than a mechanical response; nevertheless, Russell's relative indifference to politics during much of his university career comes as no surprise and cannot be entirely attributed to the rigours of the wrangler's life.

In his *Autobiography* Russell claims that between the ages of eleven and thirty-eight mathematics was 'my chief interest and chief source of happiness'[13] – a statement which, though probably true, loses some of its force when we consider just how unhappy he was for much of this time. It also does scant justice to his first wife, Alys Pearsall Smith, who, though the source of much of his misery, was certainly responsible for at least some of the happiness he experienced between going up to Trinity College, Cambridge in 1890 and completing *Principia Mathematica* in 1910. The Pearsall Smiths were wealthy Philadelphian Quakers with three children all of whom are remembered more for their relationships than their achievements. Alys, the youngest, married Russell, Mary married Bernard Berenson, and Logan sponsored young men of talent, the most notable being Cyril Connolly, though Russell himself has some claim to be regarded as the original protégé. From 1889 Russell was a regular visitor at the family's country house, Friday's Hill, and it was there he first met the Webbs, Shaw, and Berenson. When away at Cambridge Russell maintained contact by sending Alys detailed accounts of his activities, involving her as much as was possible in his intellectual life.

He also joined Logan's (largely imaginary) 'Order of Prigs' and for several years observed the rules and meticulously confessed to any minor extravagance or indulgence. That membership necessitated self-mockery is obvious, but he was not inhibited by this awareness and continued to assume moral superiority. Alys's defects were, of course, dutifully attended to and while Russell's strictures usually related to tolerable imperfections – her diffidence, her grammar – he did on occasion detect the unacceptable, such as incipient worldliness:

> I know myself well enough to be sure (though it is a confession of weakness) that if thee insists on my having a lot of experience, on my seeing a heterogeneous society and going out into the world, and perhaps having episodes of an utterly different, worldly sort of life, my nervous force will be unequal to the strain; I shall either have to give up the work my conscience approves of, or I shall be worn out and broken down by the time I am thirty.[14]

In this extract Russell displays the characteristic evangelical traits (reliance on conscience, use of talents, and so on) emphasising that Cambridge had reinforced rather than eroded the central features of his upbringing. This was, in part, connected with his election to the Cambridge 'Apostles', a society which, as Noel Annan points out in his biography of Leslie Stephen, retained many of the qualities of the early evangelicals.

However, though he remained upright, disciplined, and vigorously censorious, Russell was at last able to exercise his intellect and wit without the risk of incurring disapproval. In fact, the Society demanded 'absolute candour' of its members, something to which – being temperamentally inclined towards intellectual ruthlessness – he could at least approximate, and for the first and arguably the last time he experienced a sense of belonging: hence the trace of nostalgia in his recollection of the period.[15] Russell's participation in the Society spanned the latter days of Sidgwick's influence to the latter days of Strachey's, and, although he eventually ceased to be popular even in this company, the friendships he formed amongst the Apostles were central to his intellectual development.

Russell's first three years at Cambridge were given over to mathematics, but in common with many of his contemporaries he found the teaching 'definitely bad'[16] and became temporarily disgusted with the subject. This dissatisfaction with his career as a wrangler probably accounts for its being marginalised in his *Autobiography* where the focus is on Apostolic interests which were mainly philosophical. Before university Russell's philosophical reading had a theological slant, and though he read Mill and Spencer in his first year, this was merely a consolidation of his work at Southgate, a continuation of his political education. That he remained for some time more comfortable in this area is indicated by the title of his initial offering to the Society in 1893, 'Can We Be Statesmen?'. His knowledge of both classical and current professional philosophy was therefore slight and an attempt to remedy this was discouraged by his tutor, James Ward, who connected a failure to be single-minded with a falling off in Russell's mathematics in the early months of 1892.[17] Following the Mathematical Tripos, however (in which he was bracketed seventh wrangler), Russell had a year in which to concentrate on philosophy. The subject as he encountered it was dominated by Idealism, and, despite being warned off by Logan, he succumbed. Amongst the British Idealists, F.H. Bradley (whose *Appearance and Reality* had been published in 1893) was the figure he most admired, but as Russell makes clear in his *Autobiography* his acceptance of the Idealist position owed more to his association with McTaggart, a fellow Apostle:

McTaggart was a Hegelian, and at that time still young and enthusiastic. He had a great intellectual influence upon my generation, though in retrospect I do not think it was a very good one. For two or three years, under his influence, I was a Hegelian. I remember the exact moment during my fourth year when I became one. I had gone out to buy a tin of tobacco and was going back with it along Trinity Lane, when suddenly I threw it up in the air and exclaimed: 'Great God in boots! – the ontological argument is sound!'[18]

Russell's revelatory experiences were to become a feature of his intellectual and emotional life, and the insights he achieved thereby were sometimes surprisingly provisional. In this case his Hegelian beliefs began to weaken when he got around to reading Hegel and were renounced when G.E. Moore departed the faith.[19] Russell's writing in an Idealist vein is suggestive of intellectual exercise; that his customary trenchant style re-emerged in the development – with Moore – of an extreme realism suggests that his uncertainty was related to temperament.[20] In some respects British Idealism can be seen as part of the late-Victorian search for consolation. Russell, by contrast, was always happiest when confronting uncomfortable truths, hence the tension between his instinctive intellectual stance and the general thrust of Bradleian metaphysics.

Along with Bradley and McTaggart, Russell took the view that professional philosophy had scant purchase on political thought – a position he always retained – and in consequence displayed little interest in the political Idealism of Green and Bosanquet. Yet while Russell – unlike many young Liberal intellectuals of the 1890s – remained outside Green's influence, he was not entirely neglectful, and the *Prolegomena to Ethics* is included on his reading list. Green's argument in this work revolves around the ideas of self-realisation and the common good, and – in a suitably modified form – they are likewise central to Russell's social thought of the war years. This is not to suggest that Green's philosophy formed a major strand of his political thinking, but merely that in this area his eclecticism embraced residual aspects of his Idealism, something which can be overlooked if we too readily assume that when as a philosopher Russell came to reject Idealism it left no trace.

Russell's Idealist beliefs were lightly held but lingered, whereas his main preoccupation – his love of Alys – was intense but transitory. In fact, while Russell's career was to be characterised by a turnover in ideas and wives many considered indecently rapid, he rarely discarded the former with quite the same finality with which he discarded the latter. This said, no one could accuse him of being casual in his approach to matrimony. Yet if he appeared grim in his pursuit of Alys this was largely because his grandmother was so resolute in opposing a match she saw as representing a betrayal of her aspirations. Her opposition, though resourceful, was somewhat lacking in subtlety and logic, involving as it did both the disclosure that the incidence of lunacy within the family was such that the Russells were in danger of requiring their own asylum, and the promise of early preferment should Bertie abandon himself to that other family aberration, namely, a weakness for running the country. Aside from its other inadequacies, her campaign suffered from his having at twenty-one inherited £20,000 from his father's estate. Thus, while troubled by the suggestion that a sane Russell was a rare phenomenon, he was not about to alter his plans, and prepared for marriage to an American by reading through the novels of Henry James. The only concession Russell made was to spend three months working in the Paris Embassy. The family's intention was that he should acquire political ambition and with luck a more sophisticated taste in women, whereas all he seemed to develop was a distaste for the French.

Alys aside, the company Russell missed most in Paris was that of his fellow Apostles, and his family failed to grasp the extent to which he now judged the world according to the standards of the Society. As we have seen, even Alys persisted in entertaining ambitions for Russell which to him smacked of the worldly and the vulgar, and this despite his having made no attempt to separate his Apostolic concerns from his courtship. The latter seems to have been conducted on strict Sidgwickian lines with *The Method of Ethics* forming the subtext to his love letters. As such, Russell indulged in lengthy displays of moral nit-picking, while Alys, who appears to have expected no more (or no less), made vain attempts to respond in kind. By the time of their marriage in December 1894, however, the balance of affection had shifted decisively, leaving her the more vulnerable partner. Russell adopted a tolerant tone and his letters chart the manner in which his devotion to Alys was gradually replaced by a devotion to his own intellect. She had anticipated a working relationship similar to that enjoyed by her friend Beatrice Webb, and in its early years their marriage did in some respects approximate that of the Webbs. Yet while Russell as suitor might have appeared potentially uxorious, as a husband he was to prove disappointing, for not only did he find Alys's intellect unimpressive, he lacked altogether that settled disposition which made Sidney such a reliable companion.

This particular deficiency could scarcely have been predicted by Alys, as Russell appeared to possess all the qualities routinely associated with the late-Victorian ideal of a well-formed character. In an early letter he had endorsed her disapproval of a too-passionate Whitman poem with the remarks

> I am glad you don't like the Walt: I don't either. It was really in excess of honesty to represent it as expressing what my feelings had ever been, but in any case I cannot see why one should be ashamed of any feeling which has not got the better of one's reason; it seems to me the stronger it is the more glad one should be to have conquered it and have made it help (as every conquered feeling does) to the formation of a stable character. Such intensity and concentration is scarcely likely to occur often so that one may feel a certain confidence of being always able to act reasonably.[21]

Russell clearly imagined that he had the matter of character well in hand and in November 1894 he delivered a paper to the Apostles which dealt with the control of the passions. In essence, he was putting forward the conventional case for the cultivation of the 'higher pleasures': 'The passions for knowledge, for beauty, for love are the very condition of all self-development',[22] a development which could be diverted by the kind of immediate and intense desires emanating from the lower self. However, he goes on to argue that it is

> very necessary to gauge one's own strength before denying any really strong craving, and the dangers involved in doing so may well make it well worth while to indulge a passion even when it seems to interfere with a wider and nobler one. It is necessary to keep the springs of desire fresh, otherwise the character dries up – the energy and life goes out of it, and it loses perhaps the very passion for which it made the sacrifice.[23]

Russell, alert to the morbid consequences of 'too great repression' is setting out sensible guidelines for character building, maintaining that excess could result in either desiccation and sterility or degeneration and insanity.

The paper issued out of a reading of William James and adopts James's genial tones, treating the problem as 'curious and interesting' rather than immediately threatening. Yet Russell's interest was not merely academic; his fear of insanity and his intellectual ambition lent an urgency to the question of how to achieve a stable character while at the same time not repressing the passion required for great achievement. Moral rectitude might well ensure a sound mind, but morality could be overdone and he was aware of his tendency towards excess. At this stage, however, he was complacent not only as to his possession of all the desirable passions, but also (and on rather weaker ground) of his ability to control them fruitfully.

Later, when faced with a choice, he opted for desiccation until degeneration lost its terrors. In general, this paper nicely anticipates not only Russell's mismanagement of his own character in the years 1901–10, but also the remedies he afterwards adopted. Russell's tendency towards excess is everywhere apparent in his letters from Paris which reveal that while his strenuous campaign against the lower self could not be faulted, there was as yet no sign of its giving up the struggle.

> I hate this place – I have been walking about at night, and the endless rows of prostitutes with their painted lips and coarse 'allure' get on my nerves and depress me terribly. The French man too is an unutterable beast: I suffer a physical pang every time I come across any coarseness even of word or feeling, and this, instead of getting less as years go by, gets greater and greater. ... I get to loathe the prettiness of everything, the pleasure-seeking air of the whole town. I should almost love to plunge into some ancient monastery and take any number of vows, to get away from the oppressive sinning of this place.[24]

Russell's Gladstonian fascination merely emphasises the fact that while he might share Mill's enthusiasm for sexual restraint, his own animal instincts were somewhat less tractable than were his godfather's. For Russell this was in some sense a bonus, for how could one manifest character by overcoming base impulses if the impulses were lacking? Character was, after all, the outward sign of a moral victory, an indication that self-development was proceeding smoothly in tandem with self-control – proof against instinct the individual was free to pursue his goals in a rational manner. In short, moral success led inexorably to other approved kinds of success, moral failure to every other kind of failure – mismanage your character and in all likelihood you ended in the ditch.

On this view marriage could be seen as necessary to the development of character, and the Webbs certainly prized it as an institution capable of efficiently seeing off the lower self. Naturally enough, when Russell's marriage failed, this was – as with all failure – put down to 'character' deficiency. Mrs Webb in particular was keen to attribute not only this disaster but every other defeat or reversal Russell subsequently experienced to his lack of a stable character – the ditch was where she usually expected to find him and in her view this was where he was increasingly to be found. For Alys and the Webbs, developing character was rather like mastering the bicycle – it might be difficult, but once done all that was required was to keep pedalling. In his case, both activities were to prove troublesome, mere mastery offering no protection against disquieting experiences.

When Russell realised his marriage had ended (while out on a spin – the favoured Wellsian means of escape) James's moderation rapidly gave way to excess, passion was eschewed and abstinence embraced. This particularly narrow concept of character was adopted with the aim of preserving his sanity while he worked on *Principia Mathematica*. However, Russell's exaggeration of the ideal of manly self-restraint into one of stoical self-abnegation was perhaps more an indication of mental instability than an effective preventative – in any case a passionless pursuit of truth lent a certain sterility to his daily life and in a wider sense went some way towards emptying existence of all meaning. His morbidity during these years is reflected in such essays as 'A Free Man's Worship' and also in his interest in eugenics which he saw as a promising method of pursuing the Liberal dream of a rational electorate. Russell's fascination with eugenics is unsurprising – it was common amongst intellectuals of all political persuasions during the period and, moreover, was easily accommodated within character discourse. Indeed, those who manifested character were thought to comprise the eugenically desirable, the main bulwark against racial degeneration.

The role of 'character' is important as it was Russell's eventual abandonment of those values which underpinned the ideal that in many respects determined the direction of his social thought. The late nineteenth-century view of character derived from a restricted conception of self-realisation – one which emphasised restraint and was to some degree measured by material success. After his diligent, not to say obsessive, exploration of its repressive potential, Russell directed his talent for excess in the opposite direction and sought a diversity of experience, adopting that generous ideal of many-sided self-development usually associated with the Romantic concept of *Bildung*.[25] The process began when he had completed *Principia Mathematica* and fallen in love with Lady Ottoline Morrell. With love came a determination to revivify his other passions and to discard a personality which had become increasingly depleted and irksome. As an Apostle Russell knew the members of Old Bloomsbury such as Maynard Keynes, Lytton Strachey, and Leonard Woolf, while at Garsington with Ottoline he also came into contact with New Bloomsbury, a more disparate assembly which inevitably drew on a more variegated culture. Yet though he had been a keen Apostle, Russell's subsequent memberships were tentative and often awkward. As such, Bloomsbury, like the Fabians, represented an elite group of intellectuals with whom he could only partially identify.

Recent scholarship has dealt exhaustively with the complexities of the two groups and somewhat undercut the assumption of antithesis by emphasising the aestheticism of the Fabians and the political seriousness of Bloomsbury. Russell, however, was drawn to dichotomy and had a weakness for intellectual caricature. From his point of view, therefore, the shift from being wary of a package comprising an enthusiasm for the state, political permeation, sociological research, and ascetic philistinism, to being wary of one comprising an enthusiasm for personal relations, cultural permeation, intuitive impressionism, and promiscuous aestheticism, marked a development. Though modern art was as little to Russell's taste as were the intricacies of welfare politics, the cultural and moral influence was undeniable, and his move from the ambience of Mrs Webb to the ambience of Mrs Woolf is reflected in a transformation in his social thought. Even in the matter of tone the contrast between the prim, chaste, 'Fabian' text *German Social Democracy*, and the eclectic vitality of *Principles of Social Reconstruction* is remarkable. Russell's aristocratic independence of mind is, however, confirmed by the fact that neither woman much cared for his cultural criticism.

CHAPTER 2

Fellow-travelling with the Fabians

> My lectures on German Socialism were published in 1896. This was my first book, but I took no great interest in it, as I had determined to devote myself to mathematical philosophy.[1]

As Russell here indicates, the publication of *German Social Democracy* marked the end of a period of indecision and the beginning of the work which culminated in *Principia Mathematica* some fourteen years later. The book on German Socialism originated in a visit Russell made with his wife to Berlin in the spring of 1895, during which he spent time considering his future. Having rejected the family profession of politics, he had thoughts of becoming an economist and was thus undecided as to whether he would write on mathematics or economics for his Fellowship Dissertation. Indeed, Russell was beset by the sheer variety of his intellectual ambitions, although his autobiographical account claims that Hegelianism gave coherence to his aspirations:

> I remember a cold, bright day in early spring when I walked by myself in the Tiergarten, and made projects of future work. I thought that I would write one series of books on the philosophy of the sciences from pure mathematics to physiology, and another series of books on social questions. I hoped that the two series might ultimately meet in a synthesis at once scientific and practical. My scheme was largely inspired by Hegelian ideas.[2]

That this plan of action sounds more Spencerian than Hegelian is perhaps immaterial, as it is doubtful whether *German Social Democracy* formed any aspect of it. The book emerged out of a part accidental part logical sequence of events, and appears slightly out of place even among Russell's various productions. This is largely due to its being a text separated by twenty years from the main body of his social and political writing, one which reflects the personality of the youthful Russell to the extent that political passion is either lacking or kept severely in check.

On his initial visit to Berlin Russell's intention was to study economics and prepare his Fellowship Dissertation while Alys investigated the Social Democrats and their attitude towards women's rights. As Marxism was at that time viewed primarily as an economic theory with Hegelian overtones, Russell's interest was aroused, and in the autumn following his election to a Fellowship he decided to utilise his expertise as a Hegelian and an economist in an examination of modern German Socialism.

Another and perhaps more speculative reason for the venture, which was (at least on the level of research) a joint affair, is to be found in Alys's conception of an ideal married life. Before Russell's own marriage he had little experience of a 'conventional' family, an approximation of which was on display at Friday's Hill, his wife's home. There he was introduced to the Webbs, whom he later referred to as 'the most completely married couple that I have ever known',[3] and it is clear that he was encouraged to model his own marriage on theirs with *German Social Democracy* forming the Russells' first project. Mrs Webb offers confirmation of this view, noting with approval that the Russells ordered their life on Webbian lines: 'The Russells are the most attractive married couple I know ... The scheme of their joint life is deliberately conceived to attain ends they both believe in, and it is persistently yet modestly carried out. The routine of their daily existence is as carefully planned and executed as our own.'[4] Whether at this stage the Webbs provided Russell with anything more substantial than a recipe for marital bliss is hard to say; what is certain is that Mrs Webb had him marked down as an acceptable acolyte. Between 1895 and 1902, therefore, the Webbs and the Russells were mutually admiring couples spending at least two summers together at Friday's Hill, and as a by-product of this relationship Russell joined the Fabian Society in 1897.

This seems to indicate that Russell was already under Fabian influence in 1896; yet in the preface to the 1965 edition of *German Social Democracy*, he claims that the book was written from the point of view of an 'orthodox Liberal'. As might be expected, Russell, in making retrospective claims, was occasionally impatient of historical complexity; therefore, while his politics in the years 1901–14 were tenaciously traditional – exhibiting an unstated, yet unmistakable, lack of enthusiasm for the New Liberalism – in the period under discussion he undoubtedly felt the attraction of certain aspects of Fabianism.

What is not in question is that *German Social Democracy* emerged out of a Fabian environment. It was written in the first instance as a series of lectures to be delivered at the London School of Economics, and Russell, as a novice in the field of political theory, gave thought to the expectations of his audience.[5] This is not to say that he attempted to ingratiate himself, but merely that these considerations set limits upon what he was willing to risk saying, and in consequence he was perhaps more cautious than if he had been writing for a less immediately threatening public. Also, the methods used by the Russells in their work on the Social Democrats probably owed something to the Webbs' study of the trade unions, although their division of labour was not as clear cut, for Russell had not only taken care of the reading but also shared with Alys the task of interviewing Party members. Little of this 'background' information found its way into the book, as a 'condition of the people' approach would have introduced a moralising element into the writing and this Russell was anxious to avoid; yet the interviews were an important component in his understanding of the movement, counterbalancing the rather impersonal stance he adopted. Russell, in the separate talk he gave to the Fabian Society, described his attitude as being 'Machiavellian',[6] in that he was not concerned with the arguments for or against Socialism but solely with the correctness or otherwise of the strategy employed by the Social Democrats in their efforts to achieve it. This approach ensured a measure of objectivity and *German Social Democracy* is, in general, also notable for academic thoroughness, a quality often absent in his later work in this field.

Although *German Social Democracy* is more scholarly than some of his later work, its subject was not of purely academic interest. The Social Democrats were attracting attention in England, as was the emergence of German state-Socialism, and Sidney Webb certainly believed that the topic would have wide appeal, a point he emphasises in a letter setting the date for Russell's lectures: 'All the powers that be seem determined to co-operate towards making the subject of thrilling interest. I suggested that there might by that time be no party to describe. Pease, on the other hand, said the whole party might be in London, prepared to crowd our largest hall!'[7] While doubtless intended to encourage, such enthusiastic anticipation only elicited caution, for Russell, though making some effort to minimise political differences with his audience and thus to some extent conditioned by their expectations, sticks fairly doggedly to self-imposed restrictions, seeking only to demonstrate historical accuracy and economic expertise. Yet his analysis is not disinterested: his preferences emerge within the text, revealing that despite the advances made by a tolerant Fabianism, he remained decidedly more Liberal than Collectivist.

In *German Social Democracy*, Russell deals with the theoretical basis of the Party, its history, current position, and future prospects, and while he begins his account with something of a rhetorical flourish: 'To judge the work of Marx, or the aims and beliefs of his followers, from a narrow economic standpoint, is to overlook the whole body and spirit of their greatness',[8] it is Marx's economics which claim most of his attention. Lacking knowledge of much of Marx's early work, Russell shared with his contemporaries an understandable inability to separate Marx from his followers. Consequently, he accepts the Social Democrats as being orthodox Marxists, when they were merely the accepted orthodoxy. In other words, Russell takes Kautsky, for example, as representing Marx's views, and then doubles back and burdens Marx with views held by Kautsky. Russell could not be expected to disentangle Marx from the positivist trend of Marxism – a trend to which Marx was in any case not entirely opposed – but his natural tendency to exaggerate, even to caricature systems of thought, led him in this instance to present Marx's position in rather crude terms. That Marx's economic theory was, if not exactly crude, then certainly outdated and lacking the sophistication of current academic economics was a view Russell shared with the Fabians. This said, he was not content to dismiss Marx as a mid-Victorian museum piece. His work clearly held a fascination for many, therefore Russell was willing to approach it in a Millian spirit and search for the kernel of truth.

Russell took the view that the two main elements in Marx's economic theory – the theory of value and the law of concentration of capital – were logically distinct: the falsity of the former not invalidating the general truth of the latter. Although Marx's notion of surplus value derived from an argument lacking theoretical validity, the existence of surplus value in the form of substantial inequalities in the distribution of wealth was, as Russell concedes, not in dispute. The demolition of Marx's argument does not therefore remove the problem, and after completing such an exercise he remarks:

> At this point it is customary for the self-satisfied German bourgeois to sing a paean of triumph, and leave Socialism to be devoured by its own inconsistencies. But economic pedantries such as the above do not suffice to answer a whole class of society just awakened to its interests; the unspeakable contempt with which Social Democrats allude to such refuters of Marx, ought to suggest that somehow there must be a kernel of truth in his doctrine after

all. And I believe that by a little more pedantry, by the magic words Rent and Monopoly, we can bring out something which, from the standpoint of the working-man, is practically the same as Marx's doctrine – with the one very important exception, however, that such methods as combination among workmen and factory legislation, without a communistic society, seem able to effect far more of the improvements which Marx desires than he is willing to admit.[9]

As a recent student of the subject, Russell is confident as to the modernity of his economics and assumes an authoritative tone. The 'surplus' is thus established as deriving from 'Monopoly Rent':

those who have a monopoly of the best conditions, obtain a rent from their advantage, and this rent is not the reward of labour, but a surplus-value which the capitalist is enabled to deduct from the labourer's produce. The skilful entrepreneur, in like manner, gets a rent from his monopoly of skill. The skilful artisan, also, gets a monopoly rent, which raises his wages above his cost of production; but the *average* working-man, so long as Marx's reserve-army of labour is kept up, cannot obtain any monopoly-value; the marginal utility of the necessities of life, to him, is infinite.[10]

In this instance, Russell follows Marshall in expanding the theory of rent to include the possibility of a 'rent of ability'. He does not, though, stray outside academic respectability by similarly following the Fabians in their argument that the 'unearned increment', being a purely social product, should be 'collectivised' through taxation. Rather, he argues that Marx's Malthusian pessimism was misplaced; that the Iron Law of Wages does not hold because a 'prudent' and organised workforce could in theory 'keep the supply down to the level of the demand and ensure the highest wages at which the trade can be carried on'.[11] Again Russell tends to confuse Marx with the Social Democrats, ignoring Marx's specific rejection of the Iron Law in his 'Critique of the Gotha Programme', a work with which he was certainly familiar.

It could of course be argued that the Social Democrats' adherence to an outmoded concept had less to do with their own selective reading of Marx than with something Russell readily accepts, namely, that the conditions which obtained in Germany made the Iron Law of Wages appear valid. Yet while conceding the point he still maintained that the Social Democrats would be more likely to achieve their aims if they curbed their inclination towards exclusively political action and instead promoted union membership. It was no part of Russell's intention to advise the Social Democrats on alternative forms of Socialism – his analysis was 'objective', his reasoning merely instrumental, aimed at indicating more efficient ways of attaining already established ends. Yet while he abstained from questioning Socialist ends, his discussion of means is distinctly Liberal rather than being purely instrumental.

Although Russell despised the nominal democracy initiated by Bismarck, he did share with many Liberals of the 1890s a preference for a 'non-political' working class. England he saw as being fortunate in possessing a 'real' democracy combined with minimal working-class involvement in politics. This had come about because the English working class had chosen to pursue purely economic ends through their trade unions, and confined their political activities to giving support to the Liberal Party. The position in Germany could not have been more different, as Socialism there was a working-class movement, whereas in England it remained a middle-class occupation. This being so, his advocacy of what amounts to 'labourist' policies for the German working class appears rather futile. Yet Russell, although he is at pains to point out that the two countries were very different, persists in offering English practice as a remedy for German ills.

In his examination of the 'Law of Concentration of Capital' Russell finds himself in partial agreement with Marx. He does, however, take issue on several points, maintaining that joint-stock companies indicated a proliferation of capitalists; that the need for technical expertise would create a new middle class, which would also help prevent the polarisation of classes; that state ownership of land, although desirable, would not necessitate state management of agriculture, and that such management would be impractical; and finally, that state ownership in industry would take place only gradually, with different industries becoming ripe for take-over at different times. Russell is intent throughout the book to eschew all value judgements and to assess Marx's theory as the science it purports to be, and to this extent he finds it less than convincing:

> As a doctrine of necessary fatality, as a body of knowledge which we know to be true, whatever men may do to help or hinder it, Socialism cannot stand criticism any better than the earlier gospel of Laissez-faire; a dogmatic denial of the possibility or desirability of a Collectivist State would, however, be equally impossible to substantiate, and the decision must therefore be left to detailed considerations of special circumstances.[12]

While he does not explicitly attack Socialism, neither does he implicitly endorse it; his Liberal orthodoxy is certainly questionable, yet he was obviously unprepared to travel the Fabian road with the enthusiasm shown by certain other progressive intellectuals, and on balance his views seem to indicate that he was at this stage a rather cautious Liberal Collectivist.

By accepting the inevitability of some measure of state control in industry, Russell, after rejecting Marx's brand of fatalism, leans towards that offered by the Fabians. Yet at the same time he explicitly denies the inevitability of Collectivism/Socialism. One explanation for this seeming contradiction is that he had succumbed to certain of the Fabian arguments without abandoning his Liberal beliefs in a reformed capitalism. Fabian efforts in the direction of 'moralising the capitalists' meant that he could identify with at least some of their aims; and they were not in the business of alienating potential converts. Another explanation would be that Russell, unlike the Fabians, did not equate a measure of Collectivism with Socialism, although he does at times write as if the terms are interchangeable.

This raises the question of what Russell understood by Socialism. He did not, for example, accept that a limited amount of government intervention in matters of welfare, factory legislation, or education sustained Harcourt's assertion that 'we are all Socialists now'. Nor did the more extensive state programme in Germany provide grounds for claiming Bismarck as a leading Socialist. In regard to Bismarck's state-Socialism, he was in total agreement with the Social Democrats, though this agreement stemmed less from his sympathy with their aims than from his Whiggish antipathy towards the state. As Russell did not accept either state control in industry or state intervention in matters of public health as Socialism, we can only conclude that he accepted the Marxist view that Socialism would only be achieved with political domination by the working class. In other words, no amount of state intervention equals Socialism so long as the existing power structure remains intact.

This is presumably the basis for Louis Greenspan's claim that Russell's 'Fabianism' was of an 'aristocratic' nature: 'In true Fabian fashion, he [Russell] held that the Bonapartes would be the upper classes of England.'[13] Yet given Russell's suspicion of the state, it seems improbable that he would find himself in detailed agreement with a Fabian Society then entering its authoritarian stage. Russell was an elitist, but primarily in the matter of intellect, and in all his discussions of Collectivism he concentrates on the problems facing the intellectuals rather than on the benefits which might accrue to the working classes. In 1894, for example, he remarks in a letter to Alys:

> The Shelleys and Darwins and so on, who couldn't have existed at all if they had had to work for their living, and all the men who spend their youth in voluntary penury over apparently unproductive work and finally produce something great, to everybody's surprise – all these would have been made to do work of generally recognised utility and perhaps ruined by it. And surely one Darwin is more important than 30 million men and women.[14]

What Greenspan appears to be arguing is that Russell, though not on his own terms a Socialist, was a Fabian – there being no contradiction here as Fabianism was hardly a working-class movement. That Russell joined the Fabians in 1897 lends support to this view; yet his membership could, as I have already indicated, be explained on personal rather than ideological grounds, and he played no large part in the Society's activities – he had of course other matters on his mind, but this does suggest that his involvement with the Fabians was less than passionate. The argument in the end revolves around the definition of Socialism, and although some of Russell's remarks in *German Social Democracy* could be interpreted in Socialist terms (especially if certain of his recommendations for the Social Democrats are confused with his own beliefs), they scarcely add up to an advocacy of Fabianism, or indeed any coherent form of Socialism. *German Social Democracy* is not intended as a vehicle for Russell's political ideas, and they are given no systematic expression. Nevertheless, the views which do emerge accord more with the Collectivist wing of the Liberal Party than with the Fabian Society.

One of the most striking things about the book and one of the main weaknesses in a work which purports to be 'Machiavellian' in intention is the number of times the word 'hope' appears in it. At these points argument is replaced by wishful thinking, and what constructive advice is offered often amounts to little more than examples of how the English conduct these matters. Russell's hopes and wishes are, therefore, cast very much in Liberal terms. For example, 'to all who believe in peace and gradual development, to all who wish the present tense hostility between rich and poor in Germany to be peacefully diminished, there can be but one hope; that the governing classes will, at last, show some small measure of political insight, of courage, and of generosity'.[15] Yet he also concedes that the German political system was well-nigh unalterable by peaceful means. The responsibility for this state of affairs was, in his view, divided equally between the autocratic government, weak Liberals, and intransigent Socialists, a combination which was preventing even the possibility of peaceful reform. For Russell, class-war was not a brute fact of historical development, but something which had been introduced into politics at the level of propaganda and was capable of infecting all parties: 'When a party proclaims class-warfare as its fundamental principle, it must expect the principle to be taken up by the classes against which war is directed.'[16] Displaying a Gladstonian distaste for the politics of class, Russell believed the English governing elite to be essentially principled – that principle and class interest coincided was convenient but should not be ascribed to base motives. In Germany, on the other hand, Russell was confronted with the realities of class politics and he found the experience unsettling: 'To an English mind, accustomed to the single division into Liberal and Conservative, and to the tactical necessity of supporting one or other of the great parties, the confusion of German politics is at first very bewildering.'[17]

The 'English mind' was also accustomed to compromise in politics, and this he found to be utterly lacking in Germany. Although determinedly optimistic Russell gives no clear idea of how Liberal solutions could be implemented in a country where Liberalism was impotent, and he merely states what was required of the various parties involved.

> If the Social Democrats can abandon their uncompromising attitude, without losing their strength; if other parties, perceiving this change, adopt a more conciliatory tone; and if an emperor or a chancellor should arise, less uncompromisingly hostile to every advance in civilisation or freedom than Bismarck or William II – if all these fortunate possibilities should concur, then Germany may develop peacefully, like England, into a free and civilised democracy.[18]

Given that his hopes for a more accommodating governing class are somewhat distant, this project for all-round compromise does not hold together logically, and the burden seems to fall on the Social Democrats to make the first move. At other times, though, Russell asserts that victory for the Social Democrats is almost certain unless the ruling class make concessions, yet 'if Social Democrats acquire the government with all their ideals intact, and without a previous and gradual training in affairs, then they may, no doubt, like the Jacobins in France, make all manner of foolish and disastrous experiments'.[19] Although not immediately apparent, this reading of the situation also encourages flexibility on the part of the Social Democrats. For if they showed themselves as being open to compromise, this might produce concessions from the other parties, thereby enabling the Social Democrats to achieve their aims, which, as Russell was aware, were essentially reformist: 'A forcible revolution would only be adopted in the last resort, as it does not accord at all with the spirit of Social Democracy, which is peaceable and orderly in the extreme.'[20]

Russell argued that the reformist inclinations of the Social Democrats were being hampered by doctrinaire Marxism in two ways. First, the revolutionary rhetoric of Marxism produced reaction on the part of Liberals and the ruling class, thereby inhibiting progress towards true democracy. Second, the conception of Marxism as a scientific theory prevented pragmatic measures, particularly in the area of agriculture, where Collectivist policies alienated the large rural population thereby undermining any hopes of parliamentary victory. On the other hand, Russell appreciated what he termed the 'religious' appeal of the fatalist element in Marxism, the certainty of victory promised by the Social Democrats being largely responsible for the massive support given to the Party. According to Russell, therefore, the Social Democrats were in the difficult position of having to alter their doctrine in such a way as to draw concessions from their opponents yet not arouse suspicion among the Party faithful. His solution to the problem is, as usual, cast in the form of a hope, yet this time it is based on something practical, namely deceit: 'it is to be hoped that, like other religious bodies, like the two chief leaders at the last Congress, they will lose something in logical acumen, and adopt, in their political activity, maxims really inconsistent with their fundamental principles, but necessitated by practical exigencies, and reconciled by some more or less fallacious line of reasoning'.[21]

Prior to this, the Social Democrats must decide on how much of Marx they could safely dispense with. Russell for his part apparently thought highly of their talents in the area of 'fallacious reasoning', as he is of the opinion that Marx's contribution could be scaled down fairly dramatically: 'There are, in my opinion, only two items which the Party could abandon without political suicide, namely:- Political Democracy and Economic Collectivism – the latter to be brought about by the natural growth of firms, until monopoly becomes the cheapest, and State-monopoly the socially most beneficial, form of every business.'[22] The influence of Sidney Webb's version of Collectivism as a natural and inevitable result of the development of capitalism is more evident here than in Russell's earlier remarks. Yet Russell's conditions – that Collectivism must be shown to be both economically sound and socially beneficial – suggest a lack of conviction, or at least a feeling that the inevitable was not necessarily desirable. Also, given his stipulations, it is difficult to see how any society could proceed by natural growth towards the complete collectivisation of industry. As a policy for the Social Democrats to pursue, his ideas appear naïve, for the Party would be unlikely to make much headway by casting its arguments in the form of 'orthodox' economics in an effort to prove to rational men the superiority of Collectivism as an economic system.

Although Russell seldom gives direct expression to his own politics in the book, some judgement as to the desirability of Collectivism might be expected. In fact, this aspect of the argument is explicitly avoided, and he concentrates his criticisms on the Social Democrats' conception of democracy. In regard to the issue of Socialism/Collectivism versus individualism, he remarks, 'I have no wish to enter on a controversial question for whose discussion I have not the necessary knowledge.'[23] Russell's modesty is both tactful and tactical, a seeming acquiescence to ideology; for he goes on to say that it was a question on which 'every reader would, in any case, retain his former opinion, to be decided by each for himself, according to his convictions'.[24] Russell's exercise in fence-sitting could be put down to his own indecision on the matter – although he saw a certain amount of Collectivism as being inevitable, he nowhere advocated it on the grounds of social justice – or it might be that he was unwilling to provoke his audience unnecessarily.

On the question of democracy, however, Russell has a great deal to say, and this was because, in his estimation, the 'excessive' democracy advocated by the Marxists posed a greater threat to Liberal values than did their Collectivist ideas. His qualified notion of democracy is very much in line with Mill's as expressed in *Representative Government.* Men were not equal, and the opinions of the intelligent and informed should carry more weight than those of the less intelligent and less well-informed sections of society. In Russell's opinion, therefore, the Marxist emphasis on equality carried with it the threat of the 'tyranny of the majority', and would, if pressed to its logical conclusion, 'make all wise and expert government impossible'.[25] If and when the Social Democrats came to power, Russell was convinced that practical considerations would compel them to moderate their 'present crude democracy, and ... to reward the real benefactors of society in any way which may be required by the public good'.[26] This represents sound Liberal doctrine, in that Russell opposes traditional or any other form of restriction upon natural ability. Yet who the real benefactors of society are, he does not specify, although as the entrepreneur would be unlikely to flourish in a Socialist society, we are forced to conclude that Russell is, as always, concerned with the intellectual, who should receive the recognition and rewards to which he is entitled.

Another point which Russell fails to clarify is how the artificial inequalities are to be distinguished from the natural, as, being beneficiaries of the artificial inequalities of class, the middle and upper classes also enjoyed a practical monopoly of 'natural' inequalities in the shape of knowledge, developed talent, and so on. Presumably Russell believed that with the removal of obstacles a form of meritocracy would evolve, but as this was likely to be a lengthy process, something in the nature of middle-class rule might be maintained even in a Socialist society, at least for the foreseeable future. The need for wise and expert government, then, rules out any question of 'primitive democracy'; therefore, in a Socialist society the educated middle class must continue to hold the responsibility of government. This seems to be self-evident, a conclusion forced on Russell by practical requirements; yet it is a conclusion which has ideological overtones, as he appears to be directing the Social Democrats towards something which looks suspiciously like Liberalism. Russell, although he sees no possibility of a classless society as such (the just reward of natural inequalities would prevent this), is arguing for government without class bias. Like Mill, he tended to believe that education helped eradicate ideology or 'interest', and that, consequently, rule by the educated middle class was to some degree neutral, whereas rule by the ignorant worker, or for that matter the aristocracy, could not be.

Russell's conclusions are hardly unexpected, as what he is recommending is compromise, and compromise between political extremes often bears a close resemblance to Liberalism. Yet in a final passage pressing for a change of heart in Germany, he indicates that even in England the governing class would be advised to make their neutrality a little more obvious:

> Friendliness to the working classes, or rather common justice and common humanity, on the part of rulers, seem, to me at least, the great and pressing necessity for Germany's welfare. I would wish, in conclusion, to emphasise the importance, for the internal peace of the nation, of every spark of generosity and emancipation from class-consciousness in the governing and propertied classes. This, more than anything else, is to me the lesson of German Politics.[27]

These remarks have a certain affinity with what Willard Wolfe, in reference to Hyndman, describes as 'the prophylactic theory of Socialism';[28] and there is ample evidence that Russell's 'Socialism' had something of this in it. As Russell was untroubled by a sense of guilt on behalf of his class (or his adopted class), and as his personal habits of austerity and industry satisfied his residual evangelicalism, the emotional content of traditional British Socialism held little appeal for him. He had in fact no sympathy with any arguments for Socialism based on justice and natural rights (in this respect his admiration for Marx was unqualified); consequently, his concerns sprang less from a desire for social justice, than from a fear that if concessions were not made to labour, the creation of a British workers' party would be inevitable.

These worries were not unique to Russell (or to the early Hyndman for that matter). Bagehot, for example (whom Russell quotes approvingly in *German Social Democracy*), made a similar point in 1872. The 'higher classes', in Bagehot's view,

> must avoid, not only every evil, but every appearance of evil; while they have still the power they must remove, not only every actual grievance, but, where it is possible, every seeming grievance too; they must willingly concede every claim which they can safely concede, in order that they may not have to concede unwillingly some claim which will impair the safety of the country.[29]

Yet Russell's concern was chiefly for the fate of the Liberal Party, and he saw a possibility that it could go the way of continental Liberalism if a workers' party produced a similar polarisation in British politics. Again he was not alone in his anxiety, as the electoral disaster of 1895 had given a new urgency to the question. Russell, along with other Liberal intellectuals, was primarily interested in keeping Liberal values alive while at the same time recognising the need for Liberalism to assimilate a measure of Socialism. 'Socialism', therefore, was seen to be necessary rather than desirable, and this appears to be one of the essential points of difference between Russell and the Fabians.

This implies that from Russell's standpoint Fabianism itself was undesirable; yet in matters of necessity it possessed convincing arguments, arguments which, as Willard Wolfe suggests, 'had the advantage of replacing the appeal to moral principles – increasingly unfashionable among secularised intellectuals in the 1890s – with the more "scientific" appeal to political and economic expediency'.[30] Also, it must be recognised that the Fabians did not emphasise their differences with the Liberals, and the transition from Liberal Collectivism to Fabianism was rendered almost painless. It would have been surprising if Fabianism had not made some appeal to Russell, so closely did he resemble Mrs Webb's idea of an ideal convert. Yet although he left no contemporary assessment of the Fabians, his lack of enthusiasm suggests fundamental differences of opinion mainly centred on their respective attitudes towards the state. The later Russell, at least, was unequivocal on the matter; he found the Fabians as offensively bureaucratic and paternalistic as he had found Bismarck's state-Socialism, which perhaps indicates that Fabian 'state-worship' was scarcely obvious in the 1890s.

Although Russell seems to have believed that the Liberals must of necessity endorse certain aspects of Fabian doctrine, his Fabianism was in general merely an adjunct to his Liberalism. There is some evidence, though, that Russell's work on the Social Democrats did shift his views towards the left, for, during a visit to the United States in the autumn of 1896, he wrote in a letter to his uncle, Rollo Russell, 'Tomorrow I am giving a lecture which I have called "Socialism as the Consummation of Individual Liberty" – I doubt whether I shall convert anybody, as Americans seem very much more opposed to Socialism than English people.'[31] The content of the lecture is unknown, but despite the title it seems unlikely that it represented any anticipation of his future 'libertarian' Socialism, as the following year he became (at least nominally) a Fabian. In the political climate of the United States, Russell's Liberal Collectivist views probably smacked of Socialism – especially as he combined them with an advocacy of women's rights and free love – and it would have been in keeping with his lifelong desire to shock if he had played up to the prejudices of his hosts by bluntly declaring himself to be a Socialist. If he had become attached to this self-image of extreme radicalism, his susceptibility to Webbian influence would obviously have been significantly increased.

Russell did, however, possess certain personal traits which were not inimical to an authoritarian Fabianism, as is clear from an exercise in 'Self-Appreciation' he completed for Logan Pearsall Smith and which was published under a pseudonym in the same year he joined the Fabians. There seems little reason for believing that Russell's responses to the questionnaire were other than seriously considered and as honest as he could make them; furthermore, they are entirely consistent with the development of his personality over the next few years:

I am quite indifferent to the mass of human creatures; though I wish, as a purely intellectual problem, to discover some way in which they might all be happy ... I believe emotionally in Democracy, though I see no reason to do so. Progress I believe in both emotionally and scientifically, though not metaphysically. I am very patriotic. I believe in several definite measures (e.g. Infanticide) by which society could be improved ... I feel myself superior to most people, and only pity myself at rare intervals when I am tired out ... I wish for fame among the expert few, but my chief desire – the desire by which I regulate my life – is a purely self-centred desire for intellectual satisfaction about things that puzzle me ... I used to try and improve my character, and I used to succeed. Now I only care for efficiency.[32]

The psychological problems which resulted from the somewhat arid nature of Russell's emotional life will be dealt with in the following chapter. At this point I wish only to comment on his political perspective, and what this list offers is some illustration of the tension between his radical inheritance and his inherent elitism. It also makes clear that certain aspects of Fabian doctrine – particularly those concerned with Imperialism and National Efficiency – were such as to make a strong appeal to Russell. In general, though, it is evident that Russell fits fairly neatly into the post-1895 pattern of Liberal uncertainty. A feature of this pattern was the temporary nature of much of the avowed Socialism, and in this, as in many other ways, Russell was a typical Liberal of the period.

CHAPTER 3

Out of the moral gymnasium

In this chapter and the next I shall offer parallel accounts of Russell's peculiarly complex development during the years 1900 to 1915: the first of these will be concerned with matters primarily psychological, the second with matters mainly political. Taken together, these chapters are intended to supply a coherent interpretation of Russell's intellectual strategy during this period and also to provide a background for what is arguably his most important theoretical text in the area of social thought, *Principles of Social Reconstruction.*

During these years changes took place in Russell's notion of character which transformed his conception of human nature in general, changes which can perhaps best be illustrated by comparing his views on education in 1902 with those he held in 1916. In 1902 he had been impressed by Graham Wallas's paper 'A Criticism of Froebelian Pedagogy' and expressed his agreement with an anti-Froebelian stance in correspondence with the author:

> The broad fact on which one would take one's stand in opposing Froebel is, I suppose, original sin, and (what is just as bad) original stupidity. I have more sympathy with Calvin than with Rousseau, if one must look to Geneva for guidance. Indeed, I have seldom known people attain a high moral level unless their childhood had been very stern and almost destitute of happiness.[1]

By 1916, Russell's Calvinistic tendencies had been replaced by a Rousseau-like 'reverence', his belief in 'rational control' by his advocacy of the cultivation of impulse: 'The man who has reverence will not think it his duty to "mould" the young. He feels in all that lives, but especially in human beings, and most of all in children, something sacred, indefinable, unlimited, something individual and strangely precious, the growing principle of life, an embodied fragment of the dumb striving of the world.'[2]

In his 'Self-Appreciation', Russell combined a high moral tone with a low estimation of the average man or woman, displaying clearly those aspects of his character which were to become dominant in the first decade of the century. His 'Journal' (1902–5) reveals an intensification of these traits, for here he is obsessively censorious, severe in the judgement of friends and acquaintances, but concerned above all with itemising what he perceived as being his wife's moral and intellectual failings. What follows is an account of how Russell's tenacious cultivation of an ascetic personality provoked a mental crisis, and his gradual development of, if not an aesthetic personality, then at least aspirations in this direction.

Scattered throughout his autobiographical writings covering the period up to 1915 are various, and varied, accounts of conversions, insights, and sudden illuminations all presented as decisive moments in the metamorphosis of the author's character. For Russell these moments of illumination were productive not only of the personality which informs his work during the First World War, but also of the beliefs which he espoused – in short they help to explain how the rather prim, self-effacing author of *German Social Democracy* became the protagonist of *Principles of Social Reconstruction.* There seems little question that his personality as manifested in his behaviour did alter significantly during this period; yet by characterising the process of change as a series of discrete events, and by seeking their causality in external happenings, Russell, even in retrospect, displayed a peculiar aversion to any notion of the unconscious being applied to himself.

The first of these events and the one which had most impact on his consciousness, if not on his subsequent behaviour, took place in 1901 when the Russells were sharing a house in Cambridge with Alfred North Whitehead (Russell's collaborator on *Principia Mathematica*) and his wife Evelyn who at the time was thought to be suffering from a 'weak heart':

> One day, Gilbert Murray came to Newnham to read part of his translation of the Hippolytos, then unpublished. Alys and I went to hear him, and I was profoundly stirred by the beauty of the poetry. When we came home, we found Mrs Whitehead undergoing an unusually severe bout of pain. She seemed cut off from everyone and everything by walls of agony, and the sense of the solitude of each human soul suddenly overwhelmed me.[3]

Russell made several references to this incident in his writings, always stressing that the experience had the mystical quality of religious conversion, and to this extent it is presented as being self-explanatory.

His response was, in his own view, purely rational – the experience was classified as mystical, the insight achieved regarded as self-evident truth, the conclusions drawn from the insight were logical and the lesson to be learned was that by confronting and dominating painful emotions one achieved wisdom. For Russell the triumph over the emotion was as significant as the emotional upheaval itself, and suggests a sense of relief that his self-control had remained intact.

Within a year, his ability to dominate pain was in daily use, for a second revelatory experience had disclosed that his marriage was in ruins; he describes the event in a famous, but rarely questioned, passage in his *Autobiography*: 'I went out bicycling one afternoon, and suddenly, as I was riding along a country road, I realised that I no longer loved Alys. I had no idea until this moment that my love for her was even lessening. The problem presented by this discovery was very grave.'[4] His daughter remarked of this incident, 'I have never really been able to believe this story. It hardly seems possible for anyone to be so totally unaware of his feelings towards someone with whom he shares an intimate daily life. Yet he was plainly unaware of being aware of them.'[5] There seems no doubt that he was remarkably 'unaware'; in consequence events in his emotional life appeared as a series of rather nasty accidents having nothing in common apart from the unfortunate fact that they all happened to him. In Russell's view, the changes in his personality were an adjustment to unexpected events and, within certain limits, subject to his control. That change of this kind might be a process over which he had no control, a process in many ways responsible for the events he found so disturbing, was an interpretation not readily available in 1901. This being so, for him to have characterised his experience in terms of psychology rather than mysticism would at that time have been singularly unhelpful.

As already indicated, lunacy was a family tradition, though one he intended to end by becoming an early practitioner of negative eugenics. Yet while the possibility of future Russells could be eliminated, doubts about his own mental stability remained and became a permanent feature of his life. For Russell, sanity was firmly linked with rational control: the more controlled he became, the more rational he appeared, therefore the more sane, and fears of insanity were only stilled when he demonstrated that he could retain control under stress. Consequently, any explanation of his 'conversion' involving acknowledgement of the irrational carried with it implications which were unacceptable. On the other hand, for someone of Russell's puritan background and ascetic inclinations, an explanation couched in terms of religious mysticism was attractive, for it linked insight not with irrationalism but with renunciation and detachment.

For the ascetically inclined to practise self-denial could be seen as a form of indulgence, but Russell's asceticism was based on a belief that austere habits were not only the basis of character but also a prerequisite for intellectual achievement and he came to regard his body as something to be kept in order so as to provide a suitable habitat for his mind. Both aesthetically and functionally, Russell's body could be described as undistinguished. His mind, though, was exceptional; therefore, in true evangelical style, he nurtured his gift and could feel virtuous in that his self-denial, far from being mere indulgence, was a public duty. Thus, even before the collapse of his marriage, Russell's habits were such as to win the approval of Mrs Webb; yet in the years 1901–10 he imposed upon himself a form of discipline which made his previous regimen appear lax.

During these years his life was dominated by the presence of Alys and his work on *Principia Mathematica*; both were oppressive, yet Russell, determined to extract every possible benefit from his situation, came to regard them as mutually necessary. In a sense this was true, for Alys functioned as hairshirt in Russell's rather self-centred scheme of things and produced the pain he thought essential if he was to work at the required pitch of concentration. *Principia Mathematica*, on the other hand, provided him with a sense of purpose and a permanent excuse for avoiding his wife's company. Russell did not endure all this for nine years merely as an aid to concentration, but his decision to renounce personal happiness, though in many ways a rationalisation of his position, prevented him from changing it. Increased asceticism was regarded by Russell as a source of inspiration and a form of therapy – it was both productive of knowledge and an insurance against insanity; in effect, it amounted to a theory of creativity which placed a grotesque emphasis upon repression: 'Abstract work, if one wishes to do it well, must be allowed to destroy one's humanity; one raises a monument which is at the same time a tomb, in which, voluntarily, one slowly inters oneself.'[6]

By 1905, he was already having doubts about the efficacy of his chosen therapy, yet was agitated by the moral and intellectual aspects of his problem rather than the psychological.

I foresee that continence will become increasingly difficult, and that I shall be tempted to get into more or less flirtatious relations with women I don't respect ... It is rather a mental than a physical feeling; it is a desire for excitement, and for a respite from the incessant checking of every impulse. Another difficulty, connected with this, is the very slight interest I take in my work and in philosophy generally. If this can't be cured, my fertility will cease. A sort of paralysis of impulse has passed from my life into my thinking, and seems to be very serious for my intellectual future.[7]

With no pleasures to be concealed Russell was hardly committed to the profound duplicity of a Henry Jekyll, but like many just emerging from the moral miasma of the 1890s with the assistance of Stevenson rather than Freud, he was troubled by the duality of his nature. With regard to his intellect Russell's fears proved groundless, but moral rectitude and a persistence in the belief that his marriage and *Principia Mathematica* were in some sense interdependent left him (if only metaphorically) entombed.

According to Russell's biographer, the 'conversion' and the break with Alys a year later were linked mainly by the fact that Mrs Whitehead was central to both events: 'Between February 1901 and February 1902, he [Russell] experienced what he later called a sudden "conversion", a change of heart which brought with it a love of humanity and a horror of force: he fell out of love with Alys: and he fell in love with someone else'[8] – this person being Mrs Whitehead. Clark's evidence for this conjecture is scarcely overwhelming, and Russell's autobiographical writings – which are not noted for being coy in these matters – offer little to support it; yet it is likely that proximity ensured a degree of affection. Mrs Whitehead was a woman for whom Russell had 'respect', therefore the 'sexual element' was firmly, even complacently, suppressed, for as he argues in a letter at the time, and possibly with Mrs Whitehead in mind, 'On the whole, real life does not consist, as Hodder would have you believe, in intrigues with those who are already married. If one wants uncommon experiences, a little renunciation, a little performance of duty, will give one far more unusual sensations than all the fine free passion in the universe.'[9] Russell's relationship with Mrs Whitehead was perhaps as much therapeutic as romantic in nature, and probably stemmed from his need of a female confidante – a role for which Alys was apparently unsuitable, and one which Ottoline Morrell accepted unwillingly, but performed satisfactorily. With regard to Mrs Whitehead, however, there is no evidence of success on either the the romantic or the therapeutic front, and Russell appeared to become reconciled to repression as a way of life.

Clark's view – that Russell's problems had little to do with his 'change of heart' and resulted instead from his being obliged by convention to suppress his love for Mrs Whitehead – seems altogether too simplistic, and reflects Russell's own preference for seeing his difficulties as circumstantial rather than psychological in nature. Also, it tends to ignore the fact that the resurrection of Russell's sexual life in 1911 – though it signified a dramatic shift in his moral outlook, at least in so far as his personal conduct was concerned – did not produce any sudden and complete transformation in his personality, for while sex was in every way preferable to self-control, as a panacea it proved scarcely more effective.

To a certain extent his shift from the kind of serious-minded austerity recommended in late-Victorian character discourse to obsessive self-control was largely fortuitous, in that it developed out of the logic of the situation rather than being a conscious programme of self-improvement. In consequence, Russell, while acknowledging the benefits unhappiness brought, was nonetheless profoundly unhappy, and refrained from suicide only because Whitehead himself was in a precarious mental state. Russell's altruism was not confined to mere self-preservation, but also involved underwriting his collaborator's compulsive overspending. Nor was Whitehead the main object of his benevolence, for Russell was concerned to ensure the completion of *Principia Mathematica*, a major work of ratiocination threatened, somewhat ironically, by the mental instability of both authors.

In view of his many burdens, it is hardly surprising that Russell's metaphysics took on a gloomy aspect, and his stoically depressive letters of the period display a measure of incredulity that people free from his constraints should choose to live in such a miserable world: 'The world seems to me quite dreadful; the unhappiness of most people is very great, and I often wonder how they all endure it.'[10] Convinced that his own condition was widespread if not universal, and having borne up under the strain himself, Russell began to proselytise, giving in 'A Free Man's Worship' the first public performance of a piece thoroughly rehearsed in private correspondence. 'A Free Man's Worship' has been described by F.R. Leavis as 'an indulgence in the dramatisation of one's nobly-suffering self',[11] and by Alan Donagan as 'insincere, faked and attitudinising'.[12] The essay is undoubtedly a stylistic oddity, an unfortunate legacy of Friday's Hill where Russell came under the influence of its resident Paterians, Bernard Berenson and Logan Pearsall Smith. Although it was begun as a therapeutic exercise – 'the construction of prose rhythms was the only thing in which I found any real consolation'[13] – the essay was largely written in the far from austere surroundings of I Tatti, Berenson's house near Florence.

This close attention to style (though doubtless symptomatic of Russell's repressed condition) is in part responsible for the failure of the essay to give adequate expression to his emotions. Also, by excluding personal revelation from the essay – even the word mysticism is avoided – he denies himself the directness of expression we find in his letters. Instead, Russell chooses as his starting point, 'the fundamental facts', 'the world which Science presents for our belief',[14] and seeks to convey the excluded experience indirectly – hence the elevation of the prose and the 'borrowings' from the Victorian literature of unbelief which add to the staginess of the overall effect by making the rhetoric appear faked, or at best an anachronistic attempt to emulate Pater: 'To abandon the struggle for private happiness, to expel all eagerness of temporary desire, to burn with passion for external things – this is emancipation, and this is the free man's worship. And this liberation is effected by a contemplation of Fate; for Fate itself is subdued by the mind which leaves nothing to be purged by the purifying fire of Time.'[15]

Although 'A Free Man's Worship' was intended to provide intellectually acceptable solace for the non-religious, it is an assemblage of austere thoughts rather than an example of rigorous thinking. Only at one point does Russell touch on the relationship of mystical insight to philosophical analysis, and anticipates his later argument in 'Mysticism and Logic' to the effect that insight is antecedent to philosophy, providing the materials upon which the philosopher works. In Russell's rather one-sided humanism, desire and emancipation take on the function of sin and salvation, and 'a purified ideal' was, he thought, possible according to the ethical position he shared with Moore and best described as 'objective intuitionism'. As a professional philosopher Russell held that questions of value were not matters of mere taste and opinion; in any dispute someone was in absolute terms right, though in practice it might remain unclear who this someone was. It was a stance not calculated to lessen the severity of his character.

Initially, his personality altered only to the extent that existing traits became somewhat exaggerated – Lawrence's much-quoted remark that Russell was 'all disembodied mind' was a potent caricature – but his aspirations in the early 1900s certainly lay in this direction, and, for someone who tended to extol the mind at the expense of the body, *Principia Mathematica* and celibacy made a pleasing combination. Gloomily complacent, he gave free rein to the priggish, self-righteous, and censorious elements in his nature; indeed he became something of a moral zealot, and Alys the main beneficiary of his zeal.

In the years leading up to 1901, Russell's reticence was linked to a complacent self-sufficiency that was largely spurious, being based on an acceptance of the various myths surrounding the aetiology of insanity in late-Victorian England, myths which, by relating morality to mental health, promoted in self-control a prophylactic he found both congenial and comforting. Russell's 'self-sufficiency' was sustained by his avoidance of 'all deep emotion' and his endeavour to lead 'a life of intellect tempered by flippancy',[16] – this attitude is reflected not only in the rather tepid relationship he had with his first wife, but also in the cool, astringent nature of his friendships. After his 'mystical' experience Russell, although relieved at the success of his preventative measures so far as his mental stability was concerned, found his self-sufficiency undermined; and his wife, who until then had performed her function with perfect adequacy, was now found to be inadequate and he began the process of disengagement – rationalised as the achievement of true insight into her character.

Although Russell later regretted his treatment of Alys, he remained convinced that he had had reasonable grounds for his criticism: 'She tried to be more impeccably virtuous than is possible to human beings, and was thus led into insincerity. Like her brother, Logan, she was malicious, and liked to make people think ill of each other, but she was not aware of this, and was instinctively subtle in her methods.'[17] By cataloguing his wife's shortcomings and claiming insight into the subtleties of her unconscious, Russell wished to demonstrate that his behaviour, though reprehensible, had never been other than impeccably rational. The ever-observant Mrs Webb would not have agreed; in her view the ascetic excesses of the young Russell exposed a fundamental weakness of character: 'I am far more concerned about the man's mental condition than about the woman's! Bertrand is going to have trouble with his own nature, of that I am convinced. His work is too abstract and inhuman to satisfy his somewhat uncontrolled emotional nature and strong tendency towards introspection of his own and others' natures.'[18] Introspective Russell may have been, but introspection does not guarantee self-knowledge, especially when the mind under inspection devotes so much of its surplus capacity to the production of rationalisations.

Russell remained psychologically incurious, his introspection bearing a closer resemblance to religious self-scrutiny than self-analysis, and he retained his belief in the therapeutic value of self-control. Consequently, he viewed with some distaste the upsurge of interest in the irrational which took place during the first decade of the century, finding its most visible form in the cult of Nietzsche. Although Russell considered Bergson and William James to be respectable antagonists, he placed Nietzsche in a category with Shaw and found both unworthy of serious consideration – his reaction to the 'Nietzschean' *Man and Superman* was therefore fairly predictable, being little more than a routine exercise in character discourse: 'I think Shaw, on the whole, is more bounder than genius ... Also he hates self-control, and makes up theories with a view to proving that self-control is pernicious. I couldn't get on with *Man and Superman*: it disgusted me.'[19] Shaw's jibe at the 'pious English habit of regarding the world as a moral gymnasium built expressly to strengthen your character in' clearly found its mark.

In extreme old age, Russell, in correspondence with D.S. Thatcher, wrote: 'I do not think that Nietzsche ever had any important influence in England. I believe that more people at Oxford than at Cambridge paid attention to him, but they were not the most able people. I should add that I consistently thought ill of Nietzsche, and I may be biased about his influence, which was certainly considerable in Germany.'[20] Russell's antipathy towards Nietzsche, though in part based on misinterpretation, remained immune from alternative assessment. Yet, even allowing for the vagaries of memory, his initial response also appears to have been coloured by a measure of cultural elitism, a belief that the admirers of Nietzsche flourished in an irrelevant sub-culture, and these associations appear to have been retained, even though Russell himself was to be found lurking in this area at the outbreak of the First World War. Also, that Nietzsche was linked in some quarters with social Darwinism did little to endear him to Russell who was, and remained, opposed to any form of evolutionary ethics.

Russell's scepticism, rationalism, asceticism, ethical views, and conception of mental health all ensured immunity from the fringe culture of 'dubious' magazines and societies through which Nietzsche and, to some extent, Freud emerged on to the English scene. He was, of course, not alone in this, for Cambridge rationalism fostered a rather smug insularity, a devotion to a restricted set of values which was, as Keynes conceded, essentially limiting: 'The attribution of rationality to human nature instead of enriching it, now seems to me to have impoverished it. It ignored certain powerful and valuable springs of feeling. Some of the spontaneous, irrational outbursts of human nature can have a sort of value from which our schematism was cut off.'[21] Yet there is no hint that Keynes found these 'limitations' psychologically disabling, whereas Russell clearly did.

A comparison between the two men is interesting, because, of all Russell's contemporaries, it is perhaps Keynes he most closely resembles, for both possessed a quality of intellect which their acquaintances assessed, somewhat ambivalently, by the use of metallic adjectives and mechanical analogies. Of Keynes, Lytton Strachey remarked, 'An immensely interesting figure partly because, with his curious typewriter intellect, he's also so oddly and unexpectedly emotional'.[22] And Strachey's brother James, in an attempt to refute Lawrence's description of Russell, manages to convey the feeling that his displays of emotion were rather quixotic, faintly comical aberrations from the norm: 'By the way, do you bring out the fact that Bertie has the most marvellous mental apparatus, perhaps, ever? I mean as a mere machine. Lawrence's view of him, incidentally, was extraordinarily obtuse. Bertie was full of passionate emotions (which led him into trouble of all sorts).'[23] There are important social and generational differences between the two figures; yet Harrod, in his biography, offers an account which suggests that Keynes experienced problems similar to those of Russell – the fact that Keynes 'appeared to some to be almost inhuman, so mechanical was the precision with which he achieved every objective',[24] erected barriers which could, as in Russell's case, have resulted in isolation. That they were overcome was, in Harrod's view, largely due to Strachey's influence: 'from time to time the woes of the world descended upon him, and his spirit would languish. It was therefore of very great value to have such a confidant as Strachey, who was not in the least frightened of him and who had a unique power of sympathetic understanding. To intellectual companionship was added a deeper communion of spirit.'[25]

Although Harrod's reticence encourages an alertness to euphemism, 'communion of spirit' suggests a relationship not entirely reducible to the sexual. Yet, for Russell, the degree of intimacy achieved among the Strachey generation of Apostles was indistinguishable from homosexuality, and this attitude is responsible for the occasional bout of rather tetchy moralising to be found in his *Autobiography*: 'After my time The Society changed in one respect. There was a long drawn out battle between George Trevelyan and Lytton Strachey, both members, in which Lytton Strachey was on the whole victorious. Since his time, homosexual relations among the members were for a time common, but in my day they were unknown.'[26] By making a false distinction between Strachey's 'time' and his own – during much of the period of his dominance, Strachey's formal relations with the Society were the exact equivalent of Russell's – he seeks to give the impression that the bulk of the Apostles at the turn of the century were practising homosexuals. Leonard Woolf is an obvious exception, yet, in his autobiography, he also acknowledges a debt to Strachey, who encouraged introspection and mutual analysis, something Russell probably found distasteful, and in retrospect associated with Strachey's brand of militant homosexuality.

In Russell's case, a conventional post-Wildean view of homosexuality was reinforced by a reluctance or inability to establish any degree of intimacy with members of his own sex. This was a consequence of his upbringing, for Russell, denied the experience of school, found life at home increasingly oppressive, and his resistance took the form of concealment. The concealment of his feelings became habitual, and although university and marriage weakened it, the habit was never broken, and after 1901 it again became something of a refuge: 'For my part', he wrote in 1902, 'I am constructing a mental cloister, in which my inner soul is to dwell in peace, while an outer simulacrum goes forth to meet the world. In this inner sanctuary I sit and think spectral thoughts.'[27] While this *doppelgänger* was protective not of Wildean excess but of a gothic monkishness derived from Poe, Russell's experiment with the 'double' does illustrate that the *fin de siècle* taste for masks was as prevalent as was the imitation of Pater's prose.[28]

The 'simulacrum' was not necessarily gloomy, and even had it been so, this alone would not have blighted Russell's relations with the Apostles, for, according to Keynes, the affectation of gloom was fashionable in the Society at the turn of the century, creating an atmosphere in which authentic depression could be indulged without detection. Russell's unhappiness did not impair the quality of his conversation, nor did it alter the methods he used in argument; for Moore in particular, the characteristics he found so irksome in the unconverted Russell continued to plague him after conversion. In his autobiography, Leonard Woolf describes Russell's customary intellectual performance as follows: 'However serious he may be, his conversation scintillates with wit and a kind of puckish humour flickers through his thought. Like most people who possess this kind of mental brilliance, in an argument a slower and duller opponent may ruefully find that Russell is not always entirely scrupulous in taking advantage of his superior skill in the use of weapons.'[29] As Woolf implies, beneath Russell's surface brilliance there lurked the possibility of intellectual dishonesty; Moore certainly took this view and Moore's views were catching.[30]

For Moore, though, it was not just a question of intellectual impropriety; he clearly had some insight into the dual nature of Russell's personality and objected to being palmed off with a mere semblance.[31] It is sometimes suggested that Russell resented the influence which Moore exerted over the Strachey generation of Apostles, and this is normally interpreted as dismay and incredulity that the young found Moore more interesting (though considering the nature of their respective work this is not altogether surprising). Yet of greater importance for Russell was that Moore continued to 'belong' in a way he no longer did. As it was, by 1903, Russell found himself not only estranged from his wife, but also (in his view) prematurely eased out of the only group of which he had ever really been a part.[32]

Although Russell was 'ousted' by Moore, there is no evidence that (despite his reservations) he disliked the new members during their time as undergraduates, and, but for Moore's discouragement, he would probably have spent more time in their doleful, but nonetheless congenial, company; for as Woolf recalls, 'In 1903 we had all the inexperience, virginity, seriousness, intellectual puritanism of youth.'[33] Russell's attitude to Bloomsbury is more complex. 'Bloomsbury' is a notoriously amorphous term, but no matter how loose the definition, he could scarcely be regarded as a member; yet, whereas Moore's intellectual relationship with the group is never confused with membership, Russell's connection, through his association with Lady Ottoline Morrell, sometimes is.

Ottoline Morrell's ties with Bloomsbury were to some extent strengthened at Russell's expense, for with her move to Garsington in 1915 began the decline in their relationship; and at Garsington, his position, though unique, became increasingly peripheral – Strachey and co. having established themselves at the centre of things with practised ease. It is unlikely, however, that Russell – fond though he was of conspiracy theories – ever felt threatened by Bloomsbury as an entity, or, for that matter, that he ever conceptualised the group in such a way. Caught up as he was in the genetic tangle of the 'intellectual aristocracy', Russell – unlike Lawrence or Wyndham Lewis – was incapable of the outsider's hostility; instead he looked on disapprovingly from within. Not desiring any closer ties with Bloomsbury than those conferred by birth, education, marriage, and mere proximity, it is scarcely probable that the animosity so evident in his recollections sprang from envy.[34] A better explanation is to be found in Russell's belief that, under Keynes and Strachey, certain 'Bloomsbury' values came to dominate the Society which had played such an important part in his life.

Russell's displeasure was clearly revealed in 1912 when he sought to dissuade Wittgenstein from becoming a member.[35] Again, his motives were held to be suspect, and Strachey, with typical exaggeration, reported that

> The poor man [Russell] is in a sad state ... He looks about 96 – with long snow-white hair and an infinitely haggard countenance. The election of Wittgenstein has been a great blow to him. He dearly hoped to keep him all to himself, and indeed succeeded wonderfully, until Keynes at last insisted on meeting him, and saw at once that he was a genius and that it was essential to elect him ... their decision was suddenly announced to Bertie, who nearly swooned. Of course he could produce no reason against the election – except the remarkable one that the Society was so degraded that his Austrian would certainly refuse to belong to it.[36]

Yet, for Russell, having Wittgenstein 'all to himself' was not as cosy as Strachey imagined; indeed, at that period in particular, it was an experience guaranteed to weaken anyone's possessive impulses. In Russell's opinion, the Society had become 'degraded' entirely because of the prevalence of homosexuality; he believed that 'Bloomsbury' influence had meant that new members were being selected as much for aesthetic appeal as intellectual ability. That Wittgenstein was himself homosexual makes Russell's protest appear somewhat eccentric, yet the intensity of their intellectual relationship suggests that he remained unaware of his protégé's sexual preferences.

At the time of Wittgenstein's election, Russell, although he still displayed traces of his evangelical background, was, under Ottoline Morrell's guidance, attempting to discard the less appealing aspects of his personality; and, as part of this particular course in self-improvement, he strove to cultivate a more tolerant attitude towards homosexuality. Yet his reluctant enlightenment did not survive Lawrence's famous visit to Cambridge in 1915 – for Lawrence also took a dim view of homosexuals, and, encouraged by this youthful support, Russell (as he reported to Ottoline Morrell) reverted to his former opinion:

> Lawrence is gone, disgusted with Cambridge, but not with me, I think. I felt that we got on very well with each other, and made real progress towards intimacy. His intuitive perceptiveness is wonderful – it leaves me gasping in admiration.
>
> Keynes came to dinner, and we had an interesting but rather dreadful evening. Keynes was hard, intellectual, insincere – using intellect to hide the torment and discord in his soul. Lawrence likes him but can't get on with him; I get on with him, but dislike him. Lawrence has the same feeling against sodomy as I have; you had nearly made me believe there is no great harm in it, but I have reverted; and all the examples I know confirm me in thinking it sterilising.
>
> Lawrence is wonderfully lovable. The mainspring of his life is love – the universal mystical love – which inspires even his most vehement and passionate hate.[37]

Lawrence (even by his own standards) was at that time in a particularly volatile state of mind, and this, together with the complex nature of what Leavis termed the 'Cambridge–Bloomsbury milieu', has caused a fairly muted confrontation to become a much-discussed episode in literary history. Russell's part in the proceedings, though, seems fairly clear, in that his role was not, as is sometimes suggested, that of mediator, but of Lawrentian advocate. His identification with Lawrence, as revealed in this letter, involved certain ironies, not least of which is that his criticism of Keynes bears a striking resemblance to Lawrence's analysis of Russell's own shortcomings. The most remarkable aspect of Russell's letter, though, is that it combines a renewed hostility towards homosexuality with a celebration of Lawrence which has distinct sexual overtones; indeed it is in his relationship with Lawrence that Russell came closest to the 'passionate mutual admirations'[38] he found so distasteful among the denizens of Bloomsbury.

In its early stages, the relationship between Russell and Lawrence was of a peculiar intensity, a 'strange almost passionate friendship' Ottoline Morrell called it, and Paul Delany remarks that 'Russell became infatuated with him [Lawrence] not sexually, to be sure, but with all the rest of his being.'[39] Two years earlier, in 1913, Russell had been overwhelmed by the personality of Joseph Conrad; and he writes as follows of his first encounter with the novelist:

At our very first meeting, we talked with continually increasing intimacy. We seemed to sink through layer after layer of what was superficial, till gradually both reached the central fire. It was an experience unlike any other that I have known. We looked into each other's eyes, half appalled and half intoxicated to find ourselves together in such a region. The emotion was as intense as passionate love, and at the same time all-embracing. I came away bewildered, and hardly able to find my way among ordinary affairs.[40]

Not only is the prose itself distinctly Wildean, the passage also recalls Lord Henry Wotton's first sighting of Dorian Gray:

I turned halfway around, and saw Dorian Gray for the first time. When our eyes met, I felt that I was growing pale. A curious sensation of terror came over me. I knew that I had come face to face with someone whose mere personality was so fascinating that, if I allowed it to do so, it would absorb my whole nature, my whole soul, my very art itself.[41]

From Russell's point of view his meeting with Conrad had a mystical quality, yet as with much mystical experience, its evocation compels a use of language which betrays an element of sexuality. It is reasonable to assume that his involvement with Lawrence had its basis in a similar experience; as such Delany's exclusion of the sexual element in the relationship seems arbitrary. Lawrence, Conrad, and indeed Wittgenstein appeared to Russell as rather exotic creatures, alien yet attractive, and as such they eluded the constraints which he normally imposed on his relationships, particularly with members of his own sex. Also, in Lawrence's case, it seems likely that his fulminations against sodomy created an atmosphere so aggressively heterosexual that Russell was able to respond to the feminine element in the other man's personality without any feelings of disquiet.[42]

The completion of *Principia Mathematica* in 1910 had meant that Russell was, in one respect at least, liberated from oppression, and, after falling in love with Lady Ottoline Morrell, he dispensed with his other burden; for Alys, now surplus to requirements, was finally abandoned. The separation came as a blow to Mrs Webb who took the view that a sound Fabian partnership had collapsed purely because Russell had been corrupted by the unclean ways of Cambridge and Bloomsbury: 'I am sorry now that Bertie went to Cambridge – there is a pernicious set presided over by Lowes Dickinson, which makes a sort of ideal of anarchic ways in sexual questions – we have for a long time been aware of its bad influence over our young Fabians.'[43] Although Russell regularly overturned convention by marrying middle-class women while choosing his mistresses from the aristocracy, he was not as yet happily mired in sexual anarchy. Indeed, his happiness was sporadic, his underlying mood continued to be fairly pessimistic, and his contacts with the rest of the world remained much as before. Russell was aware of the disparity between his private feelings and his public face, yet his need for concealment persisted; for in 1912, after writing a fragment of autobiography, he toyed with the idea of publishing it, but only anonymously, remarking in a letter to Ottoline Morrell: 'No-one would guess it was me. That's not at all the sort of person I am supposed to be.'[44] In the following years, however, Russell did make a determined effort to escape the 'moral gymnasium', and in many respects his development up to the end of the war kept pace with that of the younger generation. Yet while the changes in his personality were in direct response to the general movement of ideas – similar development can be observed in certain members of the Bloomsbury Group for example – the transformation in his case seems so extreme as to be atypical and to require further explanation.

From being severely repressed, with an almost morbid regard for conventional morality, and concerned above all with his role as professional philosopher, Russell, by 1917, had achieved such notoriety as to be regarded in some quarters as the most 'mischievous crank in the country'. This dramatic change cannot be reduced to a mere matter of falling in and out of love in unpropitious circumstances; nor can it be written off by reference to the 'complex' nature of his personality, as revealed both in Clark's biography and in his own writings – a view which has in recent years replaced the original stereotype, and created in its stead a popular image of Russell as an exotic hybrid, a cross between Sherlock Holmes and a licentious Mad Hatter. Neither Clark nor Russell himself are able to offer a coherent account of his life at this time, largely because both depict change as a matter of adaptation to external events. Russell's *Autobiography*, though 'confessional' in style, is remorseless in its search for rational motives, and the result is a procession of fragments, connected only by transforming experiences.

In order to achieve coherence, any account of Russell's life during this period must include some discussion of his mental condition, and this in turn can perhaps be best understood in terms of adult developmental psychology. Without wishing to become entangled in the problems of psycho-history, it is perhaps illuminating to offer a comparison of the particular psychological difficulties Russell experienced with those addressed in the first instance by Jung. Although

Jung's theories may not have general validity (as with Freud he has been accused of generalising too much from his own experience), in Russell's case there are reasonable grounds for considering some aspects of Jungian psychology to be applicable. Jung and Russell were, after all, contemporaries, with parallel experiences, and careers which followed the same trajectory from academic respectability to suspect popularity; and although their personalities were in some ways dissimilar, there are several points of resemblance. In the main, though, Russell invites Jungian interpretation because he displayed, in almost a classic sense, many of the symptoms which typified Jung's patients, and his development between 1911 and 1918 can be seen as characteristic of the process of 'individuation'.

According to Anthony Storr,

> The first thing to realise about individuation is that it is essentially a process which takes place in the second half of life. Moreover, it is an esoteric process which engages only the few. It would be a great mistake to suppose that this is the path every neurotic must travel, or that it is the solution at every stage of the neurotic problem. It is appropriate only in those cases where consciousness has reached an abnormal degree of development and has diverged too far from the unconscious. This is the *sine qua non* of the process. Nothing would be more wrong than to open this way to neurotics who are ill on account of an excessive predominance of the unconscious. For the same reason, this way of development has scarcely any meaning before the middle of life (normally between the ages of thirty-five and forty), and if entered upon too soon can be decidedly injurious.[45]

In Russell's case, identification of self-control with mental health allowed him to rationalise his condition in such a way as to preclude consideration of any psychological middle term between rational autonomy and insanity. In the event, a misguided attempt to ward off insanity went some way towards achieving the opposite of his intentions, for, by increasing both the tendency towards extreme rationality and the poverty of his emotional life, Russell, by more or less conscious effort, developed markedly schizoid characteristics.

For Jung, the psyche constitutes a self-regulating mechanism, which ensures that if any of its various functions achieve undue dominance, this imbalance is automatically corrected. Consequently, the over-development of one side of the personality – often necessary in order to achieve the goals of the first half of life – can, in certain cases, produce in middle life something in the nature of a backlash from the unconscious, usually triggered by what Jung terms an 'archetypal experience'. There seem reasonable grounds for assuming that this was very like what happened to Russell in 1901, and was probably triggered as much by the impact of Euripides' play as by Mrs Whitehead's suffering. Although Russell makes little of the 'Hippolytos' in his account of the 'conversion' – he merely remarks that he was 'profoundly stirred by the beauty of the poetry' – in 'A Free Man's Worship', which he maintains was written as a direct result of his experience, his references to drama indicate that he was at least partially aware of the role of the play in producing that attitude of mind Arthur O. Lovejoy was later to characterise as 'metaphysical pathos'. Euripides' plays seem calculated to produce just the effect they had upon Russell; for as one commentator remarks, 'The human action he [Euripides] reveals is the extremely modern one of the psyche caught in the categories its reason invents, responding with unmitigated sharpness to the feeling of the moment, but cut off from the deepest level of experience, where the mysterious world is yet felt as real and prior to our inventions, demands and criticism.'[46] Russell's response to the experience can also be attributed to the play, for there seems little doubt that he strongly identified with the character of Hippolytos, who was, as Ronald Bagg explains, 'sophron' – 'to be sophron is to be so strong of character, so free of guilt and clear of mind that you are not even tempted to do the wrong or weak or greedy action. Etymologically speaking sophron means "having a mind that is sound and safe" ... Hippolytos avoids sex, among other reasons, that he might never lose control and harm others.'[47]

If, as Jung suggests, the process of individuation is directed towards the development of a personality which is balanced, integrated, in some sense 'whole', then Russell could not be described as having embarked upon this path in the years immediately following his crisis. In his case, although he began to question certain of his previous assumptions, he 'misread the signs', seeing in the emotional upheaval not (as Jung would have it) a rebuke from the unconscious, but a threat to his self-control and therefore to his autonomy. Also, Russell was barely thirty; he had yet to complete the tasks of 'the first half of life', and the demands of his work prevented any possibility of development until 1910.

The major changes in Russell's personality – or at least in his behaviour – took place after this date, changes he attributed largely to Ottoline Morrell (who in many ways conformed to Jung's notion of an 'anima' figure): 'Ottoline had a great influence upon me, which was almost wholly beneficial. She laughed at me when I behaved like a don or a prig, and when I was dictatorial in conversation. She gradually cured me of the belief that I was seething with appalling wickedness which could only be kept under by an iron self-control.'[48] It seems unlikely, though, that Ottoline would have agreed with Russell's assessment of her achievements, for she appeared to detect no such transformation in his personality. In 1914 she comments on a journal entry, 'This sounds all very priggish – perhaps I am catching it from Bertie',[49] and in 1915 writes, 'Bertie and I had a walk in the rain yesterday. He gets dreadfully on my nerves, he is so stiff, so self-absorbed, so harsh and unbending in mind or body, that I can hardly look at him, but have to control myself and look away.'[50]

Antecedent to Ottoline's influence was Russell's increasing dislike of his own personality; and there seems little doubt that he was drawn to Ottoline because she embodied many of the qualities he felt lacking in himself. Ottoline was aware of this, and viewed her relationship with Russell as being mainly therapeutic. During this period, Russell was regularly attracted to the intuitive, creative personality, people who fascinated him precisely because they appeared to have access to areas of experience which remained closed to him: flamboyant figures typified by Ottoline Morrell and the actress Lady Constance Malleson; writers such as Lawrence, Conrad, and Katherine Mansfield; and the slightly unbalanced, such as T.S. Eliot's wife Vivien and an American girl, Helen Dudley, both of whom eventually became insane.

Russell's psychological approach to his problems in some ways resembles that of his godfather, Mill, who in similar circumstances imbibed the poetry of Wordsworth for what appears to have been medicinal purposes only. Russell, though, had the advantage in not only having recourse to the literature, but also to the source; and in regard to Lawrence he writes, 'What at first attracted me to Lawrence was a certain dynamic quality and a habit of challenging assumptions that one is apt to take for granted. I was already accustomed to being accused of undue slavery to reason, and I thought perhaps that he could give me a vivifying dose of unreason.'[51] Yet while Russell may have cultivated creative individuals in order to redress the balance in his own personality, his remark about Lawrence is misleading, because from Russell's point of view, 'unreason', in the crude sense in which he uses the word, was by 1915 in plentiful supply both in terms of intellectual products and historical events. Instead, what he hoped to obtain was a sense of certainty, and he was, according to Ottoline Morrell, at least for a time, utterly convinced of Lawrence's powers of intuitive understanding.

In his essay, 'Mysticism and Logic', published the year before he met Lawrence, Russell had compared intuition with empirical analysis as a form of knowledge, this essay being just one of several attempts he made during this period to defend the idea of objective truth against both pragmatism and Bergsonian intuitionism. In 1914, Russell viewed mysticism rather differently than he had done in 1901: then, moments of insight had been associated with the subjection of the body; his later opinion was that 'Intuition, in fact, is an aspect and development of instinct'[52] – an essentially primitive capacity which civilisation erodes. Russell's attitude towards instinct and intuition in the essay is critical but by no means entirely negative: he writes, 'Even in the most purely logical realm, it is insight that first arrives at what is new.'[53] Yet while intuition had its place and could to some extent inspire the philosophical enterprise, it had no part to play in the practice of philosophy, not at least as conceived by Russell: 'philosophy is not one of the pursuits which illustrate our affinity with the past: it is a highly refined, highly civilized pursuit, demanding, for its success, a certain liberation from the life of instinct, and even, at times, a certain aloofness from all mundane hopes and fears'.[54]

The transition from the views which he had espoused in 'A Free Man's Worship' (that good and evil were objective features of the universe and as such amenable to philosophical analysis – analysis capable of providing a 'purified ideal') was brought about by Santayana's criticism of his 'Elements of Ethics' in 1912, which resulted in Russell's partial conversion to relativism. Just how unsettling Russell found this conversion is difficult to say, yet it is from this point that he began to cultivate those individuals who seemed to possess that sense of certainty which he himself had fleetingly experienced in 1901, for he comments in 'Mysticism and Logic', 'It is true that intuition has a convincingness which is lacking to intellect: while it is present, it is almost impossible to doubt its truth.'[55] When he had associated mysticism with the ascetic, Russell had conceived of it in both therapeutic and epistemological terms; and now, when he began to link mysticism with the instinctual, intuitive, irrational side of human nature, it retained its dual potentiality. On the one hand, he was consciously striving to develop the emotional side of his personality, and on the other (especially after the outbreak of war), he was hoping to transcend a fairly pessimistic relativism, and there seems little doubt that he expected assistance from Lawrence on both fronts.

The publication of 'Mysticism and Logic' preceded both the outbreak of war and his meeting with Lawrence, and in that essay there is no hint that he considered the instinctual side of human behaviour as being at all threatening; his views were, for example, far more sanguine than those put forward by Graham Wallas in *The Great Society* which came out the same year. Whereas Wallas was preoccupied with the dangers of atavism, there is an unstated assumption in Russell's writing that, as civilisation progresses, intellect would increase its dominance, and, as a consequence, instinctual behaviour, far from being a threat, would need (as in Russell himself) artificial cultivation.

At the outbreak of war, Russell was in a rather strange position, in that as the conception of 'normality' altered, his own 'abnormality' was accentuated. What little progress he had made did nothing to alter the fact that his excessive rationality began to appear perverse, even non-rational, though, from his own point of view, it regained its status as a virtue. At the same time, a purely rational stance would have been entirely inadequate; Russell, therefore, sought to understand the war in psychological terms, and he produced a spate of articles which display the influence of current psychological thinking. Nevertheless, as much of this literature took a rather negative view of the instincts, he was able to maintain an essentially intellectualist position, seeing instinctual behaviour and ideology as related problems, and both as being amenable to rational understanding and control.

By the time he wrote *Principles*, he had come to regard the instincts or 'impulses' in a more positive light, viewing them as a creative and potentially liberating source of energy, a standpoint in many ways similar to that of Jung but derived in Russell's case from Lawrence. Russell, of course, found Lawrence's 'philosophy' of blood consciousness fairly incomprehensible, not only because of its incoherent nature, but also because it represented an outlook which, to be even partially understood, required, to use Russell's own term, 'knowledge by acquaintance'. In consequence their friendship was brief. Lawrence's writing at this time was pervaded by the image of the shell, and it makes its appearance in the first letter he wrote to Russell: 'There comes a point when the shell, the form of life, is a prison to the life.'[56] Lawrence's notion of 'the shell' has affinities with Jung's theories of the mid-life crisis and individuation, and in Russell this image found its ideal object, a fact which Lawrence was not slow to seize upon, and he began to lecture Russell on the topic of his one-sidedness: 'the tragedy of this our life, and of your life, is that the mental and nerve consciousness exerts a tyranny over the blood consciousness and that your will has gone completely over to the mental consciousness and is engaged in the destruction of your blood-being or blood consciousness, the final liberating of the one, which is only death in result. Plato was the same.'[57] Despite the flattery Russell began to resist, and then to disengage – his scepticism with regard to the certainty intuition provides having returned – yet he did assimilate some of Lawrence's ideas, which eventually found their way into *Principles*. Lawrence's theories gave substance to Russell's own sense of dissatisfaction and offered a conception of psychological development which made more tangible the goal he had been groping towards since 1910.

Whether Russell's personality as perceived by his acquaintances altered to any great extent is hard to say; what is evident, though, is that the realisation of his own deficiencies and of the failure of repression to solve these problems, enabled him to take (with Lawrence) a far more positive view of instinctual behaviour, and to see in the solution to his personal difficulties a remedy for the ills of society in general.

CHAPTER 4

Political science

By Russell's own account *Principles of Social Reconstruction* made its appearance as an unexpected event; as with other aspects of his life and work he declined to accord it a history, preferring to see in it a variant of revelation or an example of authentic creativity in the Romantic tradition: 'During the summer of 1915 I wrote *Principles of Social Reconstruction* ... I had no intention of writing such a book and it was totally unlike anything I had previously written, but it came out in a spontaneous manner. In fact I did not discover what it was all about until I had finished it.'[1] Russell here seems to be confusing two distinct phases in his work on the book, for what he wrote in the summer of 1915 was merely an outline presented to D.H. Lawrence as a basis for their collaboration on a series of lectures. In the event, this initial exercise – although couched in terms calculated to appeal – failed to please, and the manuscript was returned resembling a piece of shoddy homework. Russell was at this time fated to suffer at the hands of former and future schoolmasters, and Lawrence's 'Don't be angry that I have scribbled all over your work'[2] recalls Wittgenstein's bland apology for his devastating criticisms of 1913: 'I am very sorry to hear that my objection to your theory of judgement paralyses you.'[3] Although made to feel something of a 'worm' by Lawrence, Russell was not in this instance paralysed, and withdrawing from the hostilities of collaboration resolved to proceed alone, producing the lectures – laboriously rather than spontaneously – between October 1915 and January 1916.[4] Despite the breach, the psychological approach characteristic of the finished work owes much to Lawrence's stimulus, and traces of the distinctive Lawrentian vocabulary remain. It also derives in part from Russell's rejection of the monastic virtues he had so obsessively cultivated in the early years of the century. Yet while these influences account for some features of what is in essence a very autobiographical piece of writing, the shift in political perspective which it represents requires separate explanation.

Published in 1916, *Principles* was Russell's first substantial work in social and political theory since *German Social Democracy* which had appeared in 1896. Although the circumstances surrounding the writing of the two books were very different, there is a certain significance in the dates of publication, in that both follow immediately upon the fall of a Liberal government. His relative silence on questions of political theory during the intervening twenty years coincided with a period when he seemed satisfied that Liberalism would survive in something resembling its traditional form. From this it could be argued that in the first half of his life, political theory engaged Russell's interest only when Liberalism itself was plainly in a state of crisis.

Principles was written partly as an exercise in self-clarification; a response to the disillusionment and political disorientation which Russell, along with other Liberals, had experienced in the first year of war – a year which ended with the fall of the Liberal government. That Britain had entered the war under Asquith was seen by Russell as conclusive evidence that traditional Liberalism was incapable of fashioning institutions able to sustain its own values; and in the opening paragraph of his book he declares its aim to be that of affording 'a basis for political philosophy more capable of standing erect in a time of crisis than the philosophy of traditional Liberalism has shown itself to be'.[5]

The relationship between *German Social Democracy* and the Liberal electoral defeat of 1895 is less clear. Conceived as a piece of research on Fabian lines, the book was, as already indicated, a product of fortuitous circumstance and Russell's indecision regarding his own future career. The few personal opinions which emerge from the rather austere text indicate not dissatisfaction with Liberalism but a concern for its future. Nevertheless, this concern of Russell's was closely linked with his choice of subject, the electoral defeat having concentrated many Liberal minds on the problems posed by Socialism. To this extent, *German Social Democracy* was prompted by anxieties similar to those which produced the New Liberalism. Unlike writers such as J.A. Hobson and L.T. Hobhouse, however, Russell did not consider the assimilation of Collectivist ideas as a natural and necessary element in the evolution of Liberal thought. Instead, he regarded some accommodation with Socialism as being probably inevitable but in no way desirable.

The long interval between the two books was not entirely due to Russell's political complacency; other factors, such as personal problems and the arduous nature of his professional work, enter into it, providing in themselves a more than adequate explanation of the twenty-year 'gap'. I am not, however, suggesting that he required excuses for not embarking on further political writing following *German Social Democracy* (the three volumes of *Principia Mathematica* are, after all, hardly an indication of idleness during this period); merely that if the political situation had been different – if, for example, final fragmentation rather than reunification had been the lot of the Liberals – he might well have been more productive in this area. In fact, Russell did, during these years, make his first forays into public life, and his political activity, sporadic though it was, set a pattern which he was to follow for the rest of his career. That this activity was not accompanied by any substantial theoretical or polemical work had perhaps as much to do with the nature of the issues involved – none of which engaged him in any fundamental reassessment of his political views – as with complacency or personal and professional preoccupations.

In the year following publication of *German Social Democracy* Russell formalised his relations with the Fabians, yet there is little evidence that the move indicated a more thoroughgoing commitment to Collectivist views than that expressed in his book – his involvement in Fabian affairs being centred on, if not confined to, the newly created London School of Economics. The text of *German Social Democracy* had formed the basis of the first series of lectures given at the School, and as well as serving as a member of its advisory committee Russell also made financial contributions. At the London School of Economics Russell made the acquaintance of its Director, W.A.S. Hewins, whose ideas were to have a strong influence upon his political thinking in the years leading up to his 'conversion' in 1901.

Hewins was not inclined towards Fabianism, nor indeed any other form of Socialism, and had been chosen for his post partly because of this; he was there as visible evidence of the School's objectivity. According to Russell, Hewins 'came of a Catholic family, and had substituted the British Empire for the Church as an object of veneration'.[6] Although there is no reason to suppose that Russell's own enthusiasm was of this order, there seems little doubt that the influence Hewins exerted was primarily on Imperialist matters. In consequence, he became almost simultaneously a Fabian and a Liberal Imperialist, a position which implied no contradiction, as the Webbs in their cultivation of the Rosebery faction within the Liberal Party were already displaying traces of the Imperialist views they were to hold after 1900. In supporting the Imperialist wing of his party – the aim of which, according to D.A. Hamer, 'was to outbid the Socialists, to devise a more attractive alternative that might eliminate and not just oppose Socialism'[7] – Russell opted for a variety of managed social reform which had decidedly elitist implications. In short, he demonstrated that he was still fearful of 'excessive democracy'.[8]

As such Russell was consciously opposing the ideas emanating from those Liberals associated with the Rainbow Circle and *The Progressive Review*, ideas which formed the basis of the New Liberalism, for although there was a tolerant pluralism within all the Liberal and Fabian groupings, and a large degree of overlap in membership, it remains true that, in general, the thinking of the New Liberals was opposed to the elitism implicit in both Fabian and Liberal Imperialist positions. If, as seems likely, Russell believed that the New Liberals went too far in the direction of democratic Socialism, and at the same time he was convinced that the Liberal Party was in need of new ideas, the Liberal Imperialist position had obvious attractions. Also, Rosebery's attempt to duplicate the tactics and success of Gladstone by promoting Imperialism as a 'great issue' was an old method of reviving Liberal fortunes which appealed to the traditionalist in Russell.

In the 1890s Russell was offered two versions of the political life, both of which he rejected: the easy entrance into high politics provided by his family connections, and the political life exemplified by the Webbs. On the face of it, high politics received the more decisive rejection, for he was, like many young Liberals, attracted by the 'scientific' pretensions of Fabianism and recognised that problems of administration were likely to bulk ever larger in all political activity. Yet at the same time Russell retained considerable affection for the Gladstonian politics of his youth when great issues provided drama on a grand scale, drama which, while being emotionally satisfying, was also pleasantly ephemeral – in short, a conception of the political life which remained somewhat aristocratic and contrasted sharply with the activities of the Webbs. The Liberal Imperialists were, as Hamer says, 'very much in the single great issue tradition'[9] and Russell, brought up in a household which had revered Gladstone above all others, certainly felt its pull, and remained throughout his career essentially a single-issue man in all his political involvements. This view of Russell as being drawn towards simplified single-issue politics is given further support when we consider that in the years leading up to the First World War, those questions which stirred him into political activity, namely Free Trade, Women's Suffrage, and the House of Lords crisis, were of this type, whereas the comprehensive programmes of social reform which absorbed the attention of both the Fabians and the New Liberals aroused little or no interest on his part.

That Russell should have passed through an Imperialist phase is only difficult to understand if one attempts to reconcile it with the notion that his political development took the form of a smooth trajectory. This (largely assumed) trajectory – kept in shape by significant silences in his autobiographical writings – follows a fairly conventional progress from radical Liberalism in the 1890s to Socialism in the 1920s, a progression which includes a period of, at the very least, fellow-travelling with the New Liberals. Against this, I would argue that any attempt to chart Russell's development in terms of a 'type' of Liberal intellectual of the period is a mistake; that the 'liberalisation' of his political views was a somewhat erratic and often idiosyncratic process; that the intellectual strategies he pursued up to 1914 usually sprang from a deeply conservative adherence to traditional Liberalism; and that, in consequence, his attitude towards New Liberal theory was – if never overtly hostile – at all times distinctly unenthusiastic.

Although Imperialism – conceived as a policy which promised an alternative method of sustaining traditional Liberalism while circumventing the threat of Socialism – was attractive, Russell's was not an entirely tactical position; for he appears to have been genuinely convinced by Hewin's arguments, and the onset of the Boer War infused this rational stance with an extremely emotional patriotism.[10] Of more lasting importance for Russell's thinking, though, was that his period as an Imperialist laid him open to the prevalent obsession with racial degeneration and eased the way for his acceptance of eugenics as a panacea.

According to Russell, his 'conversion' of 1901 caused a profound change to take place in his political thinking. 'Having been an Imperialist, I became during those five minutes a pro-Boer and a Pacifist.'[11] It might be assumed from this that the experience effectively ended his relationship with both the Liberal Imperialists and the Fabians, but this seems not to have been the case. Perhaps inevitably, this change of heart was slow in producing concrete results in either expressed opinion or political activity. Judging by his correspondence with G.M. Trevelyan in 1904, Russell's pacifism was as yet a rather tentatively held personal view – at least, it does not appear to have led to any involvement with the various pacifist movements which flourished in the pre-war period.

His new political principles were likewise of a somewhat abstract nature, for in the year after his conversion, we find him as a member of the Co-efficients, a group formed by Sidney Webb and devoted to questions of Imperial policy and national efficiency. G.R. Searle states that, 'The twelve original Co-efficients can be classified as belonging to one of three main groups: Roseberyites, Milnerites and Fabians.'[12] Whether Russell would have regarded such classification as appropriate at the time is difficult to say; nevertheless, he was there as the representative of Science and among the other members – representing Economics – was his former mentor, W.A.S. Hewins. Although Russell did not long remain a member of the Co-efficients (Literature's representative, H.G. Wells, writes that Russell 'flung out of the club ... like the ego-centred Whig he is'),[13] he cannot have been ignorant of the group's aims upon joining, and must to some extent have shared certain of their views, or at least regarded them with a measure of sympathy.[14] In this respect, the treatment given in his *Autobiography* to his dealings with the Co-efficients appears rather disingenuous, for although there is little reason to doubt that he found something grossly distasteful about the manner in which certain of his fellow members embodied Imperialist ideas, the brevity of his career as a Co-efficient seems, as Wells implies, to have had as much to do with temperament as with principle.

Russell's defensive work in his *Autobiography* is both unconvincing and unnecessary as his Imperialist affiliations were scarcely unusual, nor, within the historical context, particularly reprehensible. Only in retrospect was the Liberal Party's flirtation with Imperialism widely regarded as a period of reaction, and Russell's distaste for his former views, prompted initially by a purely emotional experience, was later supplemented and reinforced by the growing absorption within Imperialist thinking of a crude form of social Darwinism. Nevertheless, his response remained for a time muted and somewhat ambiguous, and here there does seem to be a direct connection between personal difficulties and political outlook. For approximately three years, from 1901 to 1903, the problems related to his work on *Principia Mathematica,* together with the depression consequent upon the failure of his marriage, produced in Russell's thinking a tendency to universalise the personal and omit the social – politics appearing as a vulgar intrusion into a rather bleak and narcissistic private world within which his own sorrows took on a cosmic significance: 'I know that grave men take it seriously, but it all seems to me so unimportant compared to the great eternal facts.'[15]

Russell's public opposition to the Imperialist view resulted not from moral uneasiness, nor even intellectual contempt for social Darwinism, but from an issue so closely bound up with the Liberal tradition as to trigger what amounted to a reflex response, and his involvement was predictably intense: 'We are all wildly excited about Free Trade; it is to me the last piece of sane internationalism left, and if it went I should feel inclined to cut my throat.'[16] Having equipped himself with a measure of economic expertise in the 1890s, Russell, in his attack on Chamberlain's Tariff Reform proposals, was able to make a telling, if unoriginal, contribution at a theoretical level. The centrepiece of an individual campaign which comprised lectures, speeches, and articles was a long essay in the *Edinburgh Review*, which argued that although Free Trade was an essential component of any acceptable form of Imperialism, it should not be considered as 'merely a question of economic loss or gain. It involves greater issues, and must be judged by reference to larger ideals.'[17]

These 'larger ideals' were, for Russell, embodied in a Liberal tradition which continued to offer ample evidence of a capacity not only to facilitate progress but to maintain an equilibrium between freedom and efficiency. By establishing that the argument for Free Trade had a moral dimension, he sought to identify it with a principled radical tradition, thus to counter the practice of opponents, which was to stress its historical association with *laissez-faire* economics. This strategy is implicit in Russell's opening remarks to the effect that Liberalism was now no longer dominated by a 'general theoretical doctrine'[18] as it had been in the time of its 'ascendency'.

In Russell's view, traditional Liberalism – although currently in need of some adroit repackaging – had provided the conditions necessary for economic efficiency, and at the same time allowed for a degree of organisation compatible with both principle and capitalist enterprise. What he feared was that this balance, which had been held throughout the reforms of the nineteenth century, would be endangered if the nature of the organisation involved were misunderstood, confused with efficiency, and the resulting distortion used as a rationale for an 'extension' of centralised control to foreign trade. Russell regarded the state's role as a restricted one: to assist, control and guide, but not to supersede self-help and voluntary work. Both classical economics and Liberal principle set limits on government intervention, and these were now so nearly approached as to necessitate extreme caution when contemplating further 'progress' in the direction of centralised organisation, for there was always the possibility that precipitate action might stifle enterprise and thus prove self-defeating:

> We in England have prided ourselves, ever since the Armada, upon our individual energy and resourcefulness; and this quality, it is hardly possible to doubt, we owe to our long tradition of freedom. At any given moment, it may be admitted, it might be possible, provided sufficient genius could be harnessed to the machine, to obtain better results by a centralised organisation than by the spontaneous efforts of unfettered enterprise. But the ultimate issue depends upon the national character, and under the debilitating influence of a governmental hothouse national character cannot maintain the highest level.[19]

Although the Whiggish tones are employed polemically in the defence of traditional Liberalism's real achievements, this does not prevent them from being genuinely expressive of Russell's deepest political instincts.

The Free Trade agitation of 1903–4 marked both a resurgence of traditional Liberalism and a revival of Russell's political interest, the election of 1906 being one of the events which momentarily alleviated his misery: 'at least public affairs in England will be more or less what one could wish'.[20] Although in respect of traditional policies this electoral triumph can be seen as something of a farewell appearance rather than the high point of a revival, for Russell, political life had assumed a familiarity which was reassuring. At one level, his support of the Imperialists had been largely tactical, and as the threat of Socialism receded he derived satisfaction from the apparent return to 'normality'. The election had, after all, been fought and won on policies which derived little, if any, of their content from the ideas of the New Liberalism; therefore he could continue to regard this attempt at reformulating Liberal thinking with indifference, if not outright antipathy, and was thus spared the effort of subjecting his own beliefs to close examination.

Just what the substance of these beliefs was is hardly clear, for the closest Russell came to defining his own Liberalism was in terming it orthodox, by which he presumably meant that on most questions and at most times he defended views similar to those prevailing in the Party. His Imperialist adventure aside, this is probably true of the period 1895–1914, though throughout Russell had a sneaking preference for the earlier rather than the later variety of orthodox Liberalism. To perhaps an unusual degree, Russell's Liberalism represented an attitude of mind rather than a set of political principles; yet to the extent to which it had a theoretical basis, this was to be found in the writings of Mill. In important respects, though, the rather amorphous nature of Russell's views allowed the ambiguities present in Mill's thinking to flourish into outright contradiction; thus, an abstract commitment to democracy co-existed with a growing conviction that some of the material to hand was congenitally inadequate – hence his enthusiastic response to the burgeoning eugenics movement.

Russell was hardly unique in experiencing increased anxiety as the actual and potential electorate began to appear statistically alarming in every way, nor in beginning to look to eugenics rather than education as the method by which the quality/equality dichotomy could be overcome. As G.R. Searle remarks, 'The Boer War panic about possible physical deterioration, the preoccupation with National Efficiency and despondency about the apparent failure of environmental and social policies, had between them created a political atmosphere highly congenial to eugenics.'[21] Although by 1906 Russell had returned to a complacent orthodoxy, his concern with the quality of the race suggests that for him degeneration had replaced Socialism as the main threat to Liberal values – the same problem, presented by the same section of society, but now taking a biological rather than a political form. The irony here is that in order to be successfully implemented as a programme of reform, eugenics, by its very nature, entails some form of state intervention; and, in consequence, it was often associated in the public mind with Socialism – an association which was given some substance by the leading eugenist, Karl Pearson, declaring himself a Socialist, and Sidney Webb affirming his belief in selective breeding.

In relation to this, it is important to remember that Russell, although he liked to think of himself as being progressive, was after all that rare phenomenon, an aristocratic member of the intellectual aristocracy, holding – perhaps inevitably – private views which were at times of a decidedly elitist nature. The linking of eugenics with Socialism had, therefore, obvious attractions, in that it offered a formulation whereby he could give expression to his anxieties and yet preserve his self-image. Nevertheless, Russell made no attempt to integrate the Socialist/eugenic element with his Liberalism, and this inconsistency in his political thinking was, if not unrecognised, to some extent compartmentalised, as in two strongly contrasting articles entitled 'The Politics of a Biologist' and 'Liberalism and Women's Suffrage', which he wrote in 1907 and 1908 respectively.

The first of these takes the form of a review of George Chatterton-Hill's *Heredity and Selection in Sociology* – a professional contribution to 'degeneration' literature marred, in Russell's opinion, by the author's attempt to provide scientific support for a version of social Darwinism which owed much to the work of Benjamin Kidd. An important aspect of Kidd's thinking concerned society's need for a 'supra-rational principle': a calculated dose of irrationalism intended to replicate the useful features of religion, producing thereby social cohesion and Imperial success. Chatterton-Hill gave the supra-rational principle (in his case, Roman Catholicism) a rather different role – one which reflected his concern with racial degeneration. A general conversion to Catholicism would, he believed, provide natural selection with that abundance of material necessary to its efficient operation; the intensification of the struggle for survival producing the progress which inevitably issues out of conflict. An argument employing what he took to be a Nietzschean vocabulary in the promotion of mass conversion to Roman Catholicism was, apart from its internal disorders, distinctly lacking in appeal for an anti-clerical rationalist such as Russell. What especially irritated him, though, was that such views should be presented as being extrapolations from legitimate science, when it was evident that they bore no logical relation to Chatterton-Hill's work in biology. Although Russell appears to be issuing a general warning against the ideological use of scientific authority: 'the unconscious embodiment of class or personal bias,'[22] he was particularly troubled by the manner in which evolutionary biology was being allowed to encroach upon other areas of thought – especially philosophy.

From 1900 to 1914 Russell, in his technical philosophy, pursued a programme which, though centred upon the 'scientific method', had little to do with the scientific pretensions of much evolutionary thought. He believed that if philosophy was to emulate the genuine cumulative progress of science it needed to restrict its area of operation, isolate specific problems, and tackle them by means of logical analysis; the 'substitution', as he put it in a later work, 'of piecemeal, detailed, and verifiable results for large untested generalities recommended only by a certain appeal to imagination'.[23] The evolutionary mode of thought, represented in philosophy by Spencer, Nietzsche, Bergson, and, to some extent, William James, and extended into social and political areas under the guise of scientific ethics, was, he contended, productive of these 'large untested generalities' because of a failure to recognise that science, while it could provide the philosopher with a methodology, had nothing useful to offer him by way of facts about the world. Russell's position was not set out with any clarity until 1914 when he gave the Herbert Spencer lecture entitled 'On Scientific Method in Philosophy'; it is, however, already evident in his earlier writing that he considered this misunderstanding of the true nature of philosophy to be behind that pervasive view of human development which he attacked variously for its abject fatalism and groundless optimism.

Although Russell could not deny that evolution had been characterised by progress in human terms, he regarded the two forms of development as having only a contingent relationship. He described Chatterton-Hill's outlook as pessimistic, seeing his reliance on the beneficent effects of untrammelled natural selection as exemplifying the moral fatalism implicit in much social Darwinist thinking. From the standpoint of civilised man, natural selection was, Russell thought, a thoroughly unsatisfactory process, being both morally objectionable in operation, and unreliable as a vehicle of progress. The evolutionary optimists, though intellectually more respectable, were, he believed, equally misguided – a good example here being Hobhouse, whose *Morals in Evolution* Russell had reviewed in the same year. Hobhouse's attempt to establish the reality of moral progress by means of a study of comparative ethics was, in Russell's view, essentially incomprehensible without the assumption of a teleological element in the argument. Russell's professional distance from evolutionism both in method and vocabulary made him a more cogent critic of social Darwinism than those Liberal intellectuals who, like Hobhouse, relied upon biological models in their own thinking. Yet, in 'The Politics of a Biologist', although he makes some attempt to maintain this distance, his views on degeneration compel him to qualify a normally forthright and dismissive approach. By relinquishing his critical position Russell inevitably becomes embroiled within the terms of the debate, disclosing in the process the manner in which he shared many of the presuppositions which had engendered it.

Russell regarded eugenics as differing from other varieties of social Darwinism in being a legitimate application of biological science and as such non-political. In holding that rational selection could be an objective, or at least a non-contentious procedure, he inclined towards the vaguely positivist aspirations of the National Efficiency campaigners, who believed that scientific administration could eliminate conflict, thereby rendering the messy business of traditional political activity unnecessary.[24] In the early years of the century, the science of eugenics had yet to assimilate Mendelism and was thus still somewhat shaky on the central question of heredity. A greater awareness of the complexities involved in this area might have resulted in a more cautious approach on the part of those promoting eugenics as a vehicle of reform; as it was, their 'science' was scarcely less ideological in content than other social Darwinisms. Eugenics, according to Greta Jones, was 'a combination of the language of natural selection with highly partial and contentious social judgements on the relative worth of different sections of the population' and was, in fact, aimed at 'the preservation and increase of the middle classes'.[25] The idea that rational selection should be guided by class divisions was perhaps inevitable at the time, being based on the prevalent assumption that the social order was, to a great extent, a just reflection of the natural order – class hierarchy representing levels of evolutionary development.

Yet the working classes were, in strictly Darwinian terms, proving themselves rather fitter than the middle classes, and Russell shared the view that the differential birthrate was in itself convincing evidence of a decline in the biological quality of the race. By any 'objective' standard of social worth the middle classes were clearly the most desirable stock; even their diminishing number was, he argued, largely the result of superior qualities, in that Imperial endeavour and economic ambition were leading members to either perish in the colonies or to restrict their families in the cause of personal advancement. The inferior races and classes were, on the other hand, flourishing because of the energetic intervention of middle-class Empire builders and social reformers. When condemning the effects of social reform, Russell occasionally takes on the tone of the Charity Organisation Society (COS), and reveals an instinctive bias which makes his reaction to the New Liberalism more comprehensible: 'it is plain that our present institutions, both where they encourage competition and where they mitigate it, tend to eliminate the best elements of society, leaving the future to the thriftless, the ignorant, and the superstitious'.[26]

Elsewhere, in his preoccupation with racial health, he displays that lack of concern for the individual which eugenic philosophy tended to share with all forms of social Darwinism: for example, in reference to the incidence of tuberculosis he remarks, 'though the death rate for young people has diminished, that for people over thirty-five has increased, owing to the fact that those who would formerly have died young are now kept alive for a number of years. Thus the weak and degenerate are increasingly able to leave children, and the race accordingly deteriorates.'[27] 'Weak' and 'degenerate' can be usefully ambiguous terms, and it is far from clear from Russell's usage whether he is restricting himself to an assessment of biological qualities. Even the examples he offers – the tubercular and those who are insane as a result of alcoholism or syphilis or both – could be seen as falling into separate categories: the merely unfortunate, and those who, because their condition can be attributed to weakness of character, are to be condemned on moral grounds. It would certainly be in keeping with Russell's usual disposition for him to adopt a censorious tone when assuming a connection between morals and mental health, for he believed that his sanity had been preserved only through rigid self-control, a personal struggle which had established to his own satisfaction the role played by 'character' in this matter, and which did nothing to elicit sympathy for signs of weakness in others.

This preoccupation of Russell's surfaced even in his technical philosophy, and his attitude is clearly spelled out in an article he published the following year, 'Determinism and Morals'. Here he writes that 'the madman may be blamed if he has become mad in consequence of vicious self-indulgence'.[28] It is, in fact, apparent that many of the judgements he makes in 'The Politics of a Biologist' as to the 'best people', the 'desirable classes', and 'the most desirable parents' transcend biological description and amount to little more than an evaluation of moral character. Russell's failure to clearly distinguish between these two components of his argument encourages the assumption that *all* his judgements derive from biological evidence, and that the moral qualities displayed by an individual are directly related to his physical and intellectual 'fitness'.

What is striking is that Russell's philosophical position as to the possibility of objective ethical judgements combines with, rather than combats, the positivistic approach characteristic of eugenics, to produce a complacent attitude towards the whole question of selection. In reality, this 'consensus', far from being derived from either accurate biological knowledge or philosophical analysis, amounted to little more than a belief that individuals selected themselves by virtue of their position in the social and economic hierarchy; hence we have Russell making confident moral/biological judgements based largely upon levels of income: 'The richer classes (which are assumed to be on the whole the better) marry later and have smaller families than formerly.'[29] The problem, then, was not one of choice, but of encouraging the self-selected (in every sense) to produce more offspring.

As the middle classes were declining because of the dysgenic effects of economic motivation, Russell – in keeping with all eugenists from Galton onwards – felt that they would only increase their number if given economic inducement to do so, and although this would entail 'Socialism of some sort'[30] the intervention by the state would be minimal:

> The birth-rate is now the main factor in selection, and the birth-rate is controlled by economic motives. These motives at present lead to a selection of the unfittest (in a non-biological sense); but the only thing needed is an economic organisation of society which shall reverse their operation. As a comparatively practicable measure, everything ought to be done to diminish the expense of bringing up children for the more desirable parents. Free education up to any grade, provided the parents reach a certain standard, would do something; free feeding of school-children, provided it were given to all, and not only to the destitute, would also do something. But more than this is necessary if the present inverse selection is to be arrested. It is necessary that desirable parents should be wholly relieved of the expense of bringing up their children not only by providing such things as education free, but by a direct payment from the State to the parents. At the same time those who are considered undesirable as parents ought to be in every way encouraged to limit their families as the desirable parents do at present, and no financial help ought to be given to them by the State in bringing up their children.[31]

By 'a non-biological sense', Russell presumably means a non-Darwinian sense, as this passage suggests that, although he may be hesitant in conceding biology a role in defining the 'unfit', he is – somewhat paradoxically – in no doubt that this category of individual derives all his undesirable qualities from biological inheritance. This stress on nature to the almost total exclusion of nurture – education being given a functional rather than a reforming role – represents the determinist position summed up by Karl Pearson in the phrase, 'good stock, good stock, good stock and then education'.[32]

Yet Russell, although plainly reliant on current eugenic philosophy, avoids any direct reference to the doctrine in his article; instead, the alignment of biological 'fact' with 'Socialism' is presented as being the logical conclusion of his argument. He clearly believed that eugenics was too readily identified with other, more disreputable, forms of social

Darwinism, and by presenting his views in such a way, he evidently hoped to gain a more sympathetic hearing from his fellow Liberals: 'social reformers', he writes, 'must not be misled by biologists into regarding science as their enemy, but must learn to take account of science, however repulsive may be the garb in which it is presented to them'.[33]

This attempt to promote eugenics as an objective science devoid of political content and therefore compatible with Liberalism involves certain evasions on Russell's part; for, although he appears to have been genuinely unconscious of any element of 'class or personal bias' in his argument, he was clearly aware that rational selection – regardless of its relationship to biological science – posed problems both for his moral philosophy and his political principles. Rather than bring these issues out into the open, Russell seeks instead to counterbalance the content of his argument by impressing upon his (largely Liberal) readership his adherence to the progressive tendencies within the current orthodoxy. To this effect, he defends – against the strictures of Chatterton-Hill – 'The position of modern Liberalism', as a middle course 'between un-restricted competition and no competition at all', seeing it as an example of 'the limitations which sensible men impose upon the application of principles recognised by them as having exceptions.'[34] Interpreted as an oblique endorsement of the trends encouraged by the New Liberalism involving an approach to 'socialism of some sort', this eases the way for Russell's own 'Socialist' recommendations to be accepted as being genuinely, rather than merely nominally, progressive.

If, however, Russell had chosen to defend his views on traditional Liberal grounds, it would have been possible to invoke the authority of Mill; for in *On Liberty* the state is held – at least in principle – to have the right to restrain putative parents. Although Mill's Malthusian advocacy of restraint stemmed from an assessment of the quality of life available whereas Russell's argument is based on predictions regarding innate ability, both are attempts to justify possible discriminatory action by the state against a broadly similar class of person. Russell, though, does not suggest the state should sometimes prohibit marriage – probably realising that such a move would have no practical effect – instead he hopes that harsh conditions will in themselves provide sufficient disincentive to procreation.

On the question of education, so far as the immediate results to be expected from their proposals are concerned, the differences are minimal. With Mill, it is the poorest section of society which will benefit from the – very limited – intervention of the state. Writing fifty years later, Russell can presuppose this minimum, and it is only in respect of further education that he would discriminate against those whose parents do not come up to scratch. Yet it is at this point that the consequences of his biological determinism become apparent; for although Mill's approach – based on the belief that individual differences are in the main due to circumstance – is equally extreme, it is one that does admit of a degree of self-correction. With Mill, social mobility as a result of individual development is clearly (if not very energetically) encouraged; whereas with Russell, it ceases to be a possibility, in that any hopes for the 'improvement of mankind' are centred upon those whose parents already give evidence of requiring little in the way of improvement.

Russell believed that the proliferation of the unfit would, if not checked, result in a society dominated by the ignorant, the credulous, and the superstitious – an increase in the number of robust Roman Catholics being for him as sure a sign of degeneration as an increase in the number of tubercular non-conformists. Degeneration, in his view, needed to be reversed, not because it signalled the decline of the race as a fighting unit, but because it threatened the Liberal ideal of a rational, intelligent electorate. Eugenics appealed to him because it appeared to offer a rational, humane, and efficient alternative to education as the means towards establishing an ideal democracy. That it seemed to involve a temporary abandonment of democratic principles was presumably a further example of those limits which 'sensible men impose upon the application of principles recognised by them as having exceptions',[35] and, to this extent, Russell would appear to be at one with Karl Pearson's view that the practice of eugenics would never come about through democracy.[36]

In certain respects, though, Russell's pragmatism is only apparent, for his interest in eugenics was – like his interest in Fabianism and Imperialism – always dependent upon the extent to which these seemingly inimical doctrines could help maintain the viability of traditional Liberalism without encroaching upon its essential values. In other words, the implementation of eugenic philosophy could be regarded as a political adjustment external to Liberalism, and not comparable to the way in which New Liberal thinking was attempting to assimilate Collectivist ideas into the main body of Liberal thought.

For Russell, an essentially Millian Liberalism could sustain its viability if the entire electorate possessed those qualities at present peculiar to the middle class. His unstated assumption was that such an electorate as would emerge following a brief bout of selective breeding would be, on account of improved intelligence and character, rational. Along with most of his contemporaries, Russell followed Darwin in believing that the instincts of persons of higher intelligence were weaker than those of lower intelligence, thus enabling the former to manifest character by overriding base and irrational impulses – on this question he was his own best example. In his belief that rational political behaviour could be ensured by eradicating low intelligence in the community, Russell was adhering to the methodological individualism of Liberalism, and displaying – as yet – little interest in the work of the social psychologists of the period, who were busy arguing that political behaviour was largely irrational.

In the years leading up to the First World War eugenic philosophy gained widespread intellectual acceptance; therefore it comes as no surprise to find the views expressed in 'The Politics of a Biologist' reiterated in *Principles*.[37] In the later version, though, Russell's argument has an added element; for, by then, he was concerned with the possibility that female emancipation was yet another threat to the quality of the race. In 1907, however, he had no such worries, and obviously regarded his eugenic position as being compatible with, even complementary to, the rather more limited aim of securing votes for women. As with Free Trade, this issue, being in accord with Russell's traditionalist inclinations, prompted action, and in the same year he stood – with no serious expectation of success – as a Women's Suffrage candidate, indicating in his public statements that he supported the Liberal government on all questions except this one.[38] The following year he wrote an article, 'Liberalism and Women's Suffrage', in support of what seemed to be a change in government thinking on the subject, and here he reverts to an entirely orthodox position in regard to the possibility of social progress within and through the democratic process. This is partly due to the fact that Russell's arguments derived – perhaps predictably – from Mill's 'The Subjection of Women'.

Although it is evident from the article that he thought of women in general as being in need of improvement as regards character and intelligence – thereby placing them on a level with working men and inferior races – he is confident as to the possibility of this being achieved through responsible involvement in periodic vote-casting.

That Russell could view the situation with such equanimity was largely because he believed that the success of the campaign would, at least initially, be limited, and in consequence amount to nothing more threatening than an addition to the middle-class electorate. He remarks that 'very few advocates of women's suffrage demand the vote for *all* women',[39] though he does express agreement with the view 'that any measure of women's suffrage would be merely a stage on the way to the enfranchisement of all women'.[40] Of course, the enfranchisement of all women, and hence the 'complete democracy which ought to be our goal',[41] might, in Russell's view, be dependent upon an intervening programme of eugenic reform.

Russell gestures towards eugenics only when he lists the benefits which will accrue from female suffrage (hinting in the process that the acquisition of the vote should in no way remove women from their accustomed role in society), maintaining that it would bring 'in the long run a greater care for questions of women's work, of the rearing and education of children, and of all those increasingly important problems upon which the biological future of the race depends'.[42] At this period Russell believed eugenics and women's suffrage could work in tandem to produce superior parents, in that a woman of suitable stock would, through her political involvement, begin to approach the levels of character and intellect manifested by her spouse. Later, when it became clear that the emancipated woman might eschew domesticity altogether, he began to have second thoughts on the subject.

In 'Liberalism and Women's Suffrage', because his argument was directed towards the extension of democracy, Russell was able to draw on the ideas and vocabulary of the Liberal tradition in a way which had not been possible in 'The Politics of a Biologist': 'The chief traditional argument in favour of democracy is that it is difficult for one class to judge of the interest of another, and rare for one class to care as much for the interest of another as for its own.'[43] This awareness of class interest, however, stemmed from a utilitarianism which could also be used – in extreme cases – to justify the sacrifice of the few in order to preserve the many:

> To inflict a special disability upon any class of the community is in itself an evil, and is calculated to generate resentment on the one side and arrogance on the other. It may be admitted that this evil, in some cases, is more than balanced by compensating advantages; but it remains an evil, and any gain for the sake of which it is to be endured must be very great and very certain.[44]

Although Russell was in this instance denying the need for 'a special disability' to be inflicted upon women, there is the implication that he has other cases in mind where such action might be necessary – the fecund feeble-minded for example.

A further point worth making about 'Liberalism and Women's Suffrage' is that it was written immediately after Russell had read the proofs of Graham Wallas's *Human Nature in Politics* yet it reflects none of the doubts concerning the efficacy of the democratic process which are expressed in that work. Self-consciously, even obsessively, a rationalist, Russell was not yet prepared to deviate from that strictly intellectualist approach to politics criticised by Wallas, and his eugenic beliefs were a feature of this rationalism. Allowing that he was at this time only mildly interested in Wallas's work, any attempt to establish the background to *Principles* must take some account of their relationship. Without ever being close friends, they had more in common than might at first be supposed; for although Russell displayed none of Wallas's enthusiasm for committee work, they had left the Fabian Society at around the same time and for similar reasons, and in addition to sharing pronounced anti-clerical views, they were almost alone in possessing the ability to arouse G.E. Moore's hostility – which suggests an affinity of sorts. Given their acquaintance, it is unlikely that the arguments contained in *Human Nature in Politics* would have been allowed to slip entirely from his mind, leaving grounds for seeing in *Principles* an attempt to fulfil – albeit in a rather limited way – certain aspects of the programme laid down by Wallas; for, if nothing else, Russell does at least begin in the preferred Benthamite manner by establishing the 'springs' of human nature.

Yet it was only when Russell had finished *Principia Mathematica* that he began to find his extreme rationalism too confining, experiencing a growing dissatisfaction with the personality which had to some degree evolved out of the writing of that work, and even then it was some years before instinct psychology had any direct influence on his thinking. Although an eclectic social psychology formed part of the theoretical basis of Russell's shift towards a form of libertarian Socialism during the First World War, this move was inextricably bound up with that change in his personality which had taken place between 1910 and 1915. Before this occurred, the only possible effect that the work of such writers as William Trotter and William McDougall could have had on Russell's beliefs would have been to confirm his fears regarding the emerging democracy, thereby reinforcing his elitist inclinations.[45]

It is often precisely this elitist tendency on Russell's part which makes his political position during this period so elusive; for it has the paradoxical effect of bringing him closer to certain 'Socialist', or at least Fabian, points of view – it was, after all, an article by Sidney Webb which had provided him with much of his material in 'The Politics of a Biologist'.[46] On the other hand, his apparent adherence to the principles of classical economics, plus a belief in eugenics, caused him to be suspicious of the alternative programmes of social reform recommended by the New Liberals – programmes which called for increased state intervention aimed at the promotion of greater social and economic equality. Added to this, we have his emotional attachment to a form of nineteenth-century Liberalism, which made it difficult for him to come to terms with change except on an opportunistic basis, yet which also provided the energy with which he took up traditional issues when they made occasional reappearances on the political scene.

The completion of *Principia Mathematica* coincided with the 1910 election, and Russell, 'being at the time very much interested in the struggle between the Liberals and the Lords about the Budget and the Parliament Act ... felt an inclination to go into politics'.[47] Exercising patrician rights, however, proved to be incompatible with intellectual integrity, for his refusal to make even a token obeisance to the Church of England secured his rejection by the Bedford Liberal Association. This brief encounter with practical politics, while offering further proof that he was temperamentally unsuited to the profession, did allow him the opportunity to make a statement of his views. Although his address to the Bedford Liberals has been interpreted as giving evidence of Russell's progressive economics, stamping him as a New Liberal of the 'Hobsonian School',[48] his main topic was the taxation of land values, a subject with a suitably extended history in the Liberal Party. Rather than establishing his credentials as a New Liberal, Russell's concentration on this question gives yet another indication of his preference for traditional issues.[49] Moreover, the election itself centred on the obduracy of the House of Lords, and one seems justified in assuming that it was the opportunity of participating in an assault on one of Radicalism's favourite targets, rather than any regard for the content of Lloyd George's budget, which captured his interest.

Although Russell's views in 1910 appear to have remained much as they were in 1908, there is some evidence that they did begin to alter in the following years, allowing him to remain 'orthodox' in the sense already suggested. This necessitated a shift to the left in his politics, for, energised by the personal ambitions of Lloyd George and Winston Churchill, the New Liberalism did, during this period, begin to gain the centre ground in the Party. That Russell, so long resistant to the idea of the New Liberalism, should appear to acquiesce to its actuality, can perhaps best be understood in terms of that change in his personality already referred to. Under Ottoline Morrell's influence, his belief in the benefits of rigid self-discipline weakened, his sympathies widened, and he was thus able to take a more sanguine view of the possible effects of social reform. A conversion to relativism in 1912 also helped in the process, by taking the philosophical edge off his moral dogmatism. A further consideration is that Russell's attempt at this time to exchange a premature middle age for delayed youth in some ways precluded his taking up anything resembling an overtly reactionary stance.

Explanations of this sort are, perhaps inevitably, somewhat speculative, and in any case tend towards circularity; yet given the nature of Russell's personality in the early years of the century, it probably required a decisive change in temperament to produce a 'liberalisation' of his political views in early middle age. There is, however, little evidence of any substantial rethinking on New Liberal lines. Although such a move on Russell's part would be in accord with his earlier tactical manoeuvres, pointed reference to the New Liberalism in books written during the war indicate that he never accepted 'its insistence on the substantive compatibility of the aims of Liberalism and labour'.[50] For example, in *Political Ideals* (1917) he writes, 'Under the influence of socialism, even progressive opinion, in recent years, has been hostile to individual liberty.'[51] These books were written after Russell's break with the Liberal Party, and give expression to his growing interest in the weak-state theories of academic Pluralism and Guild Socialism; yet my contention is that they do not signify any dramatic change in his assessment of the New Liberalism, but instead have their origins in his long dissatisfaction with that trend in Liberal thinking. Viewed in this way, Russell's use of Guild Socialist and Pluralist ideas can be related to his use of Imperialist and eugenic thinking, in that it represents an exploration of yet another alternative strategy seeming to offer the possibility of sustaining certain Liberal values.

Although Russell's approving references to Syndicalism began to appear only at the outbreak of war, a letter written to Ottoline Morrell in 1912 gives some indication that even at this early date he was at least emotionally receptive to the kind of extra-parliamentary agitation which Syndicalism represented, for in it he expresses extravagant support for the current miners' strike: 'The strike is likely to do good all round especially if it spreads and becomes universal revolution.'[52] Without suggesting that he was at this time approaching a Syndicalist position, there were aspects of the movement which were in line with his current programme of self-development, particularly its criticism of an exclusive reliance upon reason and its emphasis on spontaneity. Even in its British manifestation, Syndicalism carried overtones of youthful vitality and idealism which Russell at this stage might easily have found attractive.

A further point in its favour (at least from Russell's point of view) was that it had provoked such hostility in the ranks of official Socialism. In 1912, MacDonald, Snowdon, and Sidney Webb all published attacks on Syndicalism, and Mrs Webb's diary of the same year contains the following assessment of the movement and its membership:

> Syndicalism has taken the place of the old-fashioned Marxism. The angry youth, with bad complexion, frowning brow and weedy figure is now always a syndicalist; the glib young workman whose tongue runs away with him to-day mouths the phrases of French Syndicalism instead of those of German Social Democracy. The inexperienced middle class idealist has accepted with avidity the ideal of the syndicalist as a new and exciting Utopia.[53]

It was some years before Russell kept anything like this sort of company, and even then he rarely found it agreeable; yet, whatever the nature of his sympathies in this early period, his remark in 1915 on declining an invitation to join the Independent Labour Party (ILP), 'I am not a socialist, though I think I might call myself a syndicalist',[54] suggests that he had taken a fairly favourable view of the extra-parliamentary agitation which had in the intervening years increased both in scope and effectiveness.

While it is clear that Russell's beliefs altered after 1910, this was a gradual process, not involving the sort of conversion or commitment which would allow us to 'place' his views with any accuracy. To this extent, the question of whether he was orthodox Liberal or Syndicalist sympathiser is perhaps not particularly meaningful, as in this period of political reorientation his views were more than usually subject to the mood of the moment. There is, though, a discernible drift in his politics which is open to misinterpretation if no clear distinction is made between the different types of Socialism then on offer. His 'official' orthodoxy, and what this entailed, can easily be combined with occasional remarks open to a 'Socialist' interpretation to place him in the vanguard of that procession of Liberal intellectuals who travelled from Radicalism through Fabianism and New Liberalism to arrive inevitably (and often in Russell's case 'appropriately') at Socialism.

Despite being at times susceptible to the authoritarian streak in Fabianism and being numbered among those succumbing to the practice of permeation, his own Fabianism was never more than merely formal. Far from converting him, prolonged exposure to the combined personalities of the Webbs left Russell with an acute and permanent distaste for their Socialist vision. There was, though, an opposing strand of British Socialism – usually associated with the work of William Morris – and this only became available to Russell in the years before the war (most notably in G.D.H. Cole's *The World of Labour*). Again, there is no evidence of direct influence at this time; yet the point I wish to make is that it seems more accurate to locate his increasingly libertarian views – these often having more to do with questions of personal morality than politics – in the kind of Socialism which Cole represents than in any other.

As Russell arrived at something like Cole's position in 1915, there is a danger here of reading the story backwards. It is, though, not improbable that he was already receptive to the political atmosphere out of which Cole's book emerged in 1913. Russell's emotional commitment was to a traditional Liberalism which expressed theoretical distaste for class-based politics; Cole's views, therefore, might be regarded as having even less potential appeal for him than the Fabianism they opposed. There are, however, two reasons why this was not necessarily the case. In the first place, Cole and other Pluralists tended to regard class as rather a loose association when compared with the cohesive nature of the group, and whereas an individual could only belong to one class, his group allegiances were many and varied. The idea of class, then, often seems secondary and rather fragmentary in Pluralist thinking, and as they regarded the actions of and relations between groups as being similar to those obtaining between individuals, their arguments often more closely resembled those of Liberal individualism than any kind of Collectivism.

Secondly, Russell's break with the conventions of Edwardian morality was associated with a weakening of ties with his own background, and this produced subtle changes in his political perspective. Though always an intellectual elitist, Russell around this time ceased to identify this elite exclusively with Cambridge rationalism – in other words, a form of genteel bohemianism broadened his idea of excellence, and made him, in one sense at least, more genuinely democratic. If we can assume, also, that his political beliefs were beginning to include a social dimension, this allowed him the freedom to explore the political territory to the left of a Liberal Party which seemed to be heading increasingly in a Fabian direction.

Russell's alienation from his own class, and his increasing distance from a political establishment he no longer regarded as being disinterested, was brought to full consciousness at the outbreak of war, by the 'revelation' that British foreign policy had over many years been conducted in a secretive and hence undemocratic manner. One cannot help feeling that Russell – despite the insights gained at Co-efficient meetings – believed he had been in some way personally deceived in the matter of Edward Grey's secret diplomacy, and in 'The Entente Policy, 1904–1915' (written alongside *Principles* in the autumn of 1915) he remarks: 'There are some among us who hold that, if our foreign policy in recent years had been conducted with more courage, more openness, and more idealism, there is a likelihood that the present European War would never have occurred.'[55]

In the passage from *Principles* quoted on p. 61, Russell voices his dissatisfaction with 'the philosophy of traditional Liberalism', yet nowhere does he attempt to define either the philosophy or the tradition; consequently, it is not altogether clear just what aspect of Liberalism he is criticising. The context, though, does suggest that the remark is addressed to the idea of the rational, autonomous individual in Liberal thought. Against this, he would wish to argue that in any adequate political philosophy the role of impulse in human action must be given greater recognition. There is, however, by implication, a wider reference to the effect that the Liberal tradition had created, as a seemingly natural end product, that which Russell regarded as a powerful and oppressive state, able and willing to subvert Liberal values.

Despite Russell's persistent reservations concerning the direction of Liberal policy, he had retained his belief that the tradition he inhabited was inherently self-correcting, and still had confidence that rational, orderly progress was possible. He was, therefore, as unprepared as any other Liberal for the outbreak of war on a scale which seemed to necessitate a degree of organisation incompatible with individual liberty. Yet, although he was not alone among Liberal intellectuals in reacting against the sudden growth in the power of the state, most New Liberals, and ex-Fabians such as Wallas, quickly adjusted, and lent their abilities to the war effort with almost the same enthusiasm as the Webbs. Russell, on the other hand, became increasingly vociferous in his opposition, and this can only be seen as a basic difference in political temperament finally making itself manifest.

The irony of Russell's position during the war was that on finally freeing himself from a severely repressed psychological condition, he felt for the first time in his life politically oppressed, a combination of feelings which are expressed in a letter to Constance Malleson in September 1915: 'Quite lately I have had a sense of freedom I never had before ... I don't like the spirit of socialism – I think freedom is the basis of everything.'[56] Russell, of course, was not living under a Socialist government at the time, yet he believed that the conditions which had been allowed to develop during the war gave a foretaste of what such a government would be like, and it was even less to his taste than he had anticipated. Opposed as he was to what Maitland described as the 'macadamising tendency' of the state, it is not surprising that Russell should view the prospect of a pervasive crazy-paving – as proposed by the group theories of Pluralism and Guild Socialism – with some favour. Yet this is not to say that Russell was, in exploring the possibilities of these theories, expecting to find in Pluralism or Guild Socialism – any more than in the official Labour Party – a political home. Groups, as such, did not interest him a great deal; what these theories did offer, though, was a fragmentation of the state which would allow a measure of Liberal individuality to flourish in the cracks.

CHAPTER 5

The sage of Caxton Hall

Reviewing William James's *Memories and Studies* in 1911, Russell declares that 'The most delightful part of the book consists of an essay and a speech on war – especially the speech, called "Remarks at the Peace Banquet".'[1] As James's address was deliberately provocative, designed to unsettle precisely those Liberal assumptions concerning the aetiology of wars which had formed the basis of Russell's own thinking since 1901, it is to be supposed that what occasioned his delight was more a matter of context than content. The gathering of pacifists was informed by James of both the nature of war and the social benefits it conferred; aside from being 'the final bouquet of life's fireworks', 'human nature at its uppermost', 'a sacrament', war was also a necessity, for 'Society would rot without the mystical blood-payment.'[2] That Russell chose to be amused by the audacity, rather than dismayed by the celebration of these values, is perhaps an indication of personal affection, for James had only recently died.

This exposure to James's ideas is interesting because it suggests that the enthusiasm of the London crowds in August 1914 should have caused Russell less astonishment than it did: 'I discovered to my amazement that average men and women were delighted at the prospect of war. I had fondly imagined, what most pacifists contended, that wars were forced upon a reluctant population by despotic and Machiavellian governments.'[3] It is, however, easy to overstate the novelty of James's remarks, which lay mainly in the fact that they were his and thus might be expected to carry more weight among English intellectuals than similar views emanating from less agreeable sources. Against this, it must be allowed that Liberal optimism was – intellectually at least – well grounded and already armed against the various exponents of social Darwinism. James's insistence on the moral value of the martial spirit as an uplifting force in society is aligned with social Darwinism in what is the definitive statement of the Liberal case,

Norman Angell's *The Great Illusion.* For Angell, 'the war clergy' (among whom he numbered James) were 'unwilling witnesses to the truth, which is that we are all alike – English, Americans, Germans, French – losing the psychological impulse to war'.[4] Although subsequent events were to lend a certain irony to Angell's remarks, his argument carried conviction, and his thesis, that war – from a strictly rational/economic point of view – was futile, remained sound.

Russell shared Angell's belief that man's struggle for survival was solely concerned with the domination of Nature; and perhaps one of the main reasons why James failed to make much of a dent in the essentially Cobdenite views of pre-war Liberals was that the proposals he put forward in 'On the Moral Equivalent of War' aimed at utilising aggression were – as both Russell and Angell demonstrated – readily translatable into conventional Liberal discourse concerning man's energies and rational progress. What was lost in translation was the conviction that irrational impulses were in themselves a valuable aspect of social life. That the initial experience of being at war was found by most people to be enjoyable could be taken as evidence supporting James's position; yet, while the martial values began to achieve prominence, few would admit to wanting war 'for itself, and apart from each and every possible consequence'.[5] Given the nature of James's analysis, it is not surprising that it found favour chiefly among those who tended to disconfirm it in their own beliefs and practices – individuals who were, like Russell, somewhat piously engaged 'in an endeavour to understand popular feeling about the War'.[6] Thus, while Russell claimed that he was driven to revise his 'view of human nature',[7] it might be more accurate to say that he revised his view as to the nature of others.

Fond of regarding himself as an alien presence, Russell during this period was prone to indulge the notion that he was the only sober man at the party. For obvious reasons this is a self-image difficult to promote, and his distinctive behaviour rarely received such a flattering interpretation. Indeed, Russell's perceived status was more closely analogous to that of the truculent intruder – the sort of person who, following his ejection, is given to shouting through the letterbox. That he should find himself misjudged by avowed Liberals baffled and annoyed Russell, until a reading of Bernard Hart's *The Psychology of Insanity* (1912) introduced him – in the theoretical sense – to 'rationalisation', a concept he was to put to vigorous use in the coming months.

Russell's active opposition to Britain's involvement began with his membership of the Neutrality Committee and continued with his work for the Union of Democratic Control: the former, as one historian remarks, spending 'less than £20 to stop a great war';[8] the latter described by Russell himself as '8 fleas talking of building a pyramid'.[9] Despairing of what was in essence a continuation of Liberal dissent, he had, by 1916, identified himself with the No Conscription Fellowship, a more militant pacifist organisation dominated by Quakers and ILP Socialists. Although the No Conscription Fellowship under Catherine Marshall worked Russell hard and often seemed to use him as an office boy, it provided comradeship and occasional excitement up to his imprisonment in 1918. By contrast, in the Union of Democratic Control, Russell had felt himself constrained by the timidity of a 'party line' which had evolved out of the Cobdenite tradition; nevertheless, for the first year of the war he toiled doggedly in the footsteps of Morel, Brailsford, and Angell, writing, lecturing, and researching a large-scale work on British foreign policy.[10] In one respect, though, he was always at odds with this tradition, for, while sharing the radical's distrust of a diplomatic service still dominated by the aristocracy – not least because of his own unhappy experience of the Paris Embassy in the 1890s – his fascination with the psychology of the electorate complicated any belief in the democratic control of foreign policy.

In most of Russell's early writing on the war there was a tension – resolved only to his own satisfaction – between the twin attractions of conspiracy theory and instinct psychology. That Russell was engaged with these questions from the outset is evident from his first published piece on the war, a letter Massingham agreed to print in *The Nation* of 15 August 1914.[11] It is clear from this that Russell failed to detect any trace of the moral uplift promised by James, or for that matter any other potential value to civilisation in this sudden breakdown of what he identified as society's repressive function. In private he had prepared by recalling his patriotic aberration at the time of the Boer War, 'fixing some things in [his] mind' which he recited in a letter to Ottoline Morrell at the beginning of August: 'not to hate anyone, not to apportion praise and blame, not to let instinct dominate. The force that in the long run makes for peace and all other good things is Reason, the power of thinking against instinct.'[12] *The Nation* letter is witness to a failed prophylactic, yet, although Russell recovered his composure, he quickly realised that a stance based on reason and self-discipline was both futile and by now temperamentally disagreeable –

having struggled so long to free himself of repression he was not about to reinstate it as a panacea. Moreover, the events he had witnessed completely upset his previous assumptions (based on his own unusual experience) concerning the relative strengths of instinct and rational control.

In an article published in the *New Statesman* the previous year he had argued that man's instinctive life was, if anything, in need of some encouragement; attacking the 'Calvinistic horror of the "natural man"' he had written that,

> although nature must supply the initial force of desire, nature is not, in the civilized man, the spasmodic, fragmentary, and yet violent set of impulses that it is in the savage. Each impulse has its constitutional ministry of thought and knowledge and reflection, through which possible conflicts of impulses are foreseen, and temporary impulses are controlled by the unifying impulse which may be called wisdom.[13]

Russell's present dilemma sprang from a Liberal tendency to domesticate the irrational and to regard much of the literature on the subject as being rather in the nature of a self-indulgent intellectual exercise. Ironically, this predisposition is most clearly evident in a work he produced in the early summer of 1914; here he remarks:

> To the schoolmen, who lived amid wars, massacres, and pestilences, nothing appeared so delightful as safety and order ... To us, to whom safety has become monotony, to whom the primeval savageries of nature are so remote as to become a mere pleasing condiment to our ordered routine ... The barbaric substratum of human nature, unsatisfied in action, finds an outlet in imagination.[14]

Finding that 'imagination' could have a certain prescience brought a change of emphasis in Russell's views on human nature; yet he was not disposed to be either pessimistic with McDougall or celebratory with James – instead, he turned to Graham Wallas who utilised both these writers in what was perhaps the most considered attempt by a Liberal to domesticate the irrational. Wallas's domesticating tendencies are evident in his preference for the milder pessimism of McDougall in contrast with Gustave Le Bon; as early as 1908, he had dismissed Le Bon's analysis of crowd behaviour as being applicable only to the Latin races.

In *The Great Society* – which Russell read in manuscript sometime in the spring of 1914 – Wallas was at pains to distance himself from anti-intellectualism while at the same time claiming that social psychology provided the means by which the quality of rational life could be improved. By substituting the term 'disposition' for 'instinct' and arguing that man had a disposition towards rational thought, Wallas avoided the determinism implicit in instinct psychology and replaced a pessimistic dichotomy with an optimistic continuum.[15] Like Russell, Wallas was doubtful as to the effectiveness of repression, remarking that, 'If we leave unstimulated, or, to use a shorter term, if we "baulk" any one of our main dispositions, Curiosity, Property, Trial and Error, Sex, and the rest, we produce in ourselves a state of nervous strain.'[16] Russell took up the term 'baulked disposition' in his article 'Why Nations Love War' written in November 1914, yet, although he states that 'The desires for triumph and power can be satisfied by the ordinary contests of football and politics',[17] this is the closest he came at the time to linking the impossibility of repression with the possibilities of sublimation. Innocent of theories regarding the unconscious, James's arguments in 'On the Moral Equivalent of War' are not in any accurate sense related to the theory of sublimation; yet there is a resemblance, and one that had been pointed up – albeit only in a footnote – by Wallas.[18]

Although Wallas's notion of disposition and something approximating the Freudian idea of sublimation are implicit in Russell's protean use of the terms 'impulse' and 'instinct' in *Principles of Social Reconstruction*, he was at this stage concerned less with the redirecting of instinctual drives than with establishing their relationship to rational thought. His preoccupation with 'rationalisation' during the first year of the war meant that the time and energy he could spare from his research work and a private life of increasing complexity were devoted to the clarification of motive. Russell's efforts in this direction tended to be mechanical, complacent, and concentrated on those former friends and fellow intellectuals who he believed should have been without need of his services. His own motives he left unquestioned until they came under the disagreeably expert scrutiny of D.H. Lawrence.

In reference to the first few days of war Russell remarked, 'At that time I was wholly ignorant of psycho-analysis, but I arrived for myself at a view of human passions not unlike that of the psycho-analysts.'[19] He was then directed by G.M. Trevelyan to Hart's popularisation of Freudian theory, and from this point Freud's influence was difficult to avoid for someone of Russell's interests and connections. That these had expanded since 1911 was largely due to Ottoline Morrell – for whether her success as a hostess is ascribed to a capacity for friendship or more cynically as collector's mania, she had the effect of involving Russell in a genteel bohemia where certain of the repressions and hypocrisies of Edwardian society were subverted not merely intellectually but by a style of living.

By 1915 Ottoline Morrell had established at Bedford Square and Garsington an attractive refuge for Bloomsbury pacifists – a floating population encompassing most areas of English political, intellectual, and cultural life. It was in a cottage on the Garsington estate that Russell completed *Principles*, and though it was his sexual rather than his pacifist inclinations which drew him into the community, it nonetheless provided him with that conception of a desirable culture which informs the finished work. Although Ottoline Morrell's diaries suggest that Russell remained 'stiff and awkward' in this company, this seems to refer to the inhibitions of a middle-aged philosopher on the dance floor, and one, moreover, whose athletic prowess – like that of many late-Victorians – tended towards endurance rather than agility. From the time he went up to Cambridge, Russell was singularly unsuccessful in pursuits favouring the physically nimble; intellectually, though, he was anything but ponderous, and a vivid account of his evenings at Bedford Square is given by Mary Agnes Hamilton. Here, in her view, Russell's was 'The dominating mind'. At Garsington too, Russell was 'God' to the young intelligentsia who seriously discussed the possibility of making him Prime Minister.[20] Such attention was, naturally enough, not displeasing, and it is evident that *Principles* was written with this particular audience in mind – indeed, at the outset, they comprised the bulk of those attending the lectures at Caxton Hall.

The opening chapter of *Principles*, that which established its psychological basis, was one of the last written; thus in the completion of the work the influence of psycho-analytic theory is unmistakable if unacknowledged.[21] That 'Freud in England' first established secure roots in Bloomsbury is perhaps not merely fortuitous, as it is difficult to think of other circles in English cultural life where personal complexities were being analysed with equal devotion. Leonard Woolf had read *The Interpretation of Dreams* and reviewed *The Psycho-pathology of Everyday Life* in 1914, while the bohemian branch of Bloomsbury had links with the 'New Age' where some of the earliest articles on Freudianism had appeared before the war. In a milieu where sex and art provided the mainstays of conversation, and where Freud was beginning to grow in influence, it is unlikely that Russell could have long remained in ignorance of the concept of sublimation. Of more direct relevance to Russell's political concerns, though, were two articles published in 1915 by Ernest Jones, Freud's disciple and future biographer, 'War and Individual Psychology' and 'War and Sublimation'. While there is no evidence that Russell read either article, the correspondence between their respective views is striking and – if nothing else – discloses that much of the argument in the early part of *Principles* was already available in systematic form.

The foregoing is not intended to indicate that *Principles* is primarily a Freudian analysis of society: it is not. Even at the level of psychology, the echoes of Freud are perhaps fewer and fainter than those emanating from Lawrence, while neither writer much influences the substance of the work which derives in the main from Liberal, Idealist, and Pluralist thought. Yet it is, on the other hand, not too much to say that Russell's hopes for post-war reconstruction are heavily (if somewhat vaguely) reliant on what could be termed institutionalised sublimation; therefore, it seems pertinent to spell out the extent to which Freud's ideas were in circulation by 1915.

Throughout his early writings on the war Russell had sought to point up the difference between rationalisation and rational thought, to clearly set out the arguments on both sides of every issue and thus to bring a measure of objectivity into the prevailing discourse. In one of the first Union of Democratic Control pamphlets, for example, he writes: 'Let us try for a moment to forget praise and blame, to forget that we are members of one of the belligerent nations, and to view the whole tragic irony from the standpoint of impartial compassion and understanding.'[22] By April 1915, however, he was beginning to feel himself to be a member of an endangered species and appealed, somewhat despairingly, to the 'intellectuals of Europe'. 'Hatred', he declares, 'is a mechanical product of biological instinct. It is unworthy of men who pretend to freedom of thought to be caught in the toils of this purely animal mechanism.'[23] In *Principles*, the stance is still that of the embattled Liberal, but the tone is softer, he is more charitable, more understanding, indeed rather serene as he contemplates those duties which fall to him as a member of the elect.

Russell's serenity stems from a realisation that he is no longer 'opposing the stream' in quite the way he had. His position on the war, though often inconsistent – a point he concedes in his preface to *Justice in War-Time* – had been that of an intellectual self-consciously inhabiting and maintaining the Liberal tradition. Although he now placed less value on self-discipline and rational control, and had begun in his private life to cultivate a spontaneity which regularly shaded into irresponsibility, in his public stance he tended to fall back on the language of repressive Liberalism, and calls for the 'victory of reason over brute instinct'[24] are not uncommon in his published work. By the time we reach *Principles*, not only is instinct accepted as a fact of human nature, but is now seen in almost Lawrentian terms as the best guide towards truly civilised behaviour.

With *Principles*, then, the public Russell begins more closely to resemble the private, and the result is a text which, though critical of the classical Liberal theory of human nature and expressing dissatisfaction with current New Liberal/Fabian convergence regarding the role of the state, does draw heavily on the Liberal/Idealist tradition. Russell's opening chapter, 'The Principle of Growth', offers a view of man's nature which is interactionist and, as the title suggests, developmental; this to counter 'the philosophy of traditional Liberalism'[25] which is, one must suppose, that 'political philosophy ... almost entirely based upon desire as the source of human action'.[26] Cultivating spontaneity and inculcating it in the lecture hall, Russell is perhaps not to be blamed for being less than specific in identifying his targets; thus 'traditional Liberalism' becomes a large gesture denoting Benthamite origins culminating in a Fabian state.

That rational man should develop a Webbian cast of mind was not a notion with any strong appeal for Russell, and the Webbs were, in the political sense, among those doing well out of the war. It would seem, therefore, that after spending months condemning the irrationality of the motives behind the war, and at the same time growing deeply apprehensive regarding the growth of rational control within the state, Russell now saw the opportunity of attacking both simultaneously by identifying the destructive aspects of the first with the oppressive aspects of the second. Thus Lawrence – one of the first in England to take a positive view of the instincts – was, for all his increasingly evident faults, at least offering a passionate opposition to the Webbs' vision of society.

If not exactly the 'two great seminal minds of their age in England',[27] Webb and Lawrence at least provided the boundaries of Russell's eclecticism in much the same way as Bentham and Coleridge had provided Mill's. Yet, like the drawing of other parallels between Mill and Russell – their precocity, mental crises, elderly radicalism, and general conception of the role of the intellectual in society – this does not mean a great deal without some indication that Russell was intent on demonstrating that the relation between godfather and godson involved an inheritable element. Richard Wollheim comes close to taking this view, regarding Russell's life work in social philosophy as being dedicated to the updating of Mill. 'It would', he writes, 'be a matter only of simplification, and not of grave distortion, to look on the whole of Russell's social philosophy as an attempt, a sustained attempt, to repair that of John Stuart Mill: to supplement its deficiencies, to relate it to new ideas, and to demonstrate its applicability to the ever-changing realities of the twentieth century'.[28]

To see *Principles* as a conscious attempt by Russell to tie up the loose ends of *On Liberty* by providing an adequate psychology does not, on the face of it, square with the fact that Mill rates just one mention in the text and this in a list of 'impracticable idealists' who began the movement against the subjection of women. On the other hand, no social theorist is mentioned twice and most likely candidates are not mentioned at all. Russell was not, it must be admitted, much given to respectful exegesis in his social writing, therefore a non-appearance in an index provides no guarantee of a non-acquaintance with the relevant collected works. In this case, however, given the supposed centrality of Mill to the text, Russell might have been expected to make an exception to his usual practice.

That Mill is central to an understanding of certain aspects of *Principles* is undeniable – given Russell's intellectual background this could scarcely be otherwise. That the loose ends of *On Liberty* were a major preoccupation at the time of writing is another matter. Indeed, nothing would have suited Russell's purposes less than to be seen by a young and self-consciously modern audience as suggesting that the country's present needs would be best served by tinkering with the finer points of J.S. Mill. The problem with Wollheim's approach to *Principles* – which is essentially that of tidying up Russell tidying up Mill – is that it does actually distort Russell's intentions and has him performing an intellectual exercise which was no part of his concern at the time. That he did not regard himself as being engaged in writing political philosophy in the accepted sense is made abundantly clear in his 'Reply to Criticisms' in the Schilpp volume.

Russell's specific complaint here is against V.J. McGill whom he rebukes as follows:

> In *Social Reconstruction*, which was not intended as a contribution to learning, but had an entirely practical purpose, I used the word 'instincts' in its popular

> sense; elsewhere, I have used vaguer words, to make it clear that I was not speaking of instinct in its technical sense. Mr McGill gives the impression that I use the word 'instinct' much more often than I do, and affects to suppose that, when I use the word 'impulse' I mean 'instinct' as it is used in scientific accounts of animal behaviour. By this means he, no doubt unintentionally, distorts my meaning, and has an easy time in showing that I talk nonsense.[29]

This particular passage has the unfortunate effect of suggesting to the reader just what an easy time McGill had, and while it is not exactly nonsense, the claim that vaguer words were used to promote clearer meaning looks fairly desperate. That clearer words had not occurred to him in the intervening period is evident from the fact that Russell ignores the opportunity to explain just what he understands by either 'impulse' or 'instinct in the technical sense', so we are to some extent still in the dark as to how they differ. The terms instinct and impulse are used interchangeably in *Principles*, and though it must be allowed that 'impulse' is the favoured term, 'instinct' is used often, and occasionally in what looks like the 'technical sense' if we are to interpret this – as presumably Russell would – as being McDougall's sense of the term.

In other words, Russell at times talks as though a specific instinct is productive of a specific activity, and also makes some points by reference to the behaviour of dogs; yet these lapses – if such they are – cannot be said to obscure his essential position as to the malleability of human nature. Russell had learned from Wallas's criticisms of McDougall that it was possible to make use of instinct psychology without being tied to a psychological determinism, and this was all the licence he needed to equip himself with a psychological theory which, if not exactly his own, was at least personally assembled.

As such, he could be said to have taken note of Wallas's notion of 'disposition' rather than taken it over, for it was, as Qualter says, a typically 'more or less' term[30] and thus too hedged around with qualifications to serve Russell's purpose in *Principles*. Instead, what is on offer is a psychology which, though it has a basis in contemporary thinking on the subject, displays a generality and looseness of terminology which smacks of Romanticism. For example, in opposing the belief that war could be avoided if 'men were more under the dominion of reason'[31] he remarks,

> If impulses were more controlled, if thought were less dominated by passion, men would guard their minds against the approaches of war fever, and disputes would be adjusted amicably. This is true, but it is not by itself

sufficient. It is only those in whom the desire to think truly is itself a passion who will find this desire adequate to control the passions of war. Only passion can control passion. And only a contrary impulse or desire can check impulse. Reason, as it is preached by traditional moralists, is too negative, too little living, to make a good life. It is not by reason alone that wars can be prevented, but by a positive life of impulses and passions antagonistic to those that lead to war. It is the life of impulse that needs to be changed, not only the life of conscious thought.[32]

Given Russell's use of the words 'desire' and 'impulse' here, his next statement, which appears as an attempt to echo Bentham whilst implicitly pointing up his deficiencies, tends to promote confusion: 'All human activity springs from two sources: impulse and desire. The part played by desire has always been sufficiently recognised.'[33]

Wollheim, pursuing his argument that Russell's intention was to supplement Mill, interprets the above as follows:

Desire takes for its object something which is distant, possibly both in space and time: and integral or essential to a desire is the belief that the object desired will somehow or other satisfy one if one gets it. Impulse, by contrast, is immediate: it is directed towards something which one wants to do or have, here and now, and it is unmediated by the belief that that towards which one has an impulse will have desirable results or satisfying consequences. Impulse lies in the moment, desire is shaped by foresight, and Russell's first point would be that any political philosophy that held that only desire had to be taken account of and that consequently overlooked impulse, like Mill's theory at any rate as I have presented it, is to that degree inadequate.[34]

This is indeed his first point, for the neglect of impulse had, in Russell's view, resulted in a rather nasty case of political impotence, and *Principles* begins with the stated aim of providing 'a basis for political philosophy more capable of standing erect in a time of crisis than the philosophy of traditional Liberalism has shown itself to be'.[35] Though in an oblique way concerned with Mill's inadequacies, Russell's is not a self-effacing text and is offered as an alternative rather than an amendment. It is also conceptually carefree to the extent of being careless and thus hardly suited to the task Wollheim has in mind.

Russell's statements concerning traditional Liberalism are in fact misleading with regard to Mill, for while his understanding of the Liberal theory of human nature was in a sense the traditional one, his actual reading of *On Liberty* was purely pragmatic. Thus Russell used Mill whenever he found Mill to be useful and he found him to be useful even in the area of his supposed inadequacy, namely, on the subject of human nature. The flavour of Romanticism which pervades Russell's psychology stems directly from his taking over as central to his argument the plant theory of human development which Mill had in his turn derived from Rousseau and Humboldt. As commentators have noted,[36] there are some difficulties in reconciling Mill's notion of 'inward force' with even a modified associationism, yet, linking impulse to a generalised 'energy', he is able to move away from an extreme environmentalism and to approach a form of interactionism. 'Impulse' for Mill is related to spontaneity and individuality, energising the self-development or self-culture which he sees as necessary if the levelling power of public opinion was to be countered. 'Society', he remarks, 'has now fairly got the better of individuality; and the danger which threatens human nature is not the excess, but the deficiency, of personal impulses and preferences.'[37]

Given their common concern for individuality, it is hardly surprising that both Mill and Russell should in their arguments come to rely upon innate qualities, for so long as these are conceived as providing large potential for man's development, the threat of conformity issuing out of an extreme environmentalism is avoided without the necessity of confronting the determinism implicit in a thoroughgoing instinct psychology. Although Mill takes refuge in a reduction of 'impulse' to 'energy', Russell, armed with Wallas's concept of 'disposition' and some knowledge of psycho-analytic theory, can confidently adapt Mill to his own uses without troubling to adopt a modern terminology. Indeed, as already indicated, it is evident that Russell's 'borrowings' from *On Liberty* determine the tone of the whole work.

Where Russell follows Mill is in regarding a social life dominated by will and purpose, with Calvinistic moralising already merging into a Tayloristic rationalism, as being debilitating and potentially characterised by intolerance of all excellence not linked to economic or material success. Like Mill, he had a self-protective concern for the intellectual, the scientist, the creative person in general, and especially for the genius, whom he always regarded as the creator of civilisation and man's best hope for future progress. Moreover, the streak of romanticism in Russell led him to cherish the myth of posthumous recognition, hence a genius must regard as natural his antagonistic relationship with society; yet, fond though he was of this theory, Russell felt it his duty to protest at its consequences and plead, like Mill, for the tolerance of originality.

Going beyond Mill, Russell was also concerned that the war was witness to the fact that the repressed actually did return, and that the institutionalised rationalisation of war was no cure for an underlying impulse towards, if not war, then to the release which war offered. Predisposed towards dualism in much of his analysis, it is natural that Russell should favour the existence of two opposing impulses. These begin as specific, 'an impulse of aggression, and an impulse of resistance to aggression'.[38] Although this is understandable given that Russell's avowed theme is war, the danger of ending up with a list of instincts to rival McDougall's is obvious. Russell adroitly avoids this by dispensing with specificity, and proceeds to divide all impulses into 'those that make for life and those that make for death'.[39] In a later chapter, these emerge in their developed state as the creative and possessive impulses. However, these two impulses would appear to end in one, the opposing manifestations of a single impulse – a concept theoretically indistinguishable from Mill's 'energy'.

The 'creative impulse' has its origin in Russell's conviction that artists and scientists were markedly less prone to 'war fever' than other members of a population:

> Any one of the impulses that make for life, if it is strong enough, will lead a man to stand out against the war. Some of these impulses are only strong in highly civilized men; some are part of common humanity. The impulses towards art and science are among the more civilized of those that make for life. Many artists have remained wholly untouched by the passions of the war, not from feebleness of feeling, but because the creative instinct, the pursuit of a vision, makes them critical of the assaults of national passion, and not responsive to the myth in which the impulse of pugnacity clothes itself.[40]

Russell, though, offers no sociological evidence for his assertion, and given the pugnacity of many intellectuals – Max Weber and T.E. Hulme spring immediately to mind – one might suppose that he would have had a hard time amassing it. There is in fact little doubt that the notion of a 'creative impulse' was a product of his Bloomsbury environment and that this environment represented an ideal of pacifism, creativity, and instinctive liking by which the effectiveness of institutions could be judged.

As always, Russell is intent on dealing the intellectual the best hand – he has lost faith in unaided reason but not in the elite who, because of the strength of particular impulses, are able to take what is in his view a 'rational' attitude towards the war. Russell is here still operating with competing impulses rather than a theory of sublimation, yet the implicit elitism has points of similarity with Ernest Jones's analysis in

'War and Sublimation'. In this paper Jones argues that successful sublimation is relatively rare and against the minority whose 'conduct is in complete accord with the ethical, aesthetic and social standards of civilised life, and that it is so without any sense of compulsion, but as a spontaneous and natural expression of the personality', we have the majority who 'when they are left to their own resources without the supporting pressure of a civilised environment, their false acquisitions fall away from them just as a parvenu loses his veneer of good manners in similar circumstances, and they revert to a lower level of conduct'.[41] It is striking that both Jones and Russell, writing during the early part of the war and from a psychologically 'realist' point of view, should still retain the Liberal belief in culture and education and refuse to consider the possibility that culture and barbarism can, and often do, go together.

As we have seen, Russell believed that impulses are not fixed but can 'within certain wide limits' be 'profoundly modified by circumstances'. Yet his contrast between 'highly civilized men' and 'common humanity' carries the suggestion that the former have innate advantages when it comes to the strength of desirable impulses. For Russell it would seem that innate qualities exist which limit the malleability of human nature – a limit which he would probably regard as being essential if variety is to be preserved. The 'highly civilized' become so because their 'exceptional mental endowment' equips them to pursue a career which in turn encourages the cultivation of certain impulses at the expense of others. The fate of the undesirable impulses is a matter not considered by Russell, but as he apparently expects no pathological consequences following upon their repression, we must presume him already to be verging on a – albeit implicit – theory of sublimation.

Whereas the 'highly civilized' have developed those desirable impulses they possess, the situation is less happy as regards 'common humanity', for what potential they have in this direction is at present 'checked and enfeebled' by the institutions under which they live. Russell is describing 'alienated man' as much as 'repressed man'; the phrase 'impulses which make for life' suggesting that these impulses are more 'natural' than are their competitors. As Russell proceeds, it becomes apparent that he regards the great majority of men as being 'alienated' from their true nature, and that although in 'essence' each man is unique to himself, a 'natural' development or realisation of this essential self would be one which gave freedom to the creative impulses (using 'creative' here in a fairly general sense as it was no part of his argument to suggest that the average man had the makings of an aesthete). The possibility of natural development is seen by Russell as being dependent on the suitability of the environment provided, for although man is able to adapt to a wide variety of conditions, in most cases he is surviving rather than flourishing.

Russell's 'Principle of Growth' is a theory of self-realisation or self-development, and although it is based on the primacy of 'blind' impulse, he sees impulse as having a natural bias towards creative endeavour. Like Wallas, he is intent on domesticating the irrational, believing it to be almost 'predisposed' towards rationally acceptable behaviour. As such, his views remain firmly within the Liberal tradition. However, while his 'Principle of Growth' is in many respects a restatement of the theories of self-development to be found not only in Mill, but also in the Idealism of Green and Bosanquet, it is notable in reflecting a change in moral and political attitudes and is thus able to display a greater generosity of spirit. With regard to Mill, although Russell follows him in placing a high value on particular pursuits, and believes that, given the opportunity, most people would prefer something more demanding than a 'certain modicum of passive pleasure', his notion of 'individuality' is less intense, less atomistic, and thus less embattled than that expressed in *On Liberty*. For Russell, self-development is to be considered, in part at least, a social product rather than a purely personal achievement.

Russell's major differences with the Idealism of Green and Bosanquet are to be found in his conception of the state, for he was far from regarding it as a moral force capable of realising man's best self. Indeed, his theory of self-realisation is aesthetic rather than moral and is not in conflict with the demands of 'social service': he can thus promote individuality without the anxiety of seeming self-indulgence. With Green in particular the notion of self-development often appears to revolve around the rather chilly prospect of guilt-ridden music lessons, whereas Russell centres his on the easy-going atmosphere of the Bloomsbury interior. Being centred on Bloomsbury aesthetics, Russell's conception is also responsive to the ideal of friendship and therefore seems closer in spirit to the ideas of Pluralists such as Figgis who regarded the group rather than the state as forming the basis for man's development.[42] Whether from Whiggish inclinations or from conversion to Pluralism, Russell would prefer the state to have only a restricted role, seeing its essential functions to be those of – and in this he is in agreement with both Mill and Green – ensuring an area of individual freedom and removing obstacles to individual development. Against the state, Russell stresses the 'community' which he sees as the harmonious outcome of natural development within groups characterised by 'instinctive liking' and 'common purpose'.

Russell – perhaps for the first time – was feeling the deficiencies of his 'community', and throughout *Principles* he stresses the need to replace an atomistic social life dominated by economic individualism with an organic culture. That Liberal society had become characterised by what he terms 'extreme individualism' is seen by him as the inevitable consequence of its historical struggle to attain freedom and justice against authority. He suggests that the process had altered human nature to the extent of 'hardening the walls of Ego, making them a prison instead of a window'.[43] This image, which he derives from Lawrence, is not dissimilar to that used by Bosanquet in criticising Mill's conception of individuality, 'a sort of inner self, to be cherished by enclosing it, as it were, in an impervious globe'.[44] Later, Bosanquet contrasts the individual as 'atom' with 'a greater individuality' – a nature 'so thoroughly one, so vital and so true to itself, that, like a work of art, the whole of his being cannot be separated into parts without ceasing to be what it essentially is'.[45]

Even in its critique of Liberalism, Russell's 'Principle of Growth' remains within the tradition, and has therefore sound Liberal credentials despite making its first brief appearance under the guise of Chinese philosophy in the 'outline' he delivered to D.H. Lawrence in the summer of 1915. There it is produced without introduction as 'The principle of Tao. Growing like a tree. The principle of growth in a man must not be crushed. It is not crushed necessarily by preventing a man from doing some definite thing, but is often crushed by forcing him to do something else.'[46] In its developed form it takes centre stage and is important as an expression of an ideal – though an ideal much modified by realism in the actual analysis of institutions:

> The more developed and civilized the type of man the more elaborate are the conditions of his growth, and the more dependent they become upon the general state of the society in which he lives. A man's needs and desires are not confined to his own life. If his mind is comprehensive and his imagination vivid, the failures of the community to which he belongs are his failures, and its successes his successes: according as his community succeeds or fails, his own growth is nourished or impeded.[47]

Read as an indirect complaint – and there is a case for saying that much of the book does appear to have been written with Russell's own requirements in mind – this reflects a change of focus brought about mainly, but not entirely, by the war. Russell's interest in the idea of 'community', like his desire for parenthood, can be linked with his being a middle-aged man who had exchanged centrality in a stable society for marginality in conditions of crisis. At Cambridge, Russell had been able to feel himself a part of the 'establishment' and at the same time a European intellectual; after 1914 he became estranged from this governing elite, from Cambridge, and – rather more drastically – from Europe. Inevitably, he suffered a certain disorientation, for, as a landless aristocrat, Russell had no place in which to locate his sense of the past. Most of his adult life had been spent shuttling between Cambridge and London – two places for which he felt affection, but were important to him not because he 'belonged' there, but because they belonged to, participated in, were even partial creators of, 'Western Civilisation' or, slightly more specifically, 'European Culture'. Thus, when Russell remarked in the outline of *Principles* that 'I feel more allegiance to mathematics than to the State',[48] he is making the standard Pluralist point concerning conflicting ties by emphasising the abstract nature of the state and hence the unreality of its demands for allegiance. He is, though, also signifying that for the duration his loyalty was restricted to that international community of intellectuals represented for him by such terms as 'European Culture'.

That Russell had before 1914 eschewed the parochial and sought to be cosmopolitan can be seen by his almost total lack of interest in matters social and industrial. His culture was high culture, his politics high politics, his economics classical, and his hopes for the improvement of mankind largely eugenist. Land Reform, Tariff Reform, Women's Rights, and the threat of social degeneration might stir him politically, but how the average person occupied his waking hours was of little concern and no importance. The war changed this perception, and Russell – a man much given to revelatory experience – now saw the mass of the ordinary as alienated, repressed, and isolated individuals, existing in a harshly competitive society dominated by material rather than spiritual values, and welcoming a war which offered that which current institutions were incapable of providing, namely, instinctual release and a common purpose.

In the early years of the century Russell had perceived the urban working class as a threat to the quality of the race, and became an enthusiastic eugenist. Now the average citizen was seen as a threat to civilisation, and, as the mass production of pacifists by genetic means was hardly practicable, Russell's attention was focused on the environmental and the institutional. As we shall see, Russell, in his new-found enthusiasm for nurture had not abandoned nature, and at times the tones of William Morris conflict with those of Karl Pearson. Morris, though, dominates, and in the 'outline' of *Principles* he sent to Lawrence the section on industrialism consists of little more than a list of 'Evils':

> Vastness of organisations and concentration in hands of capitalists, prevents employees from feeling any *pride* in their work. There is no result in which they can feel the satisfaction of the creator. A railway porter who has a little garden will work in his garden with a joy he never can feel in working for a railway company. There is no use in merely more money. Miners earn good wages but are too uncivilized to enjoy them. No use in shorter hours, unless accompanied with means of rational enjoyment, and with education. No use abolishing poverty if ennui remains.[49]

Russell's remarks concerning railway porters' gardens and miners' culture are not, one must assume, examples drawn at random from an encyclopaedic knowledge of industrial life; rather, they can be taken as indicating that at this period his research on the subject was restricted to empirical observations on the Cambridge to London line and the recording of Lawrence's anecdotes.

On the theoretical side, it is more likely that Russell was acquainted with Cole than with Morris, but his shorthand for any influence coming from this direction was 'Syndicalism'. He was considering at the time the possibility that he might consider himself a Syndicalist – the label 'Socialist' he refused outright; therefore he was not among those whom A.D. Lindsay described in 1914 as 'The men who five years ago would have called themselves Socialists and given everything to the State, now call themselves Syndicalists and can find no place for it.'[50] Russell had taken some interest in Syndicalism in 1913, seeing the movement as a possible alternative to the projected New Liberal/Fabian state. After the war began, Pluralist thought, whether academic or political, offered arguments regarding the sovereignty of the state which could be of use to the pacifists in their claims to freedom of conscience. Now, in his concern for the psychological health of the community, he was drawn towards the Syndicalist and, by implication, the Guild Socialist position on industrial democracy and creativity within the workplace.

As part of what Ernest Barker termed 'a general reaction against "the State" ',[51] the Guild Socialist 'position' was by 1915 established but hardly fixed. Originating with the medievalism of A.J. Penty and the recoil from Fabian collectivism of A.R. Orage, Guild Socialism was nurtured by the 'New Age' until 1914, when G.D.H. Cole, another Fabian defector, began to take personal charge of its further theoretical development. In *The World of Labour* (1913) Cole had envisaged a role for a 'purified' state, claiming that 'The State of the future will not be the centralised bureaucratic mechanism of today; it will be the alert and flexible instrument of the General Will.'[52] Yet as the war progressed and the state expanded to meet its needs, Cole became less confident as to the possibility of purification, and in the years 1914–20 he devoted much of his time to elaborating Guild Socialist doctrine in an ultimately unsuccessful attempt to revise the state out of existence. In some respects, Guild Socialism can be seen as a moderate home-grown Syndicalism, but this would be to deny its roots which were essentially middle class, and it is as a reaction to Fabianism and a putative Fabian state that it was likely to attract Russell; for although recent work on the Webbs emphasises their pluralism and humanism, these features were less apparent to their contemporaries, and the Webbian viewpoint tended to be equated with centralisation, bureaucracy, and philistinism.[53]

Throughout *Principles*, Russell's hostility towards Fabianism/state-Socialism is explicit, as is his promotion of a brand of Pluralism. Yet, while his argument for the relative autonomy of groups takes the form of a hazy Syndicalism tempered by a neutral state, and his demand that work should involve the creative capacity of individuals attacks the problem of alienation very much in the manner of William Morris, the book invites a Guild Socialist label rather than claims it, for the term is never used. Russell's advocacy of Pluralism, like his psycho-analytic interpretation of society, anticipates serious study, and groups as such, while having a stated importance, are in *Principles* peripheral in terms of analysis. It could, therefore, be argued that the Pluralist background to the book should be regarded as yet another strategic move on Russell's part, enabling him to put a positive gloss on his dissatisfaction with current political culture.

Strategic or not, group theory was seen by Russell as forming the 'least worse' basis for the political future,[54] and his views were bolstered by a programme of reading which can, to some extent, be traced in the footnotes of those books he published between 1917 and 1923. In *Political Ideals*, the first of these works, the lectures of *Principles* were remodelled for an audience with a broader class base, but published initially only in the United States. They are notable, however, for the first mention by Russell of the Guild Socialism of Orage and the 'New Age'. His next, *Roads to Freedom*, was commissioned by an American publisher and written in the weeks before his imprisonment in 1918. It is here that Russell expressly favours Guild Socialism and that he begins to argue within a specific intellectual framework, rather than indulging the prophetic tone of personal reflection in a political wilderness. By the time he wrote *The Prospects of Industrial Civilization* in 1923, Russell possessed a fairly comprehensive knowledge of Pluralist thought from Sorel to Laski, taking in each of Cole's annual reworkings of Guild Socialism. In relation to Russell's 'involvement', however, what must be kept in mind about Cole's project is that it was a political theory which rarely left the drawing-board, and though Russell at one time belonged to the short-lived National Guilds League, the very nature of Guild Socialism ensured that his was, in most respects, a position held rather than a membership demanding activity.

The one constant in Cole's work was his commitment to 'community' or 'fellowship', while Russell, despite important though sporadic use of an organic vocabulary in *Principles*, was too much a product of the Liberal intellectual tradition to do otherwise than foreground the individual in all his political writing. Yet, as we have seen, Russell was as much concerned with the problems posed by economic individualism as he was with state domination, as much with social atomism as with what Laski – in reference to what he regarded as the Hegelian state made manifest in 1914 – termed 'mystic monism'.[55] In short, Russell was becoming aware of the existence of two distinct Liberalisms: the one promoting the materialistic individualist, the other centred on the problem of the moral and aesthetic development of individuality.[56]

Although Russell's radicalism was beginning to extend beyond the limits of traditional Liberalism, it was developing in a manner which suggested an intensification of the radical temperament rather than a change of direction and was from the first more likely to end in a form of what he himself termed 'aristocratic anarchism' than in a devotion to the ends of state-Socialism. Thus the reaction to the state which Barker outlined in 1914 offered Russell an opportunity, enabling him to operate outside the confines of party politics yet at the same time to feel himself to be a part of a movement, and a movement moreover which was authentically progressive. The progress of the New Liberalism was a political phenomenon with which he had little sympathy but that had allowed no sensible alternative save reaction; therefore, it was obviously with some sense of relief that Russell was able to make the following assertion in *Principles*:

Under the influence of socialism, most liberal thought in recent years has been in favour of increasing the power of the State, but more or less hostile to the power of private property. On the other hand, syndicalism has been hostile both to the State and to private property. I believe that syndicalism is more nearly right than socialism in this respect, that both private property and the State, which are the two most powerful institutions of the modern world, have become harmful to life through excess of power, and that both are hastening the loss of vitality from which the civilized world increasingly suffers.[57]

In the opening chapter, Russell, in a statement which approaches the tautological, had advanced the opinion that 'The impulses embodied in the war are among those that make for death.'[58] Now he makes a direct connection between the growth in the power of the state and a cultural entropy which resembles Bergsonism in reverse. Instinct, as he remarks later, is 'the source of vitality', but only potentially so, and at present he sees it as being denied, or directed into 'life-denying' channels by a state devoted to the needs of industrialism and war. Russell's growing tendency to interpret the world in terms of psychology carries over into his brisk analysis of state sovereignty. 'The power of the state', he writes, 'is only limited internally by the fear of rebellion and externally by the fear of defeat in war'.[59] Russell's conception of the state as an institution rational only as to means, tyrannical, and of a size and complexity which renders individual protest futile, suggests a loss of belief in the steady development of representative democracy.

Despite his Whiggish inclinations, an adoption of the often apocalyptic tones of the anti-state movement represents a new departure for Russell. His experience of political power had always been fairly intimate, therefore his criticisms had previously been directed not merely at governments, but at individuals within governments, and individuals, moreover, with whom he was often personally acquainted. Russell's critique of the state, therefore, is rarely coterminous with his critique of government; it is closer to cultural than purely political criticism and is concerned with the state as a product or manifestation of the way men in general conduct their lives. However, rather than seeing the state in the manner of the Idealists as the embodiment of 'Reason', Russell is close to regarding it as being the expression of a pervasive pathological condition. This did not prevent him from considering the government of the day as being 'conspiratorial'; for, unlike Wallas, who – rather optimistically – envisaged the voter as keeping one step ahead of the political use of social psychology,[60] Russell continued to believe that political and other 'interested' parties successfully manipulated a highly suggestible populace. This combination threatened, in Russell's view, a 'tyranny of the majority', a hegemony of the alienated and repressed. In holding power, those who had accommodated themselves to materialism and industrialism were now in a position to ignore or repress the wishes of dissenting minorities:

> Even in a democracy, all questions except very few are decided by a small number of officials and eminent men; and even the few questions which are left to the popular vote are decided by a diffused mass psychology, not by individual initiative ... This state of things leads, not only in America but in all large States, to something of the weariness and discouragement that we associate with the Roman Empire. Modern States, as opposed to the small city States of ancient Greece or mediaeval Italy, leave little room for initiative and fail to develop in most men any sense of ability to control their political destinies.[61]

The drawing of dispiriting analogies (usually between the British and Roman Empires) warning that elephantiasis of the state meant inevitable decline, was becoming commonplace, as was the corresponding attempt to seek solace in the idea of the city state, both exercises being indicative of a sudden loss of faith in progress and a suspicion – new to many Liberals – that parts of the past might be considered preferable to much of the present and most of the future. Although Russell later dismisses such analogies as 'vague theories', his does tend to be a backward-looking, even occasionally nostalgic Liberalism; and yet he also felt himself to be confronted, not by ineluctable cultural decline, but by an entirely new phenomenon – the state suffering a loss of rational direction. At the same time, his use of such terms as 'mass psychology' and 'tribalism' does not appear to connect up with a view of the Edwardian citizen as being alienated, materialistic, entirely self-interested in his desires and thus atomistic. Yet the unity produced by war, apparently giving evidence of tribal loyalties, was, he believed, due to most people being 'dwarfed by knowledge of their own impotence'[62] and in danger of being 'organised into despair'.[63] People denied a community were, he argued, prone to seek release from a sterile self-hood: 'To very many men, the instinct of patriotism, when the war broke out, was the first instinct that had bridged the gulf, the first that had made them feel a really profound unity with others.'[64]

Russell connects tribal feeling with patriotism in its religious aspect, and offers it as an example of the way in which instincts necessary to a healthy community have suffered institutional repression only to exhibit morbid intensification in times of crisis. The treatment of patriotism offers the clearest indication of a shift in his views; for it is not merely a question of his making a careful distinction between the jingo and the high-minded patriot, but of refusing to attack the question on purely rationalist grounds. In discussing patriotism Russell talks of 'an element of worship, of willing sacrifice, of joyful merging of the individual life in the life of the nation ... Like all sincerely believed religions, it gives an outlook on life, based upon instinct but sublimating it, causing a devotion to an end greater than any personal end, but containing many personal ends as it were in solution.'[65] Russell had a habit of describing all 'mass' phenomena in terms of 'religion', and the word usually carries pejorative connotations. Patriotism is no exception, but as the only example to hand of an 'instinct towards unity', he had to give a qualified endorsement, though one which was effectively negated by his criticism of its level of intensity, lack of control, and absence of universality.

Russell's feelings in this area were uncertain; although fascinated by the social/psychological phenomenon of the 'group mind', he was himself incapable of direct experience in the matter, and while he at times regretted this, there is no doubt that he interpreted his incapacity as being indicative of superiority.[66] Though the concept of a 'group mind' was the object of much discussion among political and social thinkers at the time, and was, along with 'vitalist' philosophies, being incorporated into some social analysis, Russell in his professional capacity found all such notions noxious. In 1911 he had written of Bergson, 'He is the antithesis to me: he universalises the particular soul under the name of *élan vital* and loves instinct. Ugh!'[67] In 1916 his view had altered to the extent of recognising a possible social value in the idea of an 'instinct towards unity', but only in those circumstances where a low level of intensity admitted of control: 'All really profound sense of unity with others depends upon instinct, upon cooperation or agreement in some instinctive purpose

... Instinct alone can do this, but only when it is fruitful and sane and direct.'[68]

From this it is to be assumed that Russell's assessment of Syndicalism as being 'more nearly right than socialism' in regard to the state is intended to refer exclusively to the comparatively prosaic question of industrial democracy rather than be seen as endorsing a Sorelian promotion of the heroic virtues. While recognising the force of the Syndicalist critique of the state as an inherently class-based institution, Russell, like the early Cole, refused to regard it as being beyond redemption. Indeed, on occasion, he appears somewhat bemused that his eloquent attacks on the state as 'the most serious menace to liberty'[69] issue in a realisation that 'many of its functions must be extended rather than curtailed'.[70]

When Russell comes to consider specific questions, however, it is clear that his conception of the state's legitimate province differed from Mill's only in that it edged towards Green's. Aside from the preservation of internal order the state's responsibilities were for Russell strictly limited and largely confined to such areas as sanitation, scientific research, and education. As an unavoidable interference with liberty, 'Compulsory education comes under the same head as sanitation. The existence of ignorant masses in a population is a danger to the community; when a considerable percentage are illiterate, the whole machinery of government has to take account of the fact. Democracy in its modern form would be quite impossible in a nation where many men cannot read.'[71] When we consider the importance attached to education throughout the rest of the book, his argument here seems oddly out of keeping. It is not only that the 'Principle of Growth' is momentarily inoperative and that he appears to be approaching a negative conception of liberty, it also represents a complete change of tone, as though his eclecticism encompasses his own past thoughts on the subject which are conjured up, vocabulary intact, at the appropriate juncture in his argument. That Russell is able to interpolate with such ease – and this feature of his writing is perhaps even more striking when he touches on eugenics – tends to point up his inherent elitism, for it is scarcely coincidental that it is at just these junctures that the existence of the working class intrudes upon the text.

One of the most striking aspects of *Principles* is that in a text which gestures towards Syndicalism the working class makes such rare appearances and then only in those cases where Russell recites the benefits of industrial democracy or displays his fear of the genetically disabled. To draw a further comparison with Mill's *On Liberty*, it becomes apparent on reading *Principles* that the requirements for self-development proposed by Russell are scarcely met by his suggestions for institutional change – the reason for this being that both Mill and Russell expect and require only an effective proportion of the population to attain individuality or self-realisation. This leads on in both cases to a seeming lack of any deep belief in democracy, whether this be political or industrial, and a near obsession with the position and influence of the intellectual in society.

Aside from the perennial land question, Russell considers only one other area of possible state intervention – the diminishing of economic injustice, a problem he addresses in impeccably COS terms:

> I think justice, by itself, is, like law, too static to be made a supreme political principle: it does not, when it has been achieved, contain any seeds of new life or any impetus to development. For this reason, when we wish to remedy an injustice, it is important to consider whether, in so doing, we shall be destroying the incentive to some form of vigorous action which is on the whole useful to the community.[72]

Surveying his proposed extensions of the state's activity, Russell appears to be overtaken by anxiety, and remarks that 'If all these powers are allowed to the State, what becomes of the attempt to rescue individual liberty from its tyranny?'[73] Within the context of an anti-state argument and taking into account that he expects – in ostensibly 'progressive' but also in typically nineteenth-century style – a good deal from voluntary organisations, Russell is perhaps entitled to feel that he has been recklessly over-generous.

It is the case, however, that throughout *Principles* Russell's argument tends to operate on two sharply contrasting levels – the real and the ideal. When he deals – if only by implication – with society as it is (incorporating the old, the sick, the poor, and the generally inadequate), he adheres to a belief in negative liberty tempered by eugenics, sidestepping even those issues involved in Lloyd George's budget of 1909. His conception of the ideal 'Pluralist' community, on the other hand, appears to consist of a collection of Bloomsbury Groups – non-materialistic, but vigorous, enterprising, and creative – a society manned exclusively by middle-class self-developers in their prime. Though theoretically harmonious, the relations between such groups might on occasion prove awkward, therefore the state is retained to hold the ring. In fact, the real and the ideal in *Principles* meet on the basic issue of whether the state should be concerned with holding a ring or holding a net. Although ostensibly realistic in his expectations regarding the realisation of his ideal, Russell nevertheless makes few provisions for failure; therefore on the question of rings versus nets he is decidedly against the latter, believing that in the short term they destroyed initiative, while in the long term eugenics might possibly render them unnecessary. In this respect, his is a ruthlessly optimistic view of human nature.

Against the New Liberal belief that some supportive action by the state was required if people were to make the best of themselves, Russell argued – rather in the manner of Hilaire Belloc in *The Servile State* – that security within vast organisations was paid for in terms of boredom, lack of enterprise, political impotence, and eventually war. In commenting on the lot of those men who 'have no exceptional talents', Russell remarks:

> Their separate lives are unadventurous and dull. In the morning they go to the office or the plough, in the evening they return, tired and silent, to the sober monotony of wife and children. Believing that security is the supreme good, they have ensured against sickness and death, and have found an employment where they have little fear of dismissal and no hope of any great rise. But security, once achieved, brings a Nemesis of ennui.[74]

Russell's disdain for what he regards as the philistinism of the average existence could be given no clearer expression; yet it is upon such people – the cautious, thrifty, security-minded middle classes – that he places his hopes for cultural change and eugenic progress.

It is perhaps worth mentioning here that Russell's grasp of the Edwardian class structure was by no means certain. The variegated working-class life depicted in recent studies was entirely outside his experience, while his jaundiced view of lower-middle-class society clearly has its origins in the novels of Wells and Gissing. In surveying the masses from his aristocratic perspective therefore, he often failed to note cultural differences glaringly obvious to those on the ground. Russell's sociological insouciance is all too evident in his analysis, for his main concern is with what he later termed the 'best parts of the population', a loosely defined middle class ranging from the artisan to the professional man; and it is to this middle order he refers when he claims that, 'in the modern world generally, it is the decay of life which has promoted the religion of material goods; and the religion of material goods, in its turn, has hastened the decay of life on which it thrives'.[75] Russell's heavy reliance on the Lawrentian motif 'life' establishes him in that line of English cultural criticism which extends forward through the influence of Leavis and 'Scrutiny' and backward to Arnold.[76] Indeed, throughout *Principles*, the echoes of Mill and Arnold are unmistakable and perhaps to be expected from a writer just embarking upon a career so closely modelled on that of the nineteenth-century cultural critics.

As with Mill and Arnold, Russell's attitude towards the middle classes is somewhat ambivalent – they may not be all he would wish, but viewed 'realistically' Edwardian society provided no other substantial body of promising material from which to engender cultural renewal. Russell at this point is involved in a paradox, in that he sees a repressed social life linked to economic security as being characteristic of the middle class. At the same time, he uses precisely this prudent pattern of life as the criterion by which to judge social classes in eugenic terms – the growth in the 'shiftless', presumably less repressed, lower classes representing a decline of the race. It is not, therefore, merely a case of the 'wrong' half of society being repressed. Russell's value judgement makes it clear that along with Freud he acknowledged the importance of repression in the civilising process, but, again like Freud, he feared that it could be overdone, and there was a danger of the tedium produced by an 'overcivilised' life resulting at moments of crisis in a regression to barbarism.[77] As the absence of repression denied the very possibility of civilisation – its outward signs, economic failure, and excessive fertility being accepted as unmistakable indications of 'inferiority' in an almost racial sense – what was obviously required was a development *from* repression.

For Russell, therefore, self-development emerges from the solid middle-class base of character and self-discipline, and instinctual release, while vital to 'natural growth', must follow approved channels. The concept of natural growth might in this context be somewhat nebulous, but, as already indicated, the notion of self-development Russell embraced on exiting the moral gymnasium had its roots in nineteenth-century cultural criticism and was oriented towards Bloomsbury values. That in terms of a viable organic self-sufficiency Bloomsbury represents an entirely inadequate model of the good society poses something of a problem for Russell. While recognising that mere absence of repression is unacceptable, energies channelled in the direction of economic gain produce equally unsatisfactory results, leading to philistinism, poor genetic productivity, and war. On the other hand, Russell appears to conceive of no middle way between that obsession with wealth he sees as being characteristic of the middle class and the condition of the artist, implying that sublimation can take only one acceptable form.

Russell no doubt admired those young writers and artists he encountered at Bedford Square and Garsington who were struggling along on an inadequate allowance; but incorporated into an argument concerning the general availability of surplus wealth, this is redolent of P.G. Wodehouse. Russell clearly assumed that the plutocratic mentality was endemic in Edwardian England, but as regards the bulk of the population this was naturally a matter of aspiration towards surplus income rather than an indication of its existence.[78] Bloomsbury developed on the basis of the small private income, and Russell's argument in large sections of *Principles* is vitiated by his apparent inability to come to terms with the fact that not everyone was similarly situated. It is only when one accepts that the 'subject' of the book is the middle class, that such remarks as 'England, except among a small minority, is almost as much given over to the worship of money as America' and 'Men postpone marriage until they have an income enabling them to have as many rooms and servants in their house as they feel that their dignity requires'[79] begin to make some sense in relation to the whole.

While Russell is concerned that in their pursuit of money men 'mutilate their own natures', his optimism in regard to human nature was not of the order to be found in Marx's early writing or the Utopias of Morris. Russell is closer to the pessimism of Freud, in that he tends to divide Western society into three main groups: the truly civilised – those who successfully sublimate great energies into creative projects; the average man, who simulates a civilised existence and provides the orderly (though precarious) framework for civilisation; and the 'uncivilised' remainder. At the time, great energies were being channelled into the making of money, a fact Russell explains as being the result of a general confusion regarding the actual and the real in respect of desires: 'Under the influence of economics, a theory has grown up that what men desire is wealth; this theory has tended to verify itself, because people's actions are often determined by what they think they desire rather than by what they really desire.'[80] Russell here offers an illustration of the argument which claims that any theory of positive liberty leads inexorably to the inculcation of certain values as being more in keeping with men's 'real' nature than the values they actually hold.[81] He, though, would question the circumstances in which individuals came to hold their present values, and, without claiming to know what a 'fully realised' human nature might look like, argue that having strong preferences in the matter, he had as much right to engage in the marketing of ideologies as anyone else.

Russell judged a society's contribution to civilisation by the work of a few 'great' men, but the *nature* of their achievement he saw as being dependent on the values which obtained in the society they inhabited. Production of the plutocrat rather than the Renaissance man was, he believed, an indication that a society held to an erroneous conception of 'success' – an error that could only be rectified by a change in 'public opinion' which 'has a great influence in directing the activities of vigorous men. In America a millionaire is more respected than a great artist; this leads men who might become either the one or the other to choose to become millionaires. In Renaissance Italy great artists were more respected than millionaires, and the result was the opposite of what it is in America.'[82]

Currently the West was dominated by the values of a repressed, status-conscious middle class, values which revolved around respectability construed as possession:

> For this purpose men and women make great moral efforts, and show amazing powers of self control: but all their efforts and all their self control, being not used for any creative end, serve merely to dry up the well-spring of life within them, to make them feeble, listless, and trivial. It is not in such a soil that the passion which produces genius can be nourished. Men's souls have exchanged the wilderness for the drawing-room: they have become cramped and pretty and deformed, like Chinese women's feet. Even the horrors of war have hardly awakened them from the smug somnambulism of respectability. And it is chiefly the worship of money that has brought about this death-like slumber of all that makes men great.[83]

Russell's close association with T.S. Eliot during this period may have suggested the Prufrockian imagery; for it is precisely the lassitude exemplified by the Eliot/Prufrock persona which caused him such concern, and engendered his fear that this type of individual was becoming too enervated even to reproduce, thereby allowing itself to be swamped by a genetic pool productive of the 'uncivilised'.[84] The term 'uncivilised' is used by Russell (as by his contemporaries) to denote both the 'backward', 'inferior' races and also the lower classes among his fellow countrymen. Although including some reference to personal habits and an absence of European high culture, remarks such as 'not highly civilised'[85] can simply mean 'not very bright', hence what appears to refer to questions of nurture often relates instead to questions of nature.

Throughout *Principles*, Russell's positive proposals are aimed at producing a 'common ideal', a community of values based on vitality and creativity. How such a common ideal can, in the short term, encompass both the 'best' and the 'worst' sections of society when the division is made on genetic grounds is unclear. I am not here suggesting that Russell considered the entire working class as being stranded on a lower evolutionary plane, for he does acknowledge that some boys from the lower classes might have exceptional ability. Many of his ideas were, after all, worked out in conversation with D.H. Lawrence, and, although he regarded Lawrence as something of an exotic, Russell could not deny that he had reasonable claims to be considered both working class and, in certain moods, fairly civilised. In fact, their 'expected' roles were in some sense reversed, with Lawrence in his rather ingratiating letters to Ottoline Morrell and Cynthia Asquith speaking of a 'natural aristocracy' and being scornful of Russell's enthusiasm for 'democratic control and the educating of the artisan'.[86] It is the case, however, that Russell did tend to draw the line at the level of the artisan – the individual component of the Guild Socialist ideal – and this raises the question of just how far down the social scale the benefits of a Pluralist organisation of society were likely to be felt.

As compared with the detailed complexity of Cole's developed position, Russell's proposals in this area are decidedly vague and intentionally so. Pluralism was seen by him as an alternative to an increasingly 'organised' society, therefore there was little incentive for him to produce an elaborate blueprint. What he had in mind was a loose structure, which – if only at the level of laxity – would help restore to individuals the personal freedom they had enjoyed in pre-war England. Russell's notion of acceptable freedom was perhaps extravagant, but then he had been that much freer than most. Also, within the terms of his argument, it is possible that Russell did not wish to examine the issues raised by Pluralism too closely. Although familiar with Wallas's view that 'Syndicalism meant sectionalism', he refuses to dwell on such matters. Nevertheless, he does lack at this stage the enthusiasm of the true convert, believing only that, with the individual helpless against the state, vigorous group activity would seem (in prospect at least) to be a good thing.

Beginning on the basis that the state should be the sole recipient of rent, Russell envisages an expansion of the co-operative movement, with the unions gaining control of certain industries, and these competing with a restricted capitalism. All industrial organisations would be watched over by the state and be made responsive to the worker equipped with a vote. Russell was hopeful that industrial democracy, together with activity in local government, professional, and voluntary groups, would enable people to exercise greater control over their lives, while at the same time providing them with a sense of community. He also emphasised the importance of not divorcing work from the creative instinct, but, where the nature of the employment renders such a divorce inevitable, the individual should, he argued, be able to opt for increased leisure. Here we have the first mention of what was to become one of Russell's favourite notions – the vagabond's wage – which, like much else in the book, appears to be premised on full employment, an adequate income, and the prevalence of bohemian or at least intellectual values.

Russell's Pluralism is based on two assumptions: that most people wanted to take part in the organisation of social, political, and industrial life; and that most people – including those 'with no exceptional mental endowment' – could lead a more creative life (creative being used in a broad sense). If we accept Russell's assumptions, there remains the question of whether being 'creative' includes – for example – the running of industry. In respect of the capitalist, he thinks not; but on the other hand, a worker suitably involved in the democratic control of his industry could hardly expect an abundance of leisure in which to develop his creativity in areas not connected with work, especially as he would undoubtedly be active in other groups representative of his other interests. There is no avoiding the fact that one of the chief characteristics of a Pluralist conception of society is that it promotes and demands extensive participation on the part of the individual; and Russell dodges the issue when he considers a separation of function whereby one section of society (presumably those with no exceptional mental endowment) busy themselves with the management of industry while the rest are engaged in the preservation of civilisation.

There remains, however, a need for the producers of commodities to share the values of the producers of culture; they must esteem cultural achievement, otherwise they could come to regard it as being parasitical and threaten its existence. For this reason, therefore, Russell is not concerned solely with an elite possessing the essential requirements for the creative life (as later set down by Virginia Woolf), but also with groups like the miners who, as he remarked in the 'outline', 'earn good wages but are too uncivilized to enjoy them'.[87] Regarded in this way, any extension of the capacity for intellectual pleasure remains a programme with a dual purpose, springing from the same hope for the individual and fear of the masses which had caused Mill to depart from a strict utilitarianism. What Russell is attempting to do is to combine two ideals: that of eagerly pursuing one's various interests through membership of groups; and that of enjoying leisure and perhaps isolation in which to develop one's creative instincts. Of the two, the latter ideal is dominant, not merely because it more closely corresponds to Russell's own conception of the good life, but because he viewed the whole industrial process with some disdain.

In a manner common among intellectuals of various political persuasions throughout the nineteenth century, Russell attacks 'the belief in the importance of production' for its 'fanatical irrationality and ruthlessness',[88] and this forms the basis of his main criticism of Socialism – that it shares with capitalism a sordid materialism, making it incapable of promoting real social change. Although sympathetic to demands for social justice, Russell did not think 'justice alone is a sufficient principle upon which to base an economic reconstruction'.[89] He saw no improvement, save perhaps increased security, in the state becoming the main employer, and security is a word used in a pejorative sense throughout the book. A realised Socialism offered, in his view, only the tedium of a 'static utopia' which would do nothing to promote the creative instinct upon which all prospects for the future development of civilisation depended. As always, it is the 'life of the mind' for which Russell fears and thinks vulnerable to any obsession with economic justice, and this leads on to some characteristic special pleading on behalf of the intellectuals:

> It may be thought unjust that some men should have larger incomes or shorter hours of work than other men. But efficiency in mental work, including the work of education, certainly requires more comfort and longer periods of rest than are required for efficiency in physical work, if only because mental work is not physiologically wholesome. If this is not recognised, the life of the mind may suffer through short-sightedness even more than through deliberate hostility.[90]

Any community which encouraged the life of the mind could not in the nature of things approximate, like an achieved Socialism, a 'static or final system', but must instead be 'a framework for energy and initiative'.[91] Thus, while he thought the labour movement to be 'morally irresistible', he was not convinced that it would 'make for life'.[92] A society was to be judged, in Russell's opinion, more by its contribution to 'civilisation' than by its level of industrial growth or state pensions; and Pluralism appealed to him as being capable of providing a diverse, loosely structured, yet in some sense unified society, which would encourage creative enterprise and scorn security:

> The most important purpose that political institutions can achieve is to keep alive in individuals creativeness, vigour, vitality, and the joy of life. These things existed, for example, in Elizabethan England in a way in which they do not exist now. They stimulated adventure, poetry, music, fine architecture, and set going the whole movement out of which England's greatness has sprung in every direction in which England has been great. These things coexisted with injustice, but outweighed it, and made a national life more admirable than any that is likely to exist under socialism.[93]

Russell's purpose throughout is twofold – to arrest what he sees as being a decay in civilised life, and in so doing release those energies which might otherwise be directed into war. As he acknowledges, he is, to some extent, following the line of thought first taken by William James, but it is also useful to compare his views with those of Wallas when addressing the same problem: 'If the life of men is not to lose its savour, their powers must be exercised, and the secrets of their nature searched by a way of living more varied, more coloured, more exhilarating than that which most of the present English governing class seems to contemplate in its legislative plans for improving the condition of the governed.'[94]

Covering much of the same ground and reaching many of the same conclusions, Wallas's *The Great Society* is the text of the period which *Principles* most closely resembles. However, while both writers deal with the psychological dimension of politics from a Liberal perspective, in that they share a view that non-rational impulses can, in the right circumstances, result in 'reasonable' actions, there is a sense in which Wallas's style reflects the substance of the argument, whereas Russell's is more in line with the subject matter. The two books reflect their author's respective political experience, with Wallas's years of doubling up as local government candidate and social researcher providing a sound basis for analysis and anecdote, while Russell, whose own appearances on the hustings had been infrequent and inglorious, is compelled to fall back on abstractions and absolutes. Of the two, *Principles* is the more radical work, with *The Great Society* the more consistently democratic, and if it was Wallas's experience which allowed him to retain some faith in democracy, it is the abstract nature of Russell's work which is responsible for its radical flavour; the avoidance of any real engagement with political reality allowing his tendency towards excess to be given free rein. The differences are also generational: Wallas's devotion to the example of Darwin preventing any stylistic flirtation with the irrational, while in Russell style and content are at times combined to a surprising degree. Though a philosopher widely regarded as the stylistic antithesis of Nietzsche, he does produce, in his call for a 'transvaluation of values' towards the end of the book, certain Nietzschean effects:

> The first and greatest change that is required is to establish a morality of initiative, not a morality of submission, a morality of hope rather than fear, of things to be done rather than of things to be left undone. It is not the whole duty of man to slip through the world so as to escape the wrath of God. The world is *our* world, and it rests with us to make a heaven or a hell. The power is ours, and the kingdom and the glory would be ours also if we had courage and insight to create them. The religious life that we must seek would not be one of occasional solemnity and superstitious prohibition, it will not be sad or ascetic, it will concern itself little with rules of conduct. It will be inspired by a vision of what human life may be and will be happy with the joy of creation, living in a large free world of initiative and hope. It will love mankind, not for what they are to the outward eye, but for what imagination shows that they have it in them to become. It will not readily condemn, but it will give praise to positive achievement rather than negative sinlessness, to the joy of life, the quick affection, the creative insight, by which the world may grow young and beautiful and filled with vigour.[95]

That Russell did not love mankind in its present manifestation was evident, and his admiration was reserved for those few who had developed their potential in a manner he found reasonable. As with Mill, a call for diversity in the abstract is circumscribed by a personal fastidiousness. There are, in other words, limits set to individuality, for although in his chapter on education Russell emphasises his belief that human potential can only be intuited in the particular case, that it requires an act of imaginative insight and a 'reverence' for the unique individual, his aim was to rescue the middle-class child from its institutionalised indoctrination in the values of the market-place.[96] Moreover, while Russell regarded it as being essential that a child be encouraged to 'think for itself', it seems improbable that he seriously considered the possibility that independent thought would differ fundamentally from his own.

The limits which Russell set on diversity are most apparent in his advocacy of a programme of eugenic reform, a programme which seems to contradict any claim to a 'reverence' for the unique human life. Although the arguments which he employs in favour of eugenics remain much the same as those contained in his articles of 1907/8 and discussed in the previous chapter, their role in *Principles* needs to be clarified, and some distinction made between his beliefs and his expectations. Russell's chapter 'Marriage and the Population Question' is the most personal in the book and arguably the most self-serving; he did not obtain his divorce from Alys until 1920, and the delay was due entirely to his being appalled by the difficulties, expense, and hypocrisy involved. In the mean time, parenthood was for him being postponed indefinitely. Partly in consequence of this, his views on eugenics are not entirely in line with any organised opinion on the subject. The Fabians, for example, considered eugenics as a possible adjunct to social reform, particularly in regard to their scheme for the endowment of motherhood. The Eugenics Society, on the other hand, opposed any welfare intervention that might enable the unfit to flourish.[97]

The absence in *Principles* of provision for anything resembling a welfare state might suggest that Russell's position was identical with that of the Eugenics Society but for the fact that his main proposals centred on the endowment of motherhood. This was favoured by Russell for both personal and social reasons. Intelligent, emancipated women, those who, from his point of view, were 'most desirable' as potential mothers, were to the best of their abilities avoiding motherhood; therefore, he thought it logical and necessary that the moral and economic barriers to their having children should be speedily removed. Yet, while the Webbs, according to G.R. Searle, 'did not advocate that their child allowances be withheld from anyone – except the feeble-minded',[98] there is a strong suggestion that Russell was contemplating the exclusion of an extensive proportion of the population:

The only condition attached to State maintenance of the mother and the children should be that both parents are physically and mentally sound in all ways likely to affect the children. Those who are not sound should not be debarred from having children, but should continue, as at present, to bear the expense of children themselves ... There is no necessity to begin such a system all at once. It might be begun tentatively with certain exceptionally desirable sections of the community. It might then be extended gradually, with the experience of its working which had been derived from the first experiment. If the birth rate were very much increased, the eugenic conditions exacted might be made more strict.[99]

That Russell at this point should be so uncharacteristically keen that the state be equipped with rights to intrude massively into private life suggests that he himself expected no bureaucratic attention, save perhaps a certificate marked 'highly desirable'. However, as a programme of negative eugenics, these proposals would seem to be seriously flawed, since it would appear pointless to discourage by economic means precisely those individuals who reproduced without consideration of economics, and the inevitable result would be a polarised society rather than the harmonious community he desired. Russell does – albeit reluctantly – conclude that his proposals were unlikely to be implemented, though he thought the Germans might well go ahead with something similar, thus assuring themselves of European hegemony. In essence, this remained Russell's position throughout his life – that eugenics was 'rational' but not politically acceptable; though, as the century progressed and German practice conformed to some extent with his predictions, the opportunities for his raising the issue became fewer.

Regardless of his expectations, Russell's eugenic beliefs do tend to confirm his political distance from the 'progressive parties', for, as Searle argues, the opposition to eugenics came in the main from 'the type of reform-minded professional who moved freely between the spheres of academia, journalism and party politics – a type especially prominent in both the Fabian Society and in "New Liberal" circles'.[100] Eugenics, in Searle's view, 'appealed less to "new" professionals than to the type of family which figures in Noel Annan's discussion of the Victorian intellectual elite. This would fit in with the emphasis placed in eugenical propaganda on genealogy, on tracing the pedigrees of "eminent" families with a long honourable tradition of professional service.'[101] In this instance, Russell would appear to conform to type, declaring that,

Whatever may be thought of genius, there can be no doubt that intelligence, whether through heredity or through education, tends to run in families, and that the decay of the families in which it is common must lower the mental standard of the population. It seems unquestionable that if our economic system and our moral standards remain unchanged, there will be, in the next two or three generations, a rapid change for the worse in the character of the population in all civilized communities, and an actual diminution of numbers in the most civilized.[102]

It is worth noting that Russell here regards the early cultural conditioning in the 'best' families as being at least as important as heredity in producing 'intelligence'. This offers a further indication that for all his quirkiness and increasing alienation, his own values (even when broadened by his contact with Bloomsbury) remained those of the essentially unalienated intellectual aristocracy – values which assert that 'real' intelligence manifests itself only in those areas of achievement typified by academic brilliance, pure science, and artistic creativity. Russell's acceptance of these values helps to clarify his political stance in *Principles*; for his claims to radicalism carry all the ambiguity of the Romantic tradition in its reaction to industrial progress, a radicalism selective in its modernity but categoric in its disavowal of the reactionary.

At this point what must be emphasised is how in a work addressed to the young 'advanced' intellectual, aimed at transforming what he took to be the entrenched and dominant value system of the bourgeoisie, Russell appears to exemplify that aristocratic conception of the civilised life which, according to Martin Wiener, was internalised by the professional classes throughout the late nineteenth century, retaining its hegemony over English elite culture well into the twentieth.[103] As we have seen, Russell was hostile to the assumption that society, whether it be capitalist or socialist, must concern itself above all else with industrial growth: an assumption grounded in the belief that the quality of life could only be improved by the increased production and consumption of material goods. While he concedes that 'Economic organisations, in the pursuit of efficiency, grow larger and larger, and there is no possibility of reversing this process',[104] he rejects the idea that technological progress necessarily advances civilisation. However, the disdain for the 'industrial spirit' which Wiener argues was so prevalent in English cultural life from the 1850s onwards, and which Russell so obviously shares, was – in his case at least – engendered less by a desire to preserve the gentlemanly ideal than by a desire to preserve the 'idea of the clerisy'.

Arguing along similar lines to Green and Bosanquet, Russell insisted that an organic society was only possible if the goals of self-realisation were intrinsically non-competitive.[105] Yet, running counter to all Russell has to say in favour of a harmonious society based on shared cultural and spiritual values is his persistent foregrounding of the middle classes, and in this, as in other ways, *Principles* tends to echo its

Victorian antecedents (particularly Mill's *On Liberty* and Arnold's *Culture and Anarchy*). Thus, for all its gestures towards modernity in the use it makes of social psychology and eugenics, it is important to stress the fact that *Principles* rarely transcends its influences, offering in the end a conception of a realised human nature which is given abstract expression in essentially Arnoldian terms. Russell would no doubt have agreed with Arnold that 'culture has one great passion, the passion for sweetness and light. It has one even yet greater! – the passion for making them *prevail*',[106] and as an ideal, his notion of a realised human nature does at least encompass the middle order of society. Yet in terms of reality, he appears (as did Arnold) to settle for much less, and although he does at one point deny the necessity of an 'aristocratic civilization', what emerges is a reliance on something resembling a Coleridgean clerisy – perhaps not an 'endowed class' in the original sense of the term, but certainly one whose position in society allowed for independent thought.[107]

As a means of preserving cultural values under threat from an expanding and potentially uncaring democracy, the idea of the clerisy was taken up by several nineteenth-century writers, including Mill and Arnold. Russell, by pinning his hopes on a relatively apolitical intellectual elite whose main preoccupations centred on art and literature, locates himself firmly within this tradition. This is not to say that Russell was already having second thoughts regarding his arguments for political reorganisation, but that his optimism seems finally dependent on the expansion of a minority culture. Writing to a friend towards the end of his lecture series, he remarks:

> As a matter of fact, my lectures are a great success – they are a rallying ground for the intellectuals, who are coming daily more to my way of thinking not only as regards the war but also as regards general politics. All sorts of literary and artistic people who formerly despised politics are being driven to action, as they were in France by the Dreyfus case. In the long run, their action will have a profound effect. It is primarily to them that I am speaking.[108]

In his final lecture, Russell can assume that he is preaching to the converted, a gathering of the faithful who have stuck it out through eight winter evenings and are now ready to take on the burdens of the elect. Rejecting 'any of the ordinary methods of politics',[109] Russell expects much from the young intellectuals, those who can yet attain to the 'integration' of their 'individual lives' if they can but avoid that 'kind of defeat' which 'most professions' inflict upon a man at the 'very outset'.[110] Casting his audience in the role of Arnold's 'chosen few' or 'the children of light', Russell takes on evangelical tones as he sketches out their tasks and responsibilities:

Those who are to begin the regeneration of the world must face loneliness, opposition, poverty, obloquy. They must be able to live by truth and love, with a rational unconquerable hope; they must be honest and wise, fearless, and guided by a consistent purpose. A body of men and women so inspired will conquer – first the difficulties and perplexities of their individual lives, then, in time, though perhaps only in a long time, the outer world. Wisdom and hope are what the world needs; and though it fights against them, it gives its respect to them in the end.[111]

Offering lectures grounded in social psychology, it would in the circumstances be odd were Russell not alert to the suggestibility of his own audience; nevertheless, he seems to have accepted at face value an adulation consequent upon the general hysteria and interpreted Bloomsbury's evanescent enthusiasm as commitment. As the 'ideal type' of Bloomsbury intellectual, Lytton Strachey was a duly appreciative member of the audience:

Bertie's lectures help one. They are a wonderful solace and refreshment. One hangs upon his words, and looks forward to them from week to week, and I can't bear the idea of missing one – I dragged myself to that ghastly Caxton Hall yesterday, though I was rather nearer the grave than usual, and it was well worth it. It is splendid the way he sticks at nothing – Governments, religions, laws, property, even Good Form itself – down they go like ninepins – it is a charming sight![112]

For Strachey – whose interest in industrial democracy one suspects was minimal – Russell's ideas had a novelty which perhaps says something about the group's insularity. It was left to Virginia Woolf to maintain the 'orthodox' attitude towards the prophetic personality – one of detached irony: 'Bertie, according to Bob Trevelyan who lunched here, takes his lectures very seriously, and thinks he's going to found new civilisations ...',[113] 'Bertie lectures on Tuesdays, and thinks to issue a new constitution, so we are told, with the help of young Cambridge.'[114] After reading the published work in late December, she commented, 'I have just finished Bertie upon Reconstruction with a melancholy feeling that this sort of lecturing does me no good, but only exasperates me with the rest of the world. However, others say they think it does good – to the working classes perhaps.'[115]

On one level Bloomsbury values were intrinsically elitist and did not easily lend themselves to incorporation in radical programmes of reform – a fact responsible for many of the inconsistencies in *Principles*. Its ideal society was to some degree self-enclosed – a superior enclave immune from a surrounding philistinism. In many ways, this is how Russell himself came to regard Bloomsbury, and it is probable that his disappointment at this time gave a certain edge to his later remarks: 'The generation of Keynes and Lytton did not seek to preserve any kinship with the Philistine. They aimed rather at a life of retirement among fine shades and nice feelings, and conceived of the good as consisting in the passionate mutual admirations of a clique of the elite.'[116] Yet this is scarcely a satisfying assessment of a group which contained both Leonard Woolf and Maynard Keynes.

In fact, it was not Russell's faith in Bloomsbury which was misplaced, but his faith in the young; for the dominant values of the post-war generation were those he himself had touched upon when attacking 'good form' and the Eton/Oxford tradition:

> The evils of 'good form' arise from two sources: its perfect assurance, and its belief that correct manners are more to be desired than intellect, or artistic creation, or vital energy, or any of the other sources of progress in the world. Perfect assurance by itself is enough to destroy all mental progress in those who have it. And when it is combined with contempt for the angularities and awkwardnesses that are almost invariably associated with great mental power, it becomes a source of destruction to all who come into contact with it. 'Good form' is itself dead and incapable of growth and by its attitude to those who are without it it spreads its own death to many who might otherwise have life. The harm which it has done to well-to-do Englishmen, and to men whose abilities have led the well-to-do to notice them, is incalculable.[117]

The impact of the Eton/Oxford generation of the 1920s upon English cultural life has been described by W.H. Auden in his essay 'As It Seemed to Us' in which he compares Leonard Woolf's Cambridge with Evelyn Waugh's Oxford. In Auden's view, 'the mental atmosphere of Oxford in this century does not seem to have encouraged gurus. It has produced dons whose wit and manner of speaking admiring undergraduates have tried to imitate, but their influence has been social and personal rather than intellectual; it has produced no equivalent of Dr Leavis.'[118]

While Russell's own attempt at reviving the Arnoldian project was hardly purposeful, and all aspirations in this direction effectively negated by the dandyism of the 1920s, the idea of a clerisy was taken up again with notable success at Cambridge in the 1930s under the direction of the 'angular and awkward' F.R. Leavis. In his style of political engagement Russell was perhaps closer to the 'Scrutiny' group than to the Bloomsbury Group, yet he shared with both an ineradicable belief that cultural values (like Liberal values) could only be preserved by an active and effective elite.

CHAPTER 6

Anarchist tendencies

Of the reception given to *Principles of Social Reconstruction* Russell later remarked, 'To my surprise, it had an immediate success. I had written it with no expectations of its being read, merely as a profession of faith, but it brought me in a great deal of money, and laid the foundation for all my future earnings.'[1] His initial expectations may have been modest, but the response rapidly overcame this uncharacteristic diffidence, producing instead a desire that he might extend his influence beyond the confines of Caxton Hall. He did not, however, expect a 'popular' success; indeed, his comments at the time suggest that he considered 'popularity' and influence as being scarcely compatible:

> My ambitions are more vast and less immediate than my friends' ambitions for me. I don't care for the applause one gets by saying what others are thinking; I want actually to *change* people's thoughts. Power over people's minds is the main personal desire of my life; and this sort of power is not acquired by saying popular things. In philosophy, when I was young, my views were as unpopular and strange as they could be; yet I have had a very great measure of success. Now I have started on a new career, and if I live and keep my faculties, I shall probably be equally successful ... In any large undertaking, there are rough times to go through, and of course success may not come till after one is dead – but those things don't matter if one is in earnest. I have something important to say on the philosophy of life and politics, something appropriate to the time.[2]

The confidence of youth gained, his putative clerisy briefed, Russell now felt himself prepared to engage with the 'rough times', for, as an intellectual taking on the role of cultural critic, he recognised his duty to be the traditional one of speaking unpalatable truths. In the short term, therefore, he could not count himself satisfied until his ideas were being widely contested. Russell's notion of the role of the intellectual was, like Mill's, dependent on an exaggerated belief in the power of ideas; and although nominally a relativist, he continued to assume, along with Mill, that, once in circulation, those ideas which have a closer approximation to 'truth' would eventually prevail over the opposition.[3] In assuming that the reception of his social philosophy would parallel that given to his technical philosophy, Russell anticipates making a major contribution to the subject, one intended to engender serious debate; and in so doing, he offers further evidence that at this time his aim was to replicate Mill's achievement. As an ambition this was perhaps already anachronistic, though given Russell's energy and ability not necessarily unrealistic; however, between his delivery of the final lecture in the series on 7 March 1916 and their publication in book form in the following November, notoriety supervened.

Following the introduction in January 1916 of compulsory military service for all unmarried men between the ages of eighteen and forty, the problems connected with being a pacifist grew serious and led Russell to become increasingly active as an associate member of the No Conscription Fellowship (NCF). His social standing was useful to the organisation, as was his journalistic ability; nevertheless, his professional reputation hardly amounted to fame, and he was practically unknown to the general public. His personal details, though, were sufficiently odd as to promise excellent copy, and his prosecution in the *Everett* case[4] was eagerly exploited by his colleagues, who were in turn ably assisted by the government. In consequence, those who shared the view Lord Newton expressed in Cabinet, that Russell was 'The most mischievous crank in the country',[5] became increasingly numerous. Achieving status as a notable crank brought its difficulties, and Russell was in short order deprived of his passport, Cambridge lectureship, and some of his freedom; for, although in this instance he avoided imprisonment, he was held by the government to be a threat to national security and banned from certain 'sensitive' areas of the country, particularly coastal regions – a decision which indicates that the 'invasion literature' produced by writers as disparate as Erskine Childers and P.G. Wodehouse had an influence beyond the confines of the 'popular' imagination.

Principles, then, acquired an author about whom the public already held opinions, and aside from a handful of left-of-centre journals, was received and reviewed as though it were a novel likely to be denounced by the higher clergy. This helped sales and delighted Russell's publisher Unwin who printed the *Spectator*'s verdict that it was a 'thoroughly mischievous book' on the dustjacket of the second edition. The reception did not entirely dismay Russell, who was by now practically bereft of income and thus more tolerant of instant success in matters ideological; but it ensured distortion, as reviewers diligently checking for traitorous remarks were not surprised to discover that the author was similarly unsound on such topics as inherited wealth and sexual relations. *The Nation*, *New Age*, and *New Statesman* produced sober assessments, the latter, predictably aggrieved over Russell's scant treatment of local government, commenting, 'No citizen of Bradford or Leicester would recognise Mr Russell's "State", the governmental organisation in which he lives and moves.'[6]

The *New Statesman* was also one of the first to voice what became a widely held view of Russell's excursions into social thought: that in a period of rapid professionalisation his work in this area appeared amateurish. Determined to see in *Principles* an attempt to do something best left to the Fabian Research Department, the *New Statesman* critic took the view that social analysts, like Cambridge philosophers, had claim to a certain technical competence and that it was in some sense discourteous of Russell to insist on severely professional standards in his own discipline and then make ill-judged ventures into other areas of thought. Despite the Fabian bias, the point is a valid one, for, in his social and cultural criticism, Russell falls naturally into a reliance on intellectual integrity and stylistic clarity, reassuming a stance which, in Noel Annan's view, typified the intellectual aristocracy:

> Their good manners appeared in their prose. At its worst it was lucid and free from scholarly jargon; and time and again they produced works of surpassing literary merit. They wrote with a sense of form, of drama, of the possibilities of language and they wrote not for a scholarly clique but for the intelligent public at large whom they addressed confident that they would be understood.[7]

Although Annan regards these traits in a positive light, there was by Russell's time already a case for arguing that in some areas they tended to preclude achievement at the highest level. Therefore, while this attitude could be said to have guaranteed the quality of Russell's work in social philosophy, making it difficult for him to write genuinely 'popular' books, and at the same time ensured that the work of the second 'career', being reasonably accessible, was reasonably successful, it from the first made it highly unlikely that he would emulate Mill, Sidgwick, and other Victorians in achieving parallel performance and indeed influence in differing fields. However, while the professional and popular reception of *Principles* combined to further reduce Russell's chances of being treated with any great seriousness as a social thinker, he had already shifted his ground by writing a series of lectures intended for a predominantly working-class audience.

This project had been suggested by Clifford Allen, following Russell's evident enjoyment in dealing with the crowds during his NCF propaganda tour of Wales in July. The original intention was to offer the lectures at numerous venues and then publish in the hope of obtaining a large readership: in the event, the banning order ensured that he spoke in only two cities, Manchester and Birmingham, and publication in England under the title *Political Ideals* was delayed until 1963.

As a true indication of Russell's development, *Political Ideals* is difficult to assess because, although ostensibly a more 'radical' version of *Principles*, it is not at all clear whether its radicalism emerges from conviction or concession. It depends to some degree on how we interpret the word 'popular', for in matters of style and reference Russell's attempts at simplification are recognisable but scarcely consistent; his 'good manners' are, however, clearly in evidence when estimating attention span – the lectures being approximately one half the length of those addressed to a Bloomsbury audience. Although conceived with the aim of providing him with an income, the work was approached with enthusiasm, even idealism, and he saw his main purpose as being educational. On balance Russell did not underestimate the intellectual level of his intended audience, expecting it to be representative of a working-class elite; but with regard to content there are changes in his position which can be explained in two ways: either he was anxious not to offend his listeners, or, being compelled to examine his ideas in a new context, had actually altered his opinion on some issues.

All of Russell's political writing up to this point had been in lecture form, and had, therefore, been written with an awareness of the likely ideological persuasion of his immediate audience. However, his previous work had demanded little constraint, for although he was never a convinced and enthusiastic Fabian or a member of Bloomsbury, he could, when writing *German Social Democracy* and *Principles*, feel at least *intellectually* at ease with the particular group he was addressing. In *Political Ideals* on the other hand, as he assumes in his audience a preference for some variety of state-Socialism, he is compelled to employ a cautionary tone which he balances with a heavily ironic and at times hostile assessment of capitalism. Seeking to inculcate an appreciation of the middle ground, Russell stresses the connection between radical individualism and the aims of Pluralism, bringing the latter sharply into focus, rather than employing it to suggest a functional background to the organic ideal as he had done in *Principles*. Whereas *Principles* had been almost Hegelian in its reification of 'civilisation', with a desire for a historically significant culture taking precedence over the claims of the mundane life, Russell shifts the emphasis in *Political Ideals* back to the Liberal orthodoxy of a methodological individualism.

While he retains the central argument of *Principles*, it is incorporated in the further development of his strategic Liberalism. Up to 1914 Russell had distrusted any approach towards Socialism while remaining tolerant of the Liberal state. In *Principles* he had opposed the state as such, holding that its very size ensured that it would always elude real democratic control, and was thus a clumsy apparatus for servicing the variety of human needs. In *Political Ideals*, the point that a Socialist state would, from most viewpoints, appear indistinguishable from a capitalist state is elaborated upon, with greater emphasis being placed on the growth of bureaucracy. In effect, Russell has reversed the stance taken in *German Social Democracy*; for it is no longer so much a question of Socialism perverting the true aims of the state, but of the state perverting the true aims of Socialism. Little of this is explicit, for Russell, still wary of the label Socialist, is only willing to indicate that there exist interpretations of the creed with which he might identify, by emphasising that it is 'state' Socialism to which he takes exception and by suggesting that even this – if only by virtue of its good intentions – is preferable to 'capitalism and the wage system'.

Attempts to define the aims of Socialism in Liberal terms were of course nothing new, but whereas the New Liberal theorists had sought to justify a Collectivist interpretation of Liberalism, Russell changes the emphasis, seeking a libertarian interpretation of Socialism. Part of his strategy is to isolate the idea of liberty as an absolute value in an effort to preclude its easy association with property-holding and the history of Liberalism, feeling that the latter – at least in the context of political argument – was now inseparable from the history of capitalism: 'Under the influence of socialism, even progressive opinion, in recent years, has been hostile to individual liberty. Liberty is associated, in the minds of reformers, with laissez-faire, the Manchester School, and the exploitation of women and children which resulted from what was euphemistically called "free competition".'[8]

Russell's main concession to Collectivist arguments (and to a working-class audience) is his acknowledgement of the need for security. While he had in *Principles* condemned the desire for security, remarking only that any industrial system should provide 'a tolerable existence for producers',[9] in *Political Ideals* at the same point, he substitutes 'security against destitution'.[10] Russell rationalises this requirement as follows, 'Fear of destitution is not a motive out of which a free creative life can grow, yet it is the chief motive which inspires the daily work of most wage-earners.'[11] He does, however, go on to make it clear that security provides only the basis of a good society and should not be regarded as the final aim of political endeavour: 'Security alone might produce a smug and stationary society; it demands creativeness as its counterpart, in order to keep alive the adventure and interest of life, and the movement towards perpetually new and better things.'[12]

Although Russell does for the first time display some interest in welfare organisations, he offers no indication of how such measures are to be instituted; his main concern remains with the able-bodied, those willing to work yet suffering through a lack of industrial retraining – the only security required here being the security of employment:

> It will be said that men will not work well if the fear of dismissal does not spur them on. I think it is only a small percentage of whom this would be true at present. And those of whom it would be true might easily become industrious if they were given more congenial work or a wiser training. The residue who cannot be coaxed into industry by any such methods are probably to be regarded as pathological cases, requiring medical rather than penal treatment.[13]

The Webbs in their Minority Report of 1908 had proposed detention colonies for those individuals shown to be stubbornly workshy,[14] and Russell here as in other places in the book is intent on demonstrating that, as compared with a Fabian desire to regulate and control, his position is more human and thus, when the occasion demands, more humane. Just what medical treatment Russell had in mind is unclear, as the science of dealing with the psychological 'abnormalities' of social misfits was barely in its infancy. It would seem, though, that as a method of 'curing' the residue, who have forfeited their right to liberty, this represents no substantial improvement upon the Webbs' proposals and reveals a similar tendency to drift towards authoritarian conclusions when confronted by problems relating to the lower classes.

To be fair to Russell, it would be unreasonable to expect from him a text consistent in its avoidance of previous assumptions, assumptions which after all still permeated much progressive opinion, and he does in *Political Ideals* make a conscious effort to apply his Liberal principles to previously ignored sections of society – even backtracking on the question of eugenics. 'It is obvious', he writes, 'that men and women would not tolerate having their wives or husbands selected by the state, whatever eugenists might have to say in favour of such a plan. In this it seems clear that ordinary public opinion is in the right, not because people choose wisely, but because any choice of their own is better than a forced marriage.'[15]

Yet while Russell is now willing to allow individuals to choose unwisely on this issue, he is less tolerant of unreasonable desires in other areas: the prime example being the hardening of his attitude towards capitalism. In *Principles* Russell had proposed what amounted to a mixed economy, believing that 'the total abolition of private capitalistic enterprise, which is demanded by Marxian socialism, seems scarcely necessary ... provided the sphere of capitalism is restricted, and a large proportion of the population are rescued from its dominion, there is no reason to wish it wholly abolished'.[16] Addressing the same question in *Political Ideals*, his own rhetoric takes on a somewhat 'Marxian' aspect: 'Capitalism and the wage system must be abolished; they are twin monsters which are eating up the life of the world.'[17] In this manner Russell establishes his radical credentials, offering clear evidence that his critical attitude towards the 'Socialist' alternative could scarcely be attributable to any lingering affection for society in its present form. In some ways, Russell considered the Socialists as being not radical enough, and the ease with which the Labour Party had adjusted to the needs of a capitalist state during war time had only confirmed his suspicion that it lacked the vision necessary to transform society. Socialism, he felt, displayed little inclination to curb the possessive instinct and the expansion of materialist desires, offering only a vast bureaucracy designed to ensure that such desires were satisfied according to the requirements of justice.

Russell's attack on the capitalist 'control' of industry remains largely within the Romantic tradition, expressing a belief that the whole enterprise was beginning to take on a monstrous life of its own, eroding men's values and destroying the environment. Yet this moral, ecological/aesthetic response (perhaps to be expected in someone recently exposed to the Lawrentian value system) co-existed with the fact that

Russell, while he believed that large-scale industrial organisation should not be allowed to expand according to some supposed inner logic without regard to human requirements, also recognised its necessity and sought ways to contain the damage – unlike Lawrence himself who merely sought environments as yet undamaged. Ideally, Russell would have preferred industrial production to be maintained on the same basis as the sewage system, and be regarded in a similar way, as an essential but profoundly uninteresting aspect of social life. His conviction that industrial life was incapable of being made interesting led him to place all his emphasis on leisure rather than creativity within the place of work.

Lacking enthusiasm for the niceties of industrial organisation himself, Russell had recourse to the work of an enthusiast, and nearly all his arguments in this area closely follow those Cole had been developing in a series of articles since 1914 and which formed the basis of his book, *Self-Government in Industry* (1917). Whereas Russell found Lawrence's growing paranoia depressing, and the Fabian/New Liberal deliberations uninspiring, Cole, in combining some recognition of instinctual need with a rational basis for action, individual freedom with organisation, and idealism with efficiency, seemed to provide grounds for a balanced optimism when addressing the problem of social change.

In *Self-Government in Industry* Cole attempts to achieve a synthesis of competing 'Socialisms', remarking that, 'Syndicalism is the infirmity of noble minds: Collectivism is at best only the sordid dream of a business man with a conscience. Fortunately, we have not to choose between these two: for in the Guild idea Socialism and Syndicalism are reconciled.'[18] At the same time he was firmly, though tactfully, disengaging the Guild movement from its medievalist adherents such as Penty, arguing, 'first, that a national system of industrial organisation is essential, and secondly that such a national system need not mean bureaucracy and centralisation'.[19] For Cole, the state should be regarded as an adaptable institution, and he compares its present capitalist form with how it might be under the Fabians and what it should be when incorporated into a Guild Socialist system. While the capitalist state suppressed freedom in order to exploit the individual, the Fabians were, he believed, intent on managing the individual in accordance with what they calculated to be his own best interests – neither allowed nor would allow people to attain independence. Cole's main aim was to establish through the relatively autonomous National

Guilds a participatory democracy in the industrial sphere, confident that this would in turn encourage greater democratic participation in the political sphere – the 'purified state' still organised on parliamentary lines. Industrial democracy could not, in Cole's opinion, restrict itself to the 'workshop unit' – this was merely the unrealisable ideal of the medievalists, and his only comfort for the craftsman is offered in the remark, 'He is now a voice crying in the wilderness; we claim that if we had our way he would at least be able to cry in a more promising place.'[20]

Russell appears to endorse this view, commenting, 'Vast organisations are an inevitable element in modern life, and it is useless to aim at their abolition, as has been done by some reformers, for instance, William Morris.'[21] Yet while Russell recites Cole's argument uncritically, even dutifully, when attacking the wage system, bureaucracy, and nationalisation, he is far from sharing Cole's certainty that a true democracy would, as a matter of course, generate acceptable ideals. *Self-Government in Industry* was, in Cole's words: 'a personal appeal to all who still hold dear the ideal of personal freedom, and watch with mistrust the growing domination of Prussian ideas in this country'.[22] There is, though, a sense in which Cole's development of the notion of 'National Guilds' was a concession to the logic of 'nationalisation' and the calls for 'efficiency'. Russell on the other hand was more concerned with the elaboration of ends than the improvement of means, and while he paid lip service to the necessity of 'vast organisations' his own conception of Pluralism was becoming increasingly atomistic – what he mainly had in mind was small vociferous groups, jealous of their liberties.

Distrustful of the monolithic state and temperamentally averse to 'commonplace people in authority',[23] Russell's advocacy of Pluralism is similar in intention to Mill's attempt to preserve an effective role for the critical intellectual by the device of plural voting. Like Mill, Russell sought to cultivate public opinion in order to give power to knowledge or, as he might have preferred it, to wisdom. Impatient of a world 'where honour and power and respect are given to wealth rather than to wisdom',[24] Russell, unwilling to consider a world where they are not given at all, attempts to further his somewhat Platonic ambitions in *Political Ideals* by pressing the claims of the intellectually exceptional individual who, being inevitably at odds with authority, is perforce a 'radical' – 'innovators', he remarks, 'are almost always, to some extent, Anarchists'.[25] Russell's stance here is quintessentially Millian, as he emphasises the necessity of providing conditions in which the exceptional, even the eccentric, can flourish: 'In every life, a part is governed by the community, and a part by private initiative. The part governed by private initiative is greatest in the most important individuals, such as men of genius and creative thinkers. This part ought only to be restricted when it is predatory; otherwise, everything ought to be done to make it as great and as vigorous as possible.'[26]

While Cole's argument for a participatory democracy stemmed from a firm belief in 'the natural genius of the people', Russell, like Mill before him, tended to hedge his bets. Although in *Representative Government* Mill expressed a faith in the beneficial effects of political participation, the electoral system he proposed was rigged in favour of the party of the intellectuals. Russell, though remaining convinced that initiative, innovation, and the elaboration of ideals necessary for progress all emanated from a gifted minority, sensed that in a society where power was diffused, the intellectuals would require little more than an even chance.

Russell's differences with Cole emerge in more explicit form in *Roads to Freedom* (1918), where he argues that, though imperfect, Guild Socialism must be accepted as a practicable second best to an ideal Anarchist society. During this period, there is an inevitability about Russell's political development which makes it seem unlikely that the Russian revolution – which occurred between the writing of the two books – had any significant impact upon his ideas, though he did – in keeping with many others – become temporarily revolutionary during the summer months of 1917, writing to Ottoline Morrell that 'The Russians have really put a new spirit into the world, and it is going to be worthwhile to be alive.'[27] Russell's participation in the United Socialist Council's conference in Leeds on 3 June – intended in some largely undefined way to support the Russian revolution and promote the British – marked one of the few moments in his life when he was caught up emotionally in a popular enthusiasm.

As the revolutionary fervour diminished, Russell was left with his increasingly dispiriting involvement in the NCF – an involvement which ended with the by now unappetising martyrdom of a jail sentence, fortuitously incurred by a piece of careless writing.[28] It was in this mood that Russell came to write *Roads to Freedom* – poised to contemplate the power of the state from the vantage point of a prison cell, and compelled by a publisher's advance to address the writings of other aristocrats who had themselves been enlightened by just such an experience. Always prone to romanticise his situation, and with his radical individualism already tending in the direction of Anarchism, it is scarcely surprising that Russell should come to adopt this position as an ideal.

According to one critic, 'The anarchists say much more clearly than liberals like Tocqueville and Mill (who shared their elitism), that authority blessed by numbers was far less tractable than authority consecrated by papal benediction and upheld by royalty.'[29] Although this remark is backed up by a quotation from the extreme individualist Stirner, and might thus be thought an exaggeration in terms of the central tradition, there is little doubt that for Russell the attraction of Anarchism was precisely this – that it so clearly articulated the threat of majoritarian authority.

It is undeniable that the rule of a majority may be almost as hostile to freedom as the rule of a minority: the divine right of majorities is a dogma as little possessed of absolute truth as any other. A strong democratic State may easily be led into oppression of its best citizens, namely those whose independence of mind would make them a force for progress. Experience of democratic parliamentary government has shown that it falls very far short of what was expected of it by early Socialists, and the Anarchist revolt against it is not surprising.[30]

Russell's 'best citizens' are apparently those members of the intellectual elite who criticise established opinion, as those serving society in some official capacity, such as politicians or civil servants, have, in his view, merely invested their abilities in the status quo.

In his professional stance, Russell was by now a relativist, a position from which any established opinion could be legitimately criticised but not one which leaves much scope for the notion of progress, and his use of the term here suggests – as already indicated – that a positivist strain still lingered in his social thought. Mill, when inclined towards positivism, had sought to ensure the expression of minority opinion in order that no aspect of the 'truth' be excluded from consideration. Independent thought in a relativist scheme of things demands a different rationale; and Russell, not content with the prospect of a perhaps stable but essentially meaningless plurality of 'equal' opinions, is inevitably drawn towards the idea of an endless approach towards unattainable truths – the general direction being suggested by values derived from the Liberal tradition.[31] Confident that the endeavours of social and moral philosophers could never equip a 'strong democracy' with objective knowledge in regard to man and society, Russell's relativism at least left him the certainty that those with 'independence of mind' would not be compelled to exhibit this attribute in mere eccentricity. On the other hand, Russell offers no suggestion that his professional conversion to relativism had produced that tolerant acceptance of a plurality of values which Santayana expected as a natural consequence of adopting this position.[32] Russell continued to assume that 'progress' was possible, in that it would always be the case that situations could be conceived of which were not only subjectively preferable but which appeared to rational men as being so obviously 'better' than those presently obtaining that they must be urged upon the population as a whole. Both the conceiving and the urging were tasks which naturally fell to the radical intellectuals.

Although this conception of society, in which a majority desire nothing more than to linger in complacency while a restless elite are obliged to spur them on towards elusive goals, does not look much like Anarchism (even in the form influenced by Stirner), it does tend to illustrate the fact that Russell was, regardless of conclusions reached in his technical philosophy, psychologically incapable of living without some notion of progress. For this reason, the very idea of an achieved utopia was repugnant because, though it might produce a culture capable of novelty and even excellence, it would be in historical terms 'complete'. Throughout much of his social writing, therefore, Russell is more concerned with preserving the possibility of change than with actually achieving change; hence his concentration on protecting elites, rather than formulating social programmes with some definite goal.

No matter how radical the surrounding rhetoric, this then remained the underlying theme in Russell's social thought, justified by a belief that, though the progress of technology and reform appeared assured – if only because of the abundance of advocates – there existed a corresponding tendency to undervalue the exceptional individual, the 'anarchistic innovator'. The link between this type of individual and Anarchism proper was, of course, suggestive rather than direct, and there was no question of Russell's accepting all that the theory implied; for, optimistic though he sometimes was with regard to the malleability of human nature, he believed the Anarchists to be overly sanguine as to the effects of social change upon behaviour – the levels of altruism and benevolence might rise significantly, but some unpleasing human traits were, he thought, intractable. Like Liberalism, Anarchism in its ideal form demanded a society of the exceptional, or at least the consistently rational, and while temperamentally drawn towards the negative side of the theory, Russell's expectations of the common run of man were severely limited, leading him to regard 'external authority' as essential, and, in consequence, Guild Socialism a more 'realistic' proposition.

In regard to Guild Socialism Russell remarks that, 'This method of diminishing the excessive power of the State has been attractively set forth by Mr G.D.H. Cole in his *Self-Government in Industry*.'[33] Cole's tone may have appealed, but Russell tended to discount the populist component in his argument, and took the view that the proposed organisations were too large and would allow, if not encourage, small groups to possess themselves of disproportionate amounts of power. In giving voice to his own doubts, Russell points up one of the main problems in the Pluralist project, namely, that as theorists developed the implications of their argument, the state remorselessly reappeared in something approaching its original form.[34] Yet what is at issue in this instance is whether the 'will of the people' could gain expression and so 'purify' the state. Cole believed so, and this gave him the confidence to construct alternative organisations. Russell did not, and wanted only to lay down ground rules which allowed for the spontaneity out of which an improved society might develop.

For all his attractive qualities, there was in Cole still too much of the Fabian for Russell's taste, and, as he revealed in *Political Ideals*, when confronted with the Fabian approach to social organisation, he could assume an almost Burkean stance. Talking of the 'energetic official' he remarks:

> If he is conscientious, he will think out some perfectly uniform and rigid scheme which he believes to be the best possible, and he will then impose this scheme ruthlessly, whatever promising growths he may have to lop down for the sake of symmetry. The result inevitably has something of the deadly dullness of a new rectangular town, as compared with the beauty and richness of an ancient city which has lived and grown with the separate lives and individualities of many generations. What has grown is always more living than what has been decreed; but the energetic official will always prefer the tidiness of what he has decreed to the apparent disorder of spontaneous growth.[35]

Progress for Russell had little to do with manipulating the machinery of the state, but resulted from cultivating spontaneity and variety, and from this point of view, while he did not advocate revolution, he could appreciate its possibilities in terms of moral regeneration.

Writing *Roads to Freedom* – which was after all commissioned as a sort of textbook of 'Socialist' theories – gave Russell the opportunity to examine and compare the varieties on offer. This naturally excited his eclectic propensities, causing the second half of the work to take on the aspect of a political cookbook concerned with improving the flavour of Guild Socialism. In the end Russell declares himself reasonably content with the basic recipe, but thinks it would be wise to cut down on the Collectivism and to add a dash of Kropotkin.

Kropotkin's Anarchism was heavily dependent on a belief that mutual aid, rather than the struggle for survival, was the chief characteristic of a 'natural' evolution: a belief which Russell, given his dismissal of Hobhouse's similarly optimistic interpretation of man's development, did not share – in any case, he entirely ignores this aspect of a theory he admits is presented with an 'extraordinary persuasiveness and charm'. In fact, Kropotkin's evolutionism provided the basis for a conception of society that was dynamic and creative, one which, shorn of its organic metaphors, accorded well with Russell's own preferences: 'The life of society itself we understand, not as something complete and rigid, but as something never perfect – something ever striving for new forms, and ever changing these forms in accordance with the needs of time. This is what *life* is in nature.'[36]

Apart from his reliance on what he saw as being in every sense a co-operative evolutionary process, Kropotkin also had faith in the development of applied science, which he touted with a Wellsian enthusiasm. This latter approach to social problems was something to which Russell could respond if convinced that the intention was eventually to transcend material concerns. In this instance, increased productivity was seen as a means to ends which Russell found attractively aristocratic. In Kropotkin's view, 'After bread has been secured, leisure is the supreme aim.'[37] The application of scientific methods in agriculture and the encouragement of technological improvements in industry could, Kropotkin calculated, result in all basic material needs being satisfied by each able-bodied individual working as little as four hours a day. Tedious and arduous occupations would in this way be rendered bearable, and a short working day make practicable that which Kropotkin thought desirable, namely, that all individuals should participate in both physical and intellectual work.

Russell was inclined to be convinced and, after sketching in a markedly pessimistic Malthusian projection, comments: 'Returning from these dim speculations to the facts set forth by Kropotkin, we find it proved in his writings that, by methods of intensive cultivation, which are already in actual operation, the amount of food produced on a given area can be increased far beyond anything that most uninformed persons suppose possible.'[38] Yet while Russell accepted that abundance could be created by a mere matter of application and organisation, he regarded as idealistic Kropotkin's view that there was no need to connect the free availability of goods with a willingness to work. What optimism Russell still possessed was certainly not derived from any faith in populist solutions, and he continued to feel that most individuals would be unlikely to exert themselves for purely social reasons; it seemed prudent, therefore, to retain some form of personal incentive. Russell suggests that everyone be entitled to a minimum not conditional upon either work or availability for work, but anything above this minimum must be earned – hence, total idleness should secure a bare subsistence; a few hours agreeable work, an adequate income; while handling unpleasant though necessary tasks results in additional benefits, possibly including some access to luxuries. Material rewards, then, are retained but contained. Given a framework of moderate incentives, Russell believed that so long as work was made tolerable, it was unlikely that many would choose to avoid it altogether, though the 'vagabond's wage' provided an opportunity for artistic independence:

> There would, of course, be a certain proportion of the population who would prefer idleness. Provided the proportion were small, this need not matter. And among those who would be classed as idlers might be included artists, writers of books, men devoted to abstract intellectual pursuits – in short, all those whom society despises while they are alive and honours when they are dead.[39]

These persons then are clearly not to be confused with the chronically workshy, the 'residue' destined for Russellian 'clinics' or Webbian detention colonies.

In the idea of a vagabond's wage, Russell's romantic conception of the artist acquires a medievalist component, which perhaps indicates that in weaker moments he indulged a picturesque notion of Guild Socialism more suggestive of Penty than of Cole:

> Under this plan, every man could live without work: there would be what might be called a 'vagabond's wage', sufficient for existence but not for luxury. The artist who preferred to have his whole time for art and enjoyment might live on the 'vagabond's wage' – travelling on foot when the humour seized him to see foreign countries, enjoying the air and the sun, as free as the birds and perhaps scarcely less happy. Such men would bring colour and diversity into the life of the community; their outlook would be different from that of steady stay-at-home workers, and would keep alive a much-needed element of light heartedness which our sober, serious civilisation tends to kill.[40]

Although the evident intention is to call to mind the world of the troubadour, this tends to read like an apologia issued by the Harold Skimpole Support Group, and merely illustrates the oddly naïve quality of Russell's romanticism. It is, however, an attempt to situate the creative person more firmly within the community and to furnish a role to augment his more typically Russellian function, that of being responsible for the continuity of an epiphenomenal 'culture' offered as society's 'contribution' to 'civilisation'. Rather than being definitively antithetical, the relations between the artist and society are now seen to be, in some sense, necessarily reciprocal, though the fear remains that a society bereft of loose ends would, no matter how benevolent its aims, allow little scope for the creative instinct.

The particular spectre haunting Russell was, of course, Webbian efficiency – a prospect rendered more ghastly by his gloomy anticipation of the epigone; any future Socialist government would, he believed, be inevitably intolerant and censorious. Russell lists three requirements for the creative life: training, liberty, and appreciation. In regard to training/education he retained the traditional Liberal suspicion of a state monopoly, and had always advocated that as much as was possible be left to voluntary organisations. It was natural, therefore, that he should consider Sidney Webb's desire to transform the educational system into a stringent meritocracy, with ability being assessed by the state and directed into suitable channels, as being both negligent of the aesthetic dimension and sinister in its aspiration to appropriate the central ideological 'apparatus'. In Russell's view,

> Much the simplest solution, and the only really effective one, is to make every kind of education free up to the age of twenty-one for all boys and girls who desire it. The majority will be tired of education before that age, and will prefer to begin other work sooner; this will lead to a natural selection of those with strong interests in some pursuit requiring a long training. Among those selected in this way by their own inclinations, probably almost all who have marked abilities of the kind in question will be included.[41]

The aim is to produce a higher education that is not a system – a creation which eludes the narrow designs of the state and relies on self-discipline to attain excellence. At a lower level, the expansion of leisure combined with some experience of a liberal education would, he believed, make the cultural consumer more numerous, thus providing the artist with a measure of recognition, and the intellectual with a measure of influence.

Russell's 'natural selection' is apparently intended to produce a meritocracy without bureaucracy, a demonstration of natural inequalities which, because removed from notions of success and failure, can be accepted with appreciation rather than resentment. The theme is the familiar one, the ambition persistently Millian – that of developing a society responsive to its 'natural' elite:

> The general good of the community is realised only in individuals, but it is realised much more fully in some individuals than in others ... Such men are more fortunate than the mass, and also more important for the collective life. A larger share of the general sum of good is concentrated in them than in the ordinary man and woman; but also their contribution to the general good is greater. They stand out among men, and cannot be wholly fitted into the framework of democratic equality. A social system which would render them unproductive would stand condemned, whatever other merits it might have.[42]

Such a view is not necessarily inconsistent with an Anarchist conception of society, though Anarchist theory – perhaps because of the fine distinction between influence and power – does tend to play down the role of the intellectual. Russell appeared confident that an elite could function without the development of 'elitism', and concludes that, 'the best system would be one not far removed from that advocated by Kropotkin, but rendered more practicable by the adoption of the main principles of Guild Socialism'.[43]

On the crucial question of transition, however, there appeared to be small cause for optimism, and Russell, noting that the working class had in outlook already 'become impregnated with capitalism', foresaw his libertarian ideals being dissolved in a bland materialistic uniformity. His mood as he prepared for prison reflected his awareness of these difficulties, and he appeared resigned to political impotence, regarding his own role as being personally inspirational while the responsibility for change devolved once again upon the shoulders of a future and necessarily youthful clerisy; as he remarked to Ottoline Morrell, 'I am not near enough in outlook to the average man to be able to have much immediate influence. One has to aim at being, like Shelley, an influence upon the comparatively few in the rising generation, not a power in the present.'[44]

Influence exerted on Russell's behalf resulted in his serving his term in the first division; he was thus equipped with a cell of his own, modest comfort, books, and a fellow prisoner assigned to valet-like duties. These conditions enabled him to return to philosophy and he worked steadily for most of the six months, yet despite efforts to idealise his situation as a monastic retreat, he became increasingly depressed. He emerged in September 1918 in a mildly paranoid condition, and his reflections on the victory celebrations offer evidence that his underlying sense of alienation had scarcely diminished since the turn of the century:

> Late into the night I stayed alone in the streets, watching the temper of the crowds, as I had done in the August days four years before. The crowd was frivolous still, and had learned nothing during the period of horror, except to snatch at pleasure more recklessly than before. I felt strangely solitary amid the rejoicings, like a ghost dropped by accident from some other planet. True, I rejoiced also, but I could find nothing in common between my rejoicing and that of the crowd.[45]

When viewed at close range, Russell found the constituent parts of a democracy dispiriting, and it would seem entirely appropriate that his first important political statement following his release, 'Democracy and Direct Action' (1919), should be yet another attack on majoritarian government.

'Democracy and Direct Action' displays to a marked degree that peculiarly hybrid quality which was becoming Russell's trademark, in that it employs a seemingly 'Socialist' rhetoric in the pursuit of aims which were almost wholly traditional. This tension between means and ends did, of course, admit of some concealment, yet it was engagingly characteristic that Russell, in expressing the view that 'minorities and subordinate groups have the right to live, and must not be internally subject to the malice of hostile masses',[46] should adopt a turn of phrase so ideologically remote from the advocacy of Syndicalist tactics further on in the piece: 'Direct action has its dangers, but so has every vigorous form of activity. And in our recent realisation of the importance of law we must not forget that the greatest of all dangers to a civilization is to become stereotyped and stagnant. From this danger, at least, industrial unrest is likely to save us.'[47] Indeed, the evident conviction in Russell's argument seems to relate more to a belief that the tyranny of the majority must be avoided at all costs than to any genuine enthusiasm for direct action, and the overall strategy remains that of securing the survival of Liberal values in the contemporary world.

The political situation, however, provided him with little room for manoeuvre. The 1918 election had only emphasised Lloyd George's dominance, and the remnants of the Liberal Party under Asquith inspired no confidence; therefore, while nominally a Guild Socialist,

Russell moved with little resistance into that cautious identification with the Labour Party so typical of the post-war radical. In other respects, Russell as he approached fifty remained atypical; at one time a caricature of convention, he retained a faintly anachronistic manner, persisted in being sartorially Victorian, yet had exchanged a principled celibacy for a rationally grounded, though increasingly opportunistic, promiscuity. By 1919 his entanglements included a legal tie with Alys, an emotional dependence on Ottoline Morrell, and concurrent affairs with Constance Malleson and Dora Black – the latter, being the first eugenically acceptable person willing to bear his children, eventually becoming his second wife after both signed a private contract to establish that theirs would be an open marriage.

As a public figure Russell was enjoying his brief spell as a hero of the radical intelligentsia, and attracting the attention of that inveterate hero-worshipper, Harold Laski. Being cultivated by Laski brought its burdens, in the shape of reading lists and book parcels, but also its pleasures, such as the inevitable and irresistible request for a 'photograph with your name on it to hang in my study. That', continued Laski, 'would be an act of genuine nobility on your part'.[48] By responding to a steady supply of literature concerned in the main with academic Pluralism, Russell seems to have led Laski to believe that he was considering taking a professional interest in the subject; hence, when in 1920 Laski was able to offer 'warm congratulations on your return to Cambridge',[49] he goes on to express the hope that 'you will not confine your lectures to mathematical logic'.[50] As Russell was now applying himself seriously to the study of political theory while at the same time encouraging moves to ensure his reinstatement by Trinity, it would seem that he entertained hopes of broadening the scope of his academic career to include his current political interests.

There seems little doubt that it was the complexity of his private life which determined the direction of his career in the following twenty years; for it was this problem alone which prevented his taking up the offer of a lectureship at Trinity. If Russell had returned to Cambridge in 1920, it is unlikely that philosophy would have absorbed all his attention, and he could then, like Hobhouse, Wallas, Cole, and Laski, have pursued his political interests from the security of an academic base. As it was, his energies were of necessity channelled into journalism, and in consequence, his long-term Millian ambitions began to suffer neglect as his career assumed a Wellsian trajectory. Although it was some time before Russell was being regularly bracketed with

Wells rather than say Moore or Keynes, he was already somewhat Wellsian in personal conduct, and the two had by 1922 become united in Beatrice Webb's mind as the 'frowsiest' of ex-Fabians, the most 'unclean' of apostates. When reluctantly 'recognising' Russell's second marriage, she consoled herself with a character sketch which, though it dwells on the signs of decline since he escaped her tutelage of the late 1890s, does display a certain prescience with regard to his future prospects:

Bertrand Russell, now nearing fifty, is physically aged with an impaired vitality, but more brilliantly intellectual than he has ever been ... I should be sorry to bet on the permanence of the present marital tie. She is a singularly unattractive little person to me ... Possibly the boy may keep them together for Bertie seems inclined to dote on this son and heir. His bad health may also be a restraining factor preserving his domesticity. But there is a strangely excited look in his eye (does he take opium?) and he is not at peace either with himself or the world. His present role of a fallen angel with Mephistophelian wit, and his brilliantly analytic and scoffing intellect, makes him stimulating company. All the same, I look back on this vision of an old friend with sadness: he may be successful as a *littérateur*; I doubt whether he will be of value as a thinker, and I am pretty well certain he will not attain happiness of love given and taken and the peacefulness of constructive work. When one remembers the Bertrand Russell of twenty years ago ... it is melancholy to look on this rather frowsy, unhealthy and cynical personage, prematurely old, linked to a girl of light character and materialist philosophy who he does not and can not reverence.[51]

Though the photographs of the time do tend to show Russell as less natty than formerly, they offer no hint of the bohemian dissipation suggested here; Roger Fry's portrait of 1923 does, however, indicate that his subject's romanticism was becoming more visible, a development perhaps responsible for Beatrice Webb's speculations on De Quinceyean predilections. In fact, the restless, slightly febrile temperament Russell displayed in the immediate post-war period expressed itself in travel rather than dissipation: the most significant of these journeys being to Russia in 1920 and China in 1921.

CHAPTER 7

Russia, China, and the West

In 1895 Russell, with his academic future undecided, had gone to Germany with his new wife to examine the prospects of a revolutionary Socialist party. In 1920, with his academic future undecided, he planned to go to Russia with if not a new wife then a likely contender for the role, to examine the prospects of a revolution. The symmetry was somewhat spoiled by his abandoning Dora Black in favour of a Labour Party delegation, but the similarities are maintained in the published results to the extent that both *German Social Democracy* and *The Practice and Theory of Bolshevism* offer a bleak perspective on possible Socialist imports. Although this suggests a certain consistency of purpose, no such consistency is to be found in Russell's choice of political labels; and whereas his later claim that he wrote *German Social Democracy* as an 'orthodox Liberal' has some substance, his assertion that he 'went to Russia a Communist'[1] can only confuse.

For the 1949 edition of *Practice and Theory* Russell 'found it necessary, in order to conform to modern usage, to alter the word "Communism" to "Socialism" in many places', maintaining that 'in 1920, there was not yet the sharp distinction between the two words that now exists, and a wrong impression would be made but for this change'.[2] In the political climate of the late 1940s, it was a wise move for someone who, like Russell, derived a significant part of his income from America, to make clear the fact that he had never been a Communist. Yet, though his explanation is plausible, it offers no clue as to why he adopted the label in the first place.

By 1920, Russell called himself a Socialist – a stance defined by membership of the National Guilds League which signalled a continuing rejection of state-Socialism. However, the NGL was itself divided on such issues as its relationship with the Labour Party and its attitude towards the Russian revolution. While supporters of the original 'Guild idea' opposed the notion put forward by Cole that 'nationalisation' might now form the most promising basis for 'encroaching control', proponents of Bolshevik methods demanded the abandonment of 'encroaching control' and set their sights on a 'dictatorship of the proletariat'.[3] Cole himself wished for closer ties with the Labour Party, and though he still had hope that the Bolsheviks were in the process of establishing Guild Socialism on a grand scale, he was temperamentally averse to revolution and already suspicious of the notion of a 'dictatorship of the proletariat'.

Throughout this controversy (which led eventually to the disintegration of the Guild movement) there was exhibited a fondness for what Maurice Reckitt termed the 'fashionable vocabulary of sovietism',[4] and it is likely that Russell, finding the contours of Socialism increasingly blurred, felt able to adopt 'Communism' as a synonym both appropriate to the Russian situation and helpful in lending a judicious air to the text. That Russell required help in this direction stemmed from the fact that he had 'loathed' his time in Russia, and thus experienced some difficulty in simulating dispassionate analysis and disinterested commentary in a hastily assembled book which he expected to provoke 'universal abuse'.[5] In letters written to Ottoline Morrell he gave expression to his true feelings:

> I loathed the Bolsheviks, the time in Russia was infinitely painful to me, in spite of being one of the most interesting things I have ever done. Bolshevism is a close tyrannical bureaucracy with a spy system more elaborate and terrible than the Tsar's, and an aristocracy as insolent and unfeeling, composed of Americanised Jews. No vestige of liberty remains in thought or speech or action. I was stifled and oppressed by the weight of the machine as by a cope of lead ... Imagine yourself governed in every detail by a mixture of Sidney Webb and Rufus Isaacs, and you will have a picture of modern Russia. I went hoping to find the promised land.[6]

Russia, to Russell, 'seemed like an asylum of homicidal lunatics, where the warders are the worst lunatics. It is very hard to keep one's sanity.'[7]

He later toned down his criticism, partly in an effort to placate Dora Black who had travelled to Russia alone and had responded in an entirely opposite way. In effect, Russell went to Russia a 'fellow-traveller', and Dora returned as one. Extreme reaction was and remained a feature of the Soviet experience; yet it was not obligatory – both Wells and Brailsford made the conducted tour at around the same time, and, as their published accounts illustrate, while the former took something like Russell's view[8] and the latter was impressed, like Dora, by the high standard of child-care and education,[9] neither entirely lost his sense of proportion. Russell, on the other hand, recalls in his *Autobiography* 'the sense of utter horror which overwhelmed me while I was there. Cruelty, poverty, suspicion, persecution, formed the very air we breathed. Our conversations were continually spied upon. In the middle of the night one would hear shots, and know that idealists were being killed in prison.'[10] The dangers were doubtless real, though not for Russell – his paranoia flourished without an enemy in sight.

Russell's defensively ironic comment about 'hoping to find the promised land' indicates that he had indulged, like Cole, visions of Guild Socialism writ large, and also that he had begun his journey in a mood characteristic of the fellow-traveller. Indeed, *Practice and Theory* might easily pass for an early example of fellow-travelling literature – though admittedly a peculiarly complex contribution to the genre. Particularly in the early chapters, Russell is at pains to balance all his criticism with protestations as to Bolshevik non-culpability, maintaining that, 'It is futile to blame the Bolsheviks for an unpleasant and difficult situation which it has been impossible for them to avoid.'[11] Russell also displays a tendency common among later fellow-travellers to regard Bolshevism as an 'interesting experiment' likely to have a salutary effect upon a primitive people – though it was decidedly uncongenial and totally unsuitable for 'civilised' countries, it was nonetheless right for Russia. Thus, while he was initially disappointed, remarking that, 'Before I went to Russia I imagined that I was going to see an interesting experiment in a new form of representative government',[12] he later concludes that

> From what I saw of the Russian character and of the opposition parties, I became persuaded that Russia is not ready for any form of democracy, and needs a strong Government. The Bolsheviks represent themselves as the Allies of Western advanced Socialism, and from this point of view they are open to grave criticism. For their international programme there is, to my mind, nothing to be said. But as a national Government, stripped of their camouflage, regarded as the successors of Peter the Great, they are performing a necessary though unamiable task. They are introducing, as far as they can, American efficiency among a lazy and undisciplined population. They are preparing to develop the natural resources of their country by the methods of State Socialism, for which, in Russia, there is much to be said.[13]

This is one of the few instances in the text where Russell attempts to make a distinction between 'advanced Socialism' (by which he presumably means Guild Socialism) and 'State Socialism'; for the rest, he supports the Bolsheviks in their desire to implement 'Communism' –

all his criticisms being centred on the question of method. While allowing for the semantic difficulties, there was obviously an opportunity here for Russell to have identified 'Communism' with state-Socialism as practised by the Bolsheviks. That he refrained from doing so suggests not a pedantic concern for the particularities of political labelling, but a realisation that the term 'Communism' might be employed, not only plausibly as a description of his own position, but tactically within the terms of his overall argument. As already indicated, it was used to simulate objectivity – not only for the benefit of Dora Black, but to anticipate and deflect expected criticism.

Had Russell formed his first impressions of Russia a few years later, when the economic conditions ensured that the British Labour movement was on the defensive, it is arguable that those aspects of his book which link it with the main body of fellow-travelling literature might well have been more pronounced and the Soviet 'experiment' accorded a more encouraging assessment.[14] What must be emphasised is that Russell's attack on Bolshevism was not engendered by his deep concern for the Russian people – empathy with the masses was never a feature of his Socialism – but by anxiety at the prospect of its possible importation in the shape of an English revolution. This despite maintaining that no revolution in the West could 'succeed' even to the extent of the one in Russia, because the power of American capitalism would effectively subdue any signs of Bolshevism in Europe. Russell's persistently ambivalent attitude towards America is here in evidence when considering its pivotal role in world revolution – though he appears to resent the power, one senses an underlying gratitude that he can base a logical dismissal of revolution directly upon it. At the same time, his central objection to revolution was that it created conditions in which American industrial methods became absolutely necessary, thus encouraging an already pervasive materialism.

There is no doubt that Russell, as David Caute acknowledges, 'quickly concluded that the light was not worth the candle',[15] yet much of the evidence indicates that he found his first-hand experience of the Russian revolution profoundly disturbing in ways not usually associated with clear-sightedness. This is not to suggest that his reaction (despite its extreme nature) can be entirely attributed to the paranoia of an aristocrat with an acute sense of history. His background, though important, cannot be made to serve as the only 'explanation' – even on a trivial level it did not require the fastidiousness of an aristocrat to find the conditions in Russia unpleasant and ultimately depressing. Indeed, most accounts reveal that he relished whatever hardships were made available. Although his warnings are often couched in terms of barbarism and chaos, what Russell found most oppressive was the prosaic quality of life, the rapid assimilation of Western ideals of efficiency and progress, the uninspiring uniformity. In an ante-dated letter to Constance Malleson, he wrote:

> I am infinitely unhappy in this atmosphere – stifled by its utilitarianism, its indifference to love and beauty and the life of impulse. I cannot give that importance to man's merely animal needs that is given here by those in power. No doubt that is because I have not spent half my life in hunger and want, as many of them have. But do hunger and want necessarily bring wisdom? Do they make men more, or less, capable of conceiving the ideal society that should be the inspiration of every reformer?[16]

For Russell, 'conceiving the ideal society' was the perpetual task of the intellectuals; by their efforts change was made purposeful, progress took on meaning – theirs was a creative endeavour which transcended the operation of merely instrumental reason, 'rationalisation' in Weber's sense of the term. In Russell's view, the Soviet system was destructive of the intellectual liberty necessary to this creative activity, because intellectuals had to function within the 'theological' restraints of Marxism and also in an atmosphere pervaded by utilitarian values. In other words, the system was marked by two extreme varieties of rationalist thought – the scholastic and that typified by Taylorism.[17] On this latter point, it is apparent that Russell's lack of enthusiasm for 'progress' measured in terms of industrial growth developed into a fully articulated aversion in a society where industrialisation was of necessity a central obsession.

In regard to Marxism, its claims to be 'scientific' are dismissed by Russell in the authoritative tones of the Cambridge professional. He remarks of 'philosophic materialism' that 'the arguments for and against it are long and complicated, and need not concern us, since, in fact, its truth or falsehood has little or no bearing on politics'.[18] While Russell concedes that Marxist theory is not without interest, he believes it to represent a narrow and outdated conception of human nature – something which Marx was unfortunate enough to acquire from the British:

> To desire one's own economic advancement is comparatively reasonable; to Marx, who inherited eighteenth-century rationalist psychology from the British orthodox economists, self-enrichment seemed the natural aim of a

man's political action. But modern psychology has dived much deeper into the ocean of insanity upon which the little barque of human reason insecurely floats. The intellectual optimism of a bygone age is no longer possible to the modern student of human nature.[19]

Yet by pointing up the variety of determinisms and the various opportunities for self-deception, Russell draws attention to the problem of ideology, and in an oblique manner acknowledges his professional relativism; for, whereas the ideological component in his own argument is passed over, there is throughout *Practice and Theory* a notable change of emphasis – the intellectuals now being reduced to the 'scientists', a group which in his view operates in areas of thought free from ideology. Russell had always been aware of ideology as a feature of political life, since it makes little difference whether we classify what he had in mind as 'conspiracy theory' (in which he was a passionate believer) or 'functional ideology'. However, much as he was ever alert to signs of the irrational in others while seemingly unable to detect any indication of it in his own behaviour, Russell was unwilling to countenance the notion that his own ideas were contaminated with ideology – no matter how little 'free' intelligence was left in the world, it could be relied upon that some of it was his.

Conforming in many ways to Gramsci's description of the 'Traditional Intellectual', Russell had always believed that ideas were *the* decisive force in history, steadfastly maintaining that 'the free intellect is the chief engine of human progress'.[20] In some respects his conception of the role of the intellectuals, while developing out of the Coleridgean tradition of the clerisy, closely approximates that later elaborated by Mannheim, for Russell shared the view of the intellectual as a marginal figure, socially unattached, 'free-floating', and thus able to offer 'objective' anticipations of future utopias.

There are, though, in *Practice and Theory* signs of diminished confidence, a certain diffidence in presenting the 'Traditional Intellectuals'' nostrums. Instead, we have a persistent stress on the 'scientific method' as being 'immeasurably important to the human race'.[21] Russell had always emphasised the importance of the 'scientific method', but he had regarded it, like philosophy, as something entirely divorced from the vagaries of political argument; yet it is here employed as the only way of asserting the importance of the intellectual within the materialist conception of history: 'intelligence', he insists, 'modifies profoundly the operation of material conditions ... the intelligence which has this profound effect on politics is not political, but scientific and technical: it is the kind of intelligence which discovers how to make nature minister to human passions'.[22] Pursuing this line of argument leads Russell on into Wellsian extravagance then to implicit recognition that if science is immune from ideology with regard to means, it is ideology which still determines ends. Acknowledging the limitations of science, Russell returns to political solutions and argues for the necessity of Communism/Guild Socialism – the diffusion of power, education for self-government, and encroaching control of industry – rather than revolution, warning that 'no swift method exists of establishing any desirable form of Socialism'.[23]

As in *German Social Democracy*, 'desirable Socialism' as described by Russell begins to look remarkably like Liberalism. Gone are the speculations on moral regeneration through revolution, also absent is any endorsement of direct action; instead, we find a notably greater stress on the merits of democracy. The Russian experience inclined Russell to be more appreciative of the peculiarly tolerant English, and reflections on the 'consequences of fanatical belief'[24] caused the residual Whiggishness to reassert itself: 'To an English mind they reinforce the conviction upon which English life has been based ever since 1688, that kindliness and tolerance are worth all the creeds in the world – a view which, it is true, we do not apply to other nations or to subject races.'[25]

Like many who followed him, Russell saw in Russia a vision of the future – in his case it was one in which the growth of bureaucracy and 'rationalisation' increasingly narrowed both the conception of 'progress' and the role of the 'Traditional Intellectual'. This Weberian pessimism conditioned his attitude to China, for he went there seemingly determined to discover an antidote to the Western 'disease' in the oriental attitude towards life. 'The Chinese', he remarks in his book, *The Problem of China* (1922),

> have discovered, and have practised for many centuries, a way of life which, if it could be adopted by all the world, would make all the world happy. We Europeans have not. Our way of life demands strife, exploitation, restless change, discontent and destruction. Efficiency directed to destruction can only end in annihilation, and it is to this consummation that our civilization is tending, if it cannot learn some of the wisdom for which it despises the East. It was on the Volga, in the summer of 1920, that I first realised how profound is the disease in our Western mentality, which the Bolsheviks are attempting to force upon an essentially Asiatic population, just as Japan and the West are doing in China.[26]

Although Russell was invited to spend a year at The Government University of Peking lecturing on philosophy, his appointment was in some sense a political one as his sponsors were Westernised Chinese intent on promoting the spread of scientific education. They had chosen Russell in the expectation that he would build on the work of his influential predecessor, John Dewey. According to Jerome Ch'en,

> In so far as empirical thinking, a commonsensical approach to reality, and individual freedom were concerned, Russell and Dewey differed little. However, the abstruseness of Russell's philosophy in the eyes of his Chinese admirers may have restricted the impact of his more academic lectures on mathematical logic, matter and mind, notwithstanding the enthusiasm his visit evoked. But his more popular lectures on freedom of thought and his criticism of Western civilisation in the wake of a disastrous war had widespread and longlasting influence. His antagonism to any attempt at the unification of thought appealed strongly to Chinese liberals, as did his praise of Chinese spiritual civilisation – '... those who value wisdom or beauty, or even the simple enjoyment of life, will find more of these things in China than in the distracted and turbulent West and will be happy to live where such things are valued' – sounding most agreeable to the ears of Chinese conservatives. In a sense, remarks like this made by Russell abetted the conservative revival that was to take place soon after his departure from China.[27]

That Russell should be seen as advising the Chinese to retain what they could of their traditional values was in no way surprising, for – in so far as he understood them – these appeared to be similar to those values he had been engaged in defending over the previous five years. From this point of view, the regular and seemingly arbitrary references to Taoism in the pages of *Principles* and *Roads to Freedom* now stood revealed as being entirely appropriate – in *The Problem of China* Chinese philosophy comes into its own. As Russell had in previous books argued that such values could be maintained only in particularly desirable types of social organisation, he was, on detecting their existence, compelled to concede that the social organisation which maintained them was likewise an admirable one. In China, in the early 1920s, this stance required a certain selectivity as to what one became aware of, and Russell proved singularly adept at developing blindspots.

He does, however, prepare his ground, confessing at the outset that, 'For my part, I think the cultural questions are the most important, both for China and for mankind; if these could be solved, I would accept, with more or less equanimity, any political or economic system which ministered to that end.'[28] The good society is thus defined according to cultural values, and these, with one exception, remain those upon which Bloomsbury was established: 'knowledge, art, instinctive happiness, and relations of friendship or affection'.[29] Anticipating critics of elitism, Russell allows as art 'the almost unconscious effort after beauty which one finds among Russian peasants and Chinese coolies, the sort of impulse that creates folk-songs';[30] but much as he had done in *Principles* he relies in the main on the 'popular' ultimate value:[31] 'Instinctive happiness, or joy of life, is one of the most important widespread popular goods that we have lost through industrialism and the high pressure at which most of us live; its commonness in China is a strong reason for thinking well of Chinese civilization.'[32]

Judging Chinese society in what might be loosely described as Benthamite terms involves Russell in providing an empirical basis for his calculations, and this he does in a manner which recalls Wallas's anecdotal sociology:

> I remember one hot day when a party of us were crossing the hills in chairs – the way was rough and very steep, the work for the coolies very severe. At the highest point of our journey, we stopped for ten minutes to let the men rest. Instantly they all sat in a row, brought out their pipes, and began to laugh among themselves as if they had not a care in the world.[33]

The point is emphasised by repetition, yet Russell's prose is, on occasion, so replete with qualifications as to suggest that even he was not overwhelmed by the weight of his evidence: 'I am inclined to think that the inhabitants of China, at the present moment, are happier, on the average, than the inhabitants of Europe taken as a whole.'[34] However, although at one stage he concedes that Chinese women might be less happy than their European counterparts, in general he persists with his argument even at the risk of appearing paradoxical: 'It seemed to me that the average Chinaman, even if he is miserably poor, is happier than the average Englishman, and is happier because the nation is built upon a more humane and civilized outlook than our own.'[35]

Establishing the existence of extensive happiness is necessary to Russell's overall aim, which is to counter those dominant Western values, exemplified by a banal conception of progress, with the example of Chinese civilisation. For Russell, those 'who suffer under the delusion that China is not a civilized country ... have quite forgotten what constitutes civilization'.[36] Throughout *The Problem of*

China Russell links 'progress' with 'Americanism', efficiency, philistinism, and utilitarianism, this latter term used in a sense which indicates that he was at one with Bentham in thinking that 'utility' was 'an unfortunately chosen word'.[37]

In *Principles*, Russell held that Elizabethan culture 'outweighed' social injustice, and he extends to Chinese culture something of this tolerance, regarding 'the capacity for civilized enjoyment, for leisure and laughter, for pleasure in sunshine and philosophical discourse'[38] as compensating for 'disease, anarchy and corruption'. His tolerance is at times quite majestic, and thus practically indistinguishable from that callousness which he found to be one of the few disquieting features of Chinese life:

> While I was in China millions were dying of famine; men sold their children into slavery for a few dollars, and killed them if this sum was unobtainable. Much was done by white men to relieve the famine, but very little by the Chinese, and that little vitiated by corruption. It must be said, however, that the efforts of the white men were more effective in soothing their own consciences than in helping the Chinese.[39]

That Chinese problems were merely an illustration of Malthus, and thus intractable in the short term, suited Russell's overall purpose in that they defied solution by Western methods. 'Americanism', which he defined as 'clean living, clean thinking, and pep',[40] was, in consequence, spreading but slowly. If it prevailed, American 'hygiene' might 'save the lives of many Chinamen, but would at the same time make them not worth saving'.[41] This is not to suggest that Russell at all questioned the need for reform, and he lists 'the establishment of an orderly government, industrial development under Chinese control, [and] the spread of education'[42] as being the main priorities; but his essential point is that all change must be in accordance with the Chinese conception of the ends of life. Russell believed that because of the traditionally high status enjoyed by Chinese intellectuals, China might prove unique in adopting the 'scientific method' while retaining 'civilized' values.

Predictably, these considerations coloured Russell's judgements on China. In writing on Russia he had emphasised the misery of the masses largely because the intellectuals were 'a class who have suffered terribly'.[43] In China, where the intellectuals were in some sense dominant, he tended to regard the suffering of the populace as a natural phenomenon, unrelated to the more 'attractive' features of Chinese civilisation:

> The intelligentsia in China has a very peculiar position, unlike that which it has in any other country. Hereditary aristocracy has been practically extinct in China for about 2000 years, and for many centuries the country has been governed by the successful candidates in competitive examinations. This has given to the educated the kind of prestige elsewhere belonging to a governing aristocracy. Although the old traditional education is fast dying out, and higher education now teaches modern subjects, the prestige of education has survived, and public opinion is still ready to be influenced by those who have intellectual qualifications.[44]

Although this might sound suspiciously Webbian, the interpretation Russell chooses to put upon it is essentially Burkean – the 'ancient city' rather than the 'rectangular town' – and the consequences are satisfyingly Millian, a society suitably deferential to its natural elite. The irony here is that in *On Liberty* Mill offers the Chinese as an awful warning, for despite the status of their intellectuals, 'they have become stationary – have remained so for thousands of years; and if they are ever to be farther improved, it must be by foreigners.'[45]

In Russell's view, China should contain its aspirations towards modernity and cultivate a suspicion of both progress and foreigners alike. In pressing this point *The Problem of China* at times functions as a piece of utopian literature, with Russell, lightly disguised as a product of the Enlightenment, 'A European lately arrived in China',[46] recounting the transformation of his values in the midst of an alien but by no means inferior civilisation: 'New arrivals are struck by obvious evils but gradually strange hesitations creep into the mind of the bewildered traveller.'[47] That he should differ so radically from Mill on the question of China stems from the fact that where Mill assumed order, Russell found an agreeable anarchy – or perhaps, more accurately, 'negative liberty' made manifest:

> The corruption and anarchy in Chinese politics do much less harm than one would be inclined to expect ... Nine-tenths of the activities of a modern government are harmful; therefore the worse they are performed, the better. In China, where the government is lazy, corrupt, and stupid, there is a degree of individual liberty which has been wholly lost in the rest of the world.[48]

In a later article,[49] Russell was to suggest that the advantages of Wells's 'Time Machine' could be enjoyed by merely travelling around the world – with Asia giving access to our past, and America providing (what was in fact a novelty for any European use of the Comparative Method) a realised future. While India gave access to the Middle Ages, he maintained that in the China of 1920 it was possible to 'see' the eighteenth century. It would appear, therefore, that Russell regarded his visit as affording an opportunity to witness a Liberalism as yet untrammelled by Collectivist accretions – an experience which confirmed him in the view that the growth in 'efficient' government intervention had meant a reduction in individual freedom. Thus, while China consolidated changes already taking place in Russell's ideas with regard to industrialisation and leisure, it could not be said that his essential values underwent a transformation. In effect, the illusion of direct acquaintance with a 'Classical' Liberalism only reinforced his traditionalist inclinations at the moment when he had finally come to accept that such inclinations were anachronistic.

Russell wrote a great deal on China throughout the twenties, and while the consistency of his opinions can, in part, be attributed to plain repetition – a necessity to recycle material in order to sustain his career as a journalist – there is also evidence of a need to believe that China was in fact 'the last refuge of freedom'.[50] To this extent, Russell's China bears a certain resemblance to Morris's Middle Ages in that both represent ideals protected from realistic assessment. Not only was Russell, like Morris, basing an often extreme radicalism on beliefs which were oriented towards the past, but the position he adopted in relation to China is in fact a mirror image of the stance later taken up by many intellectuals with regard to the Soviet Union. In both cases, the act of investing one's political beliefs in the prospects of a foreign country contained a religious element – the promised land was far away and in most instances was visited but once, and that visit usually brief. There existed a clear link between the phenomenon of fellow-travelling and the numerous instances of religious conversion among the intellectuals of the twenties and thirties; for these were but two methods by which individuals sought to regain that sense of assurance previously provided by the apparent stability and continuity of the Liberal tradition. In Russell's case, religion was never an available option, and in the twenties he reacted sharply against Ottoline Morrell's influence in this area – his occasional tendencies towards mysticism being replaced by an increasingly obsessive anti-clericalism.

Aside from his established antipathy towards the Soviet Union, it was typical of Russell to be so untypical as to seek assurance by contemplating the image of the past in China, rather than the image of the future in Russia. Although explicable in terms of general trends, Russell's choice of China as the exemplary Liberal society remains fairly quixotic, even on the level of what he was prepared to recognise. He was not entirely unaware of this, for, when commenting on Conrad's response to his book, he remarks: 'I felt that he was showing a deeper wisdom than I had shown in my somewhat artificial hopes for a happy issue in China.'[51] If Russell accepted the 'artificiality' of his views in 1922 as this suggests, it did little to deter their promulgation, for as late as 1930 he was still turning out articles with such titles as 'China's Philosophy of Happiness'.

China in fact became associated in Russell's mind almost exclusively with happiness, yet while this was appropriate with regard to a Liberal ideal, he was too much of a Millian to consider happiness the supreme value; his main interest remained that of protecting freedom as a necessary basis for self-realisation and creativity. The problem here is that while China *appeared* to provide all the prerequisites for a significant culture, allowing Russell to indulge the practice of making unfavourable comparisons of Western and Chinese civilisations, he also acknowledged that the latter, in terms of artistic creation and scientific innovation, supported a traditional culture which had become practically moribund.

While a seemingly less than enthusiastic assessment of Western culture might appear odd in someone who was personally acquainted with many major European intellectuals of the early twentieth century, and who was peculiarly well equipped to appreciate the value of a wide range of contemporary achievement, a man of Russell's age would be hard pressed to have kept pace with innovations in every area in which he had an interest. Thus, while he was familiar with the work of, say, Einstein, Wittgenstein, and Keynes, there is scarcely a mention in his writing of, for example, Proust, Picasso, or Stravinsky. Despite his Bloomsbury contacts Russell never got on terms with the modernist movement, and for the first time became noticeably adrift from contemporary high culture.[52] As such, his low opinion of Western 'culture' (conceived in a narrow sense) would seem to have its basis in a personal taste which was grounded in the 'Classics' of European literature and probably reached the limits of its development in the Edwardian period.

Given the overall bias of his expertise, it is ironic that Russell – remaining untouched by European sociology – should derive significant features of his social thought from a literary culture, especially as those writers who perhaps had most influence upon him were, in varying degrees, both modernist in technique and often less than progressive in political outlook. On the other hand, it was in some ways natural, not only because he remained somewhat in awe of the 'creative' personality and thus tended to look to artists rather than sociologists for insight into social/cultural problems, but also because, of the three writers in question, two, Lawrence and Conrad, were men with whom he had formed intense, even passionate friendships, while the third, Eliot, was at one time friend, tenant, flat-mate, and the husband of Vivien, in whom Russell took a personal interest. Because of the nature of these relationships, the written word was relatively unimportant, though in Lawrence's case, letters eventually negated the effects of conversation.

In *Principles* Russell had sought to rectify a perceived deficiency in contemporary political thought by emphasising the need to cultivate instinct/impulse. Like Wallas, he was putting forward an argument open to misinterpretation, yet his work was never intended as a celebration of the irrational – the 'natural' manifestation of the 'creative impulse' was, as he described it, practically indistinguishable from rational, or at least reasonable, behaviour. By 1923, however, the vocabulary of instinct psychology was less in evidence, the stress now being placed on reason and the scientific method – spontaneity is retained as a major value, but study of the irrational side of human nature advocated explicitly as a means to anticipation and circumvention. Although with regard to what Russell wrote this represents only a change of emphasis, it is indicative of a less tolerant attitude towards the promotion of the irrational.

This change of tone denoted a rejection of all Lawrence appeared to stand for, and the level of Russell's hostility can be judged by his – to put it mildly – uncharitable assessment of the novelist in the mid-fifties. In this piece (later incorporated into his *Autobiography*) Russell practically denies any involvement with Lawrence's ideas, distancing himself by means of stark contrast: 'I was a firm believer in democracy, whereas he had developed the whole philosophy of Fascism before the politicians had thought of it.'[53] Substantiating his remarks by way of selective quotation from private correspondence, Russell acknowledges only a 'certain stimulus' from the proto-Fascist Lawrence, whose notion of 'blood-consciousness' led 'straight to Auschwitz', and whose social thought lacked 'any merit whatever'.[54] Things were, of course, rather more complex than this, for while Russell was never tempted by the idea of charismatic leadership, he was at times elitist in precisely the way Lawrence was, and, as such, Lawrence's 'Socialism' was often indistinguishable from his own. Indeed, shortly after Russell's attempt to establish Lawrence's Fascist credentials, Raymond Williams was to claim that in certain respects Lawrence was 'very close to the socialism of a man like Morris, and there can be little doubt that he and Morris would have felt alike about much that has subsequently passed for socialism'.[55]

Williams's treatment is no less selective, but what is interesting is that the text he relies on in his endeavour to locate Lawrence within that tradition of cultural criticism he was in the process of retrieving is 'Democracy', an essay probably written in the late twenties and one which replicates many of the main features of Russell's social writing up to and including *Prospects of Industrial Civilization* (1923). Not only does Lawrence offer a version of Russell's 'Principle of Growth' more decisive in its rejection of Idealist teleology, but he also emphasises – as Russell had done in *Prospects* – the need to regard the political and industrial structure of society as having only one important function – that of providing a material basis for human freedom and creativity. As it is highly unlikely that Lawrence was engaged in plagiarism, the conversations of 1915 must be regarded as being the main source for both writers; and what this seems to make clear is that Russell's rejection of Lawrence's 'irrationalism' had little to do with Lawrence's actual contribution – a contribution which had been gradually, and probably unconsciously, appropriated as genuine Russellian insight and eventually balanced by a more 'reasoned' perspective.

Traces of Russell's renewed suspicion of the irrational can be found in *Practice and Theory*: for there traditional liberties, tolerance, stability, and the scientific method are valued above anything provided by the fanaticism of revolutionaries. As Russell had interpreted the war in essentially Lawrentian terms, so he interpreted the Russian revolution in essentially Conradian terms; indeed, Russell's antipathy towards Russia can in part be attributed to his having been primed on the subject by a Polish aristocrat. Of Conrad Russell remarks: 'He was very conscious of the various forms of passionate madness to which men are prone and it was this that gave him such a profound belief in the importance of discipline.'[56] This would not be a gross distortion of Russell's stance before 1911 and he was in some respects moving in this direction again by the early twenties. Tradition, stability, standards, discipline, and even duty are words which begin to creep back into

Russell's vocabulary in this period, as Lawrence's influence was countered by that of Conrad and Eliot. The two writers are in fact united with Russell in connection with what was perhaps the only modernist text he ever read, *The Waste Land*; for apart from providing the central image of a disintegrating London,[57] there is every likelihood that it was Russell who focused Eliot's attention on *Heart of Darkness*, and was thus indirectly responsible for the original epigraph to the poem.[58] That Russell both admired *The Waste Land* and had been expected by the Eliots to have some insight into its meaning is plain from correspondence, and suggests a certain similarity of outlook with regard to the fragmentation of cultural authority in the post-war world.[59]

Like Russell, but more explicitly, with a greater consciousness of developing a tradition, Eliot as cultural critic was eventually drawn towards the idea of an intellectual elite functioning as a clerisy.[60] There were, of course, sporadic revivals of the idea of the clerisy throughout the inter-war years, particularly in the work of such writers as Benda, Mannheim, Ortega y Gasset, as well as Eliot himself, but Russell's own brand of elitism was – as already indicated – perhaps closest in tone to that of F.R. Leavis; something which, when we consider that both derived inspiration from Lawrence, Conrad, and Eliot, and were defensive of Cambridge values while being at odds with Cambridge itself, is scarcely remarkable. Russell's contribution to the Arnold/Leavis tradition has rarely been stressed – even Williams, who was at once its historian and end product, consulted *Prospects* when writing *Culture and Society*, apparently without feeling the need to gather Russell into his somewhat disparate collection of intellectuals. One of the reasons for this is that in the 1920s the Wellsian features of Russell's work were much the easiest to identify, and so it was with these that he came to be identified.

CHAPTER 8

The Wellsian trajectory

Russell and Wells were beneficiaries of class backgrounds which enabled them to operate at a tangent to middle-class culture, and, having scientific interests and sexual predilections in common, they covered much of the same ground in their writing. Although increasingly out of touch with the avant-garde, they exhibited none of that defensiveness which was becoming a characteristic of the middle-aged Liberal intellectual;[1] rather they expanded into the 1920s with a certain amount of gusto, their Socialism often taking the form of a militant rationalism intended to override convention. That Wells had greater influence on Russell than had the literary intellectuals mentioned above is largely because he offered not only ideas, but an example of how the Edwardian mind could make itself effective in the modern world. In later life Russell remarked: 'In spite of some reservations, I think one should regard Wells as having been an important force towards sane and constructive thinking both as regards social systems and as regards personal relations.'[2]

Yet while Wells's extraordinary success illustrated the potential rewards of a provocative rationalism, it was the problems of rational belief which continued to exercise the post-war Liberal mind; and Russell's attempt to analyse the psychological tactics necessary to the pursuit of objectivity bears obvious comparison with arguments advanced in, for example, Wallas's *Our Social Heritage* and Hobson's *Free Thought in the Social Sciences*.[3] After being demoted in the war years, reason was promoted – in both senses – by Russell thereafter. The confirmation of Einstein's General Theory of Relativity in 1919 had rekindled his admiration for pure science; in Russia he had detected signs of thought being overtaken by dogma; in China he had been enchanted by an apparent, all pervasive tolerance, and texts such as *Heart of Darkness* and *The Waste Land* had served to convince him that the continuance of Western civilisation could only be sustained by the 'scientific temper' being inculcated in political, social, and cultural life.

The 'scientific temper' thus replaced the 'creative impulse' as Russell's key term and assumed a central position in *Prospects of Industrial Civilization*, his main theoretical text of the period, and in the series of essays which both preceded and derived from it. In one of the earliest of these, 'Free Thought and Official Propaganda', given as the Moncure Conway lecture for 1922, he concludes as follows:

> My plea throughout this essay has been for the spread of the scientific temper, which is an altogether different thing from the knowledge of scientific results. The scientific temper is capable of regenerating mankind and providing an issue for all our troubles. The results of science, in the form of mechanism, poison gas, and the Yellow Press, bid fair to lead to the total downfall of our civilization. It is a curious antithesis, which a Martian might contemplate with amused detachment. But for us it is a matter of life and death. Upon its issue depends the question whether our grandchildren are to live in a happier world, or are to exterminate each other by scientific methods, leaving perhaps to negroes and Papuans the future destinies of mankind.[4]

Russell's claims here are large, and *Prospects* is correspondingly ambitious in scope, taking the civilised world as its object of analysis, an analysis sustained by a – albeit makeshift – philosophy of history. Although in the early pages he appears uncertain as to whether contemporary civilisation is at a point of climax or 'growing decrepit and ready to fall',[5] he is in no doubt that the seemingly repetitive succession of civilisations has a cumulative result: 'when we compare any one of these civilizations with its predecessors, we become aware of a definite advance, particularly in two respects: first, the increase of knowledge; and secondly, the growth in the extent of organization, more particularly of States. From past progress in these two respects a definite though perhaps not very immediate hope for the future is seen to be justified.'[6]

Russell's 'philosophy of history', though optimistic as regards mankind (negroes and Papuans being on hand to progress to the next stage of development), provides little comfort for 'our own civilization'. Not being content with the role of fatalistic bystander, however, and having, one suspects, little faith in the potential of current 'inferior races', he produces proposals intended to avert the crisis, circumvent decline, and establish a stable and presumably permanent civilisation. Russell's argument is aimed at accelerating the progress of reason by means of logical progression. The two main factors responsible for the ultimate failure of past civilisations were, in his view, the not unrelated phenomena of war and irrational belief. Both were susceptible to final eradication by the historical process – states growing ever larger, thus diminishing (at least in numerical terms) the opportunities for war, and 'knowledge' gradually eroding irrational beliefs. It seemed, therefore, logical to anticipate progress by establishing something approximating to a world state secure in beliefs, which, being based on reason, would prove resistant to the destructive effects of the sceptical intellect.

From this it might be allowed that Keynes was justified in citing Russellian rationalism as exemplifying that narrow view of human nature habitually held by many Bloomsbury intellectuals. It could be argued, however, that Keynes's strictures were: applicable to the pre-Lawrentian Russell; inapplicable to the Lawrentian Russell; and only partly applicable to the post-Lawrentian Russell now under discussion, for while there is no doubt that he consistently underestimated the difficulties of both identifying and containing the irrational, his was not by this stage a 'thin rationalism skipping on the crust of the lava, ignoring both the reality and the value of the vulgar passions'.[7] In Russell's post-war work the irrational is not so much ignored as taken for granted – no longer a neglected aspect of human nature, it seemed to require little further in the way of recommendation. It had been assimilated by 'reason', becoming an area of knowledge which offered a theoretical basis for the further extension of rational thought. In his essay 'Can Men Be Rational?' Russell states his 'very high respect for psycho-analysis'[8] while at the same time seeking to remind his readers of Freud's rationalism. What he opposed was 'that lazy acquiescence in irrationality which is sometimes urged by those who only know that psycho-analysis has shown the prevalence of irrational beliefs'.[9] Not only did Russell believe that 'the ideal of rationality remains unaffected by the ideas that have been thought fatal to it',[10] but also that a knowledge of psycho-analysis 'enables man to become aware of a bias which has hitherto been unconscious'.[11]

Relativism, which in theoretical terms had been steadily extending its province, was similarly transformed by Russell. While accepting that 'None of our beliefs are quite true; all have at least a penumbra of vagueness and error',[12] he was not prepared to discard as meaningless such words as 'objectivity' and 'fact'. He also believed that conceding the 'fact' of moral and cultural relativism was but another instance of 'lazy acquiescence'. What he perceived in his travel and in his reading were contradictions and he believed that contradictions should breed rational doubt which would in turn issue in either agnosticism or something approaching knowledge. What he found incredible was that in those areas of discourse where contradiction was self-evident (such as politics), dogmatic certitude, even fanaticism, was increasingly in evidence, whereas, 'In science, where alone something approximating to genuine knowledge is to be found, men's attitude is tentative and full of doubt.'[13]

Science, therefore, which, in the shape of the new physics, allowed the certainty that uncertainty, indeterminacy, and relativism disallowed all claims to absolute knowledge, was reinstated by Russell as a model for social analysis. What it offered was an example of how rational doubt could issue in consensus. Although these sporadic attempts by Russell to develop a methodology are distinctly sub-Weberian in terms of analytic rigour, his pursuit of objectivity has – perhaps inevitably – certain Weberian overtones. In essence, though, they amount to a belief that psychoanalysis 'combined with a training in the scientific outlook' could 'enable people to be infinitely more rational than they are at present'.[14] At their most modest, his expectations ran in the direction of a retrieval of the Liberal ideal, expressed in a hope that self-analysis could provide the means to ensure that self-interest be established on a rational basis.

In *Prospects*, Russell, possessed of both a sceptical disposition and at least the theoretical basis for self-knowledge, was by now adequately prepared to 'consider these questions dispassionately, not as one of the fighters, but as a scientific investigator'.[15] The questions under consideration relate to the 'forces' shaping the contemporary world – the most significant being, in his view, industrialism and nationalism. As a scientist, Russell, in the first half of the book, is intent on tracing the manner in which science had been appropriated by instrumental reason and divorced from a rationality which should be linked to human values. He sees science as being 'behind' both industrialism and nationalism, 'non-political itself, yet controlling all political occurrences'.[16] With regard to the former, his argument is obvious; as to the latter, it is rather less compelling, and he himself discusses nationalism largely in terms of herd instinct. In effect, he is intent upon demonstrating that science/industrialism provides the means to transcend the 'two forms' of nationalism (imperialism and self-determination) by facilitating the growth in size of social structures, thus making a world state – or at most two or three immense and secure states – feasible.

Yet, while 'internationalism' is a prerequisite for the continuity of civilisation in its Western form, Russell's main aim is to examine the inherent tendencies of industrialism in 'isolation' as by a 'physicist'.[17] He takes the view that 'industrialism makes society more organic'[18] – individuals become interdependent rather than self-sufficient, communities grow highly organised, complex, and vulnerable to disruption by the uncooperative member, thus forcing governments to extend their interventions which in turn result in a reduction of liberty. Though actual liberty contracts however, potential liberty expands, for 'Man is rendered freer by industrialism, since his bondage to nature is diminished; but each separate man may not be freer, since there is an increase in the pressure of the community upon the individual.'[19] Industrialism, which could – if organised rationally according to human rather than economic ends – issue in a true democracy and a genuinely civilised society, has, in accordance with its own inner logic, produced instead a mass society – mass production creating the necessity for, and the possibility of, mass education, which results in a mass electorate agitated by mass circulation newspapers.

That the Arnoldian tones were revived in the twenties and thirties was, in part, due to apprehension and resentment aroused by the realisation of American power. America seemed to have exceeded all Tocqueville's expectations and provided the material for most pessimistic anticipations of the 'inherent' tendencies of Western civilisation. For the first time in Russell's writing, the by now conventional image of mass society makes its appearance, and it is, inevitably, an image of America: 'In a thoroughly industrialised community, such as the United States, there is little appreciable difference between one person and another; eccentricity is hated, and every man and woman endeavours to be as like his or her neighbours as possible.'[20] Russell sees such uniformity being reinforced by other factors, in particular 'the break-up of the family resulting from the employment of women',[21] a phenomenon created by the war and thus currently more noticeable in Europe than elsewhere. He believed that women would increasingly 'share their children with the State rather than with a husband',[22] thereby eradicating many peculiarities and idiosyncrasies presently located in the family.

Although Russell is intent on the dispassionate analysis of tendencies, his preferences are everywhere in evidence – secularisation is applauded, a pervasive utilitarianism denounced, and his conclusion is emphatic: the only rational development of industrialism is one which takes the form of Socialism. In Russell's view, 'the future of mankind depends upon the action of America during the next half century'.[23] The class war would, in fact, take place between what he terms the capitalist and proletarian nations, and such a war, conducted with modern technology, might be expected to bring European and American civilisations to an end, thus preparing the ground for the next cycle of history. According to his logical extrapolation, therefore, no future exists for Western civilisation unless America can be drawn into an international Socialism. Socialism presents itself as the alternative, because monopoly capital has already created an industrial structure which presupposes a Collectivist society.

For this reason, 'Liberalism, with its insistence upon the individual, is unable to find the cure for the evils of capitalism.'[24] Liberalism was not only 'utterly inapplicable to the modern world'[25] in terms of its economic individualism, but also with regard to the question of national self-determination. According to Russell, a rational organisation of the world would take the form of three land-based states, centred on America, Russia, and Europe respectively – each being materially self-sufficient and possessing armed force adequate for defence only. In pressing this point, he takes a firm Fabian line with small nations and their aspirations towards autonomy: 'Such rights can, unfortunately, be exacted by the strong; but that they should be voluntarily conceded to the weak is an example of Wilsonian liberalism run mad.'[26] He believed that the ground for Socialism had already been prepared in advanced industrial societies where the populations were educated, disciplined, and stable. In under-developed countries industrial discipline would need to be enforced by a state-Socialism on Soviet lines. The 'uncivilised' nations were, on the other hand, in a state of unreadiness:

> The Asiatic races will be longer and the negroes still longer, before their birth rate falls sufficiently to make their numbers stable without the help of war and pestilence ... Until that happens, the benefits aimed at by socialism can only be partially realized, and the less prolific races will have to defend themselves against the more prolific by methods which are disgusting even if they are necessary. In the meantime, therefore, our socialistic aspirations have to be confined to the white races, perhaps with the inclusion of the Japanese and Chinese at no distant date.[27]

Although its internationalism was strictly limited and its potential foreign relations somewhat dubious, Socialism – defined by Russell as the state ownership of all land and capital combined with a 'true' democracy safeguarded by extensive group autonomy – was the 'rational' system for all modern societies and as such should prove, like reason itself, irresistible in the long term. Russell believed that 'The spread of socialistic opinion in the United States is likely to be analogous to the spread of free thought in Europe.'[28] Capitalism would go the way of Christianity, which he saw as being 'practically confined to clergymen and maiden ladies',[29] because 'gradually the thing taught grows incredible, and even those who do not explicitly reject it are no longer influenced by it'.[30] Yet, although in respect of structure a Socialist society is rational, or, put another way, a rational society is Socialist, the values Russell wishes to inculcate and which he elaborates upon in Part Two of *Prospects* remain, despite his dismissal of Liberalism as a doctrine, decidedly Liberal values centred on the rational, autonomous individual.

Russell, while dividing the book into what he describes as its 'analytical' and 'ethical' parts, does not in Part Two abandon the pursuit of objectivity with an ostensible change of subject matter, insisting that 'the advocate of fundamental change, more obviously than anyone else, needs to find ways of judging a social system which do not embody merely his individual tastes'.[31] He felt that 'The only way to make people's political judgements more conscious, more explicit, and therefore more scientific, is to bring to the light of day the conception of an ideal society which underlies each man's opinion, and to discover, if we can, some method of comparing such ideals in respect of the universality, or otherwise, of their appeal.'[32] An 'ideal type' society cannot be constructed unless the irrational beliefs which produce cultural relativism are exposed, and among these he lists religion and the 'sacredness of private property'. Excluding the 'obviously' irrational, Russell is also wary of the merely aesthetic – intellectual creations elegant in conception but likely to displease actual citizens – for he had a personal loathing of 'tight systems', an expression which suggests his own occasional sense of claustrophobia in the modern world. In producing his own 'ideal', therefore, Russell is alert to subjective preferences which might inhibit its 'universal appeal', and in what might be seen as a rare moment of self-criticism he mentions the 'fallacy of the aristocrat' which 'consists in judging a society by the kind of life it affords to a privileged minority'.[33] Nevertheless, what we are offered is, if not a straight summation, then a fairly comprehensive assemblage of the ideas he had been expounding over the previous five years – scrupulous self-examination having produced only confirmation of his apparent ideological immunity, indicating that the consistency of his conclusions sprang from his being consistently disinterested in his analysis.

In fact, since 1896, what had been remarkable about Russell's social thought was not the consistency of his opinion but the tenacity of his endeavour to provide a suitable container for a peculiarly distilled form of Liberalism. At what might be termed the level of ideology, therefore, Russell's views took on a certain predictability – it was only the strategies which had been various. The signs of stability in Russell's political opinions becoming evident by the mid-twenties have, in most respects, little to do with a final conversion to 'Socialism'; rather they emerged from a settled conviction that 'Socialism' was the rational instrument with which to produce 'rational' values. Indeed, what changes there were in Russell's thinking manifest themselves in an increasing bifurcation: as he becomes more emphatic as to the need of a Socialist framework, so he becomes more insistent on the need for individuals who are sceptical, critical, rational – 'Socialism' providing not a 'collective', but a prosaic background to an ideal Liberal society. There is a sense in which it might appear perverse to quibble with Russell's self-proclaimed Socialism as he had from 1917 advocated the state ownership of the means of production and stood twice in the early twenties as a Labour candidate; yet there can be no doubt that even his ostensible political views tended towards the idiosyncratic.

'Guild Socialist' has always seemed the most appropriate label to attach to Russell, as it would appear to encompass both his radicalism and his individualism, but in most ways his later Guild Socialism was as equivocal as his earlier Fabianism. By the time he came to write *Prospects*, Guild Socialism, though on the decline politically, was, in the shape of Cole's *Social Theory* and *Guild Socialism Restated*, well provided for in the theoretical sense. This being so, Russell's response to the criticisms levelled at the theory by Wallas in *Our Social Heritage* is, coming from the pen of a Guildsman, if not exactly heretical, then distinctly odd. Wallas took the view that vocational organisations were 'technically conservative', 'suspicious of individual merit', and sought to absorb potential state revenue as wages. In regard to the first point, Russell was 'convinced that a certain amount of this was desirable'.[34] As to the second, he thought it irrelevant, as real achievement could only be expected outside the 'tedious and disagreeable'[35] sphere of industrial production. The last is dealt with in a manner which recalls his enthusiasm for the Chinese variety of negative liberty, and reflects his seeming total indifference to whole areas of social organisation: 'the purposes of the State are in the main evil, and anything which makes it harder for the State to obtain money is a boon'.[36] His attitude towards the state is, if a touch cavalier, not totally dissimilar to that taken by Cole; for although Cole was becoming interested in the idea of nationalisation, he was still resistant to the welfarism and bureaucracy of the Fabians, and Guild Socialism, as he conceived of it, remained primarily a theory of democracy.

When analysed, however, the resemblance between Russell's Guild Socialism and Cole's proves to be merely superficial – a point which can be illustrated by the following quotation from *Guild Socialism Restated*:

> democracy in industry and in every sphere of social life has for its supreme justification its power to call out in the mass of men the creative, scientific and artistic impulses which capitalism suppresses or perverts, and to enable the now stifled civic spirit to work wonders in the regeneration of human taste and appreciation of the good things of life.[37]

Aside from the fact that Cole stresses the collective while Russell invariably talks in terms of the individual, there would appear to be much here with which the latter would agree. Yet whereas Cole sought to overcome the problem of 'alienation' by way of work and politics – craft, creativity, and the imagined delights of self-expression through political participation – Russell increasingly emphasised both the relative unimportance of politics and the futility (at least for the great majority) of seeking fulfilment in work, stressing instead the perhaps less imaginary delights of leisure. Productivity and political participation were for Cole the central concerns of any vigorous community; for Russell they were peripheral to the 'true ends of life'.

Distanced from Cole, Russell was no closer to other influential positions in the 1920s – Laski's academic concern with sovereignty and objective rights had scarcely any bearing on his own interests and the tone of Tawney's brand of functionalism made works like *The Acquisitive Society* somewhat inimical. Russell was not alone in arguing for increased leisure, but he was certainly untypical in his reduction of work to a sterile time-wasting. While others followed Morris in seeking ways to change the nature of work, the attitude towards work, the control over work, and to reduce its monotony by increasing its variety, Russell flatly remarks, 'Four hours' boredom a day is a thing which most people could endure without damage; and this is probably about what would be required.'[38]

His views on industrial growth and leisure are in most respects interrelated, for it is only by supposing that needs are recognised to be finite and that in consequence increased leisure will be valued above superfluous goods that he can sustain his central argument. Although Russell's period of rigorous self-denial was behind him, he retained a tendency (which he shared with certain other intellectuals of the first half of the century) to generalise about social needs from what might be regarded as a personal asceticism. For some (Beatrice Webb, George Orwell, and F.R. Leavis are clear examples) disdain for a gross materialism was reinforced by personal eccentricities which might take the form of a meagre and largely vegetarian diet and/or a disregard for household amenities and personal comfort. Russell on the face of it would appear to reject such a stance; indeed he states clearly that 'I do not think it worthwhile to preach difficult virtues or extremes of self-denial, because the response is not likely to be great. But I have hopes of laziness as a gospel.'[39] Yet this is plainly spurious – a man who suffered a few hours of boredom in order that he could avoid all unnecessary activity for the rest of the day hardly fits Russell's image of the true 'Socialist' – what he wanted was a curb on material desires to release time and energy for something more worthwhile than work. Although he had no enthusiasm for industrial growth he was scarcely an advocate of aimlessness, believing that a 'good society' must be 'progressive', 'it must lead on to something still better'.[40]

While Russell recognised that the 'essential' requirements of his own life exceeded a strict conception of need, he chose to regard this as an unavoidable consequence of his particular vocation. He interpreted 'need' as a physical minimum, rather than as a historical concept undergoing rapid expansion and absorbing 'superfluities' almost daily. His demands on life had remained relatively unchanged, his 'excesses' were professional, hence he was prone to consider novel wants as trivial, and initially expressed a marked contempt for innovations such as the cinema and the gramophone. If leisure were extended, he thought it would and should be filled with pursuits similar to his own. At the time Russell was engaged in arguing that material wants should be contained at a low level, he possessed a house and servants in Chelsea and a coastal retreat in Cornwall. In respect of professional efficiency these were doubtless entirely necessary, but his manner of life was so remote, both intellectually and materially, from that of the average as to provide no basis for his assumption that trade union agitation for shorter hours indicated that the working class shared his feeling of sufficiency and would be prepared to moderate a passion for goods in exchange for more leisure. Freed from the irrational demands of capitalism, members of a Socialist community would, according to Russell, order their affairs on a rational basis, balancing a necessary boredom with the necessities of life. Conceived in such terms, Socialism, he maintained, could become a 'creative faith which the modern man can believe'.[41]

Somewhat late in the book Russell decides that 'It might be well to define "reason" before going farther', and continues, 'I do not mean by "reason" any faculty of determining the ends of life. The ends which a man will pursue are determined by his desires; but he may pursue them wisely or unwisely.'[42] What he does not consider is that the desire for leisure might be overridden by other, stronger desires – instead, leisure is allocated its place in the rational organisation of society as an area of freedom in which man can live his 'true life' which 'does not consist in the business of filling his belly and clothing his body, but in art and thought and love, in the creation and contemplation of beauty and in the scientific understanding of the world'.[43] As we have seen, Russell's rationalism was tending towards imperialism and desires were not exempt from being judged wise or unwise, rational or irrational. When compared with *Prospects*, *Principles* begins to seem the work of a thoroughgoing relativist, for there 'natural growth' was at least ostensibly spontaneous, while here Russell asserts that acceptable values might be inculcated by establishing a 'positive morality': 'Our natural impulses, properly directed and trained, are, I believe, capable of producing a good community, provided praise and blame are wisely apportioned.'[44]

The values which are to be inculcated comprise the by now familiar Russellian quartet: 'instinctive happiness', 'friendship', 'enjoyment of beauty', and 'love of knowledge'.[45] In discussing instinctive happiness and friendship Russell momentarily strays into Edward Carpenter territory, extolling sexual freedom and the rural life while relying on an approximate material equality to cement the bonds of good fellowship. On the other hand, his treatment of beauty and the love of knowledge suggests a desire for a culture which acknowledged an authoritative elite suitably equipped to encourage excellence, maintain standards, and restore a stable tradition.[46]

Russell's internationalist ambitions are vitiated by a fairly parochial concept of culture, one distinctively English in a manner suggestive of both Morris and Leavis, yet narrower than either in that it excludes as irrelevant both the creative and the social aspects of work. Also, his readoption of an overt rationalism serves only to entrench him more firmly in the clerisy tradition along with Eliot and Leavis; indeed, his rational stance bears an obvious resemblance to the 'impersonal' and 'disinterested' approach of the new literary critics. The connection between the New Criticism and the idea of the clerisy is that judgements which claim a measure of objectivity have a natural tendency to claim 'authority' also. As we have seen, Russell was prone to seek sociological insight from what was supposedly a purely literary discourse, while Leavis in particular had ambitions for literature which were undeniably 'political', and to this extent the aspirations of the Scrutiny group were, in essence, not so very different from Russell's own.[47] Yet where Leavis sought to 'retrieve' an organic society, Russell placed his hopes in a radical bifurcation, transcending a class-based culture by making leisure a common property. For Leavis the relation between work and leisure was an intimate one; vacuous work led inevitably to a vacuous use of leisure. In Russell's view most work eventually issued in vacuity, not excepting that variety dignified by the term 'craft': 'Owing to our belief that WORK is what matters, we have become unable to make our amusements anything but trivial ... People whose outlook on life is more leisurely have a higher standard for their amusement; they like good plays, good music, and so on, not merely something that enables them to pass the time vacuously.'[48]

With regard to both art and science Russell believed that 'our prevailing habits of mind, and our so-called moral ideals, are destructive of what is excellent. If excellence is to survive, we must become more leisurely, more just, less utilitarian, and less "progressive".'[49] His remedy is the familiar one: the authority of the 'exceptional individual' must be recognised, an authority given extra weight by his access to a historically irresistible 'reason'. By producing through education a sceptical disposition in society at large, ideological thinking would be rapidly disposed of and rational solutions embraced. A 'Socialist' structure would provide the material basis and leisure, while the 'rational' intellectual is offered the freedom to inculcate the 'true ends of life'.

Russell retained a conviction that 'in the long run those who control opinion rule the world'[50] yet thought this did not apply to the capitalist press – it controlled not 'opinion' but 'propaganda' which 'does not make people alter their opinions, but ... makes them hold their opinions more excitedly'.[51] Russell's argument here (that propaganda only serves to excite the collective ideology) is in line with his belief in the historical role of reason – genuine changes of opinion are in this view always the result of rational argument. The war, regarded by Russell's generation of Liberal intellectuals as the historical event which had effectively negated any belief in rational progress, is now treated as an aberration, thus allowing belief to be retrieved:

> Men who genuinely believe in reason, and at the same time possess a vigorous intellect, have a power over opinion which is incalculable, because it is more lasting than any other power. It is to them and their influence that we must look if a better civilization is to emerge from the present chaos, not to a mixture of passion and propaganda leading to a dreary round of violence and disenchantment. To save the world requires faith and courage: faith in reason, and courage to proclaim what reason shows to be true.[52]

The tones are suggestive of an embattled authority and as such similar to those employed later by Q.D. Leavis in *Fiction and the Reading Public* (1932): 'If there is to be any hope, it must lie in conscious and directed effort. All that can be done, it must be realised, must take the form of resistance by an armed and conscious minority.'[53]

Despite his occasional participation as a party candidate, Russell's distaste for the political process increased in the 1920s. Far from being a vehicle of rational progress, he believed the party system merely sustained the 'dreary round', producing only propaganda which an unprincipled press dispensed to an uneducated electorate. He states his position most forcibly in an address to the Students' Union of the London School of Economics in 1923, later published as 'The Need for Political Scepticism'. In Russell's view, party competition allowed 'the existing democracy' to determine the level at which political discourse was conducted: 'The power of the politician, in a democracy, depends upon his adopting the opinions which *seem* right to the average man ... an honest politician will not be tolerated by a democracy unless he is very stupid, ... because only a very stupid man can honestly share the prejudices of more than half the nation.'[54] The central point of Russell's address was that the current system excludes the possibility of rational or enlightened opinion being offered for consideration. Yet as we have seen, his tolerance of 'unreasonable' opinion was declining and it is entirely in keeping with both his occasional rationalist elitism and the initial rationale of the host institution that he should demand a greater political role for the 'expert' whose skill 'consists in calculating what really *is* advantageous, provided people can be brought to think so'.[55] 'If', writes Russell, 'measures were framed by experts after international deliberation, they would cut across party lines, and would be found to involve far less division of opinion than is now taken for granted'.[56]

Russell's view that even in the political sphere 'knowledge exists' and should therefore be allowed to claim some authority invites the rebuttal Maurice Cowling gave to what he saw as being Mill's similarly elitist conclusion.[57] It was during the 1920s that Russell came closest to exhibiting those tendencies in his political thinking which (at least in the Cowling version) represent the authoritarian component in the Millian inheritance. As we have seen, the idea of the clerisy was implicit in much of Russell's writing from *Principles* onwards – the body of exceptional individuals being conceived variously as literary intellectuals and/or scientists. In *Prospects*, he promotes the notion of a starkly bifurcated society: a culture which sustains excellence, supported by the scientific organisation of production. The cultural aspects of this society he sees as being guided by an Arnoldian elite, whereas the transition towards such a society would seem to require the services of the Millian sociologist armed with the authority of a consensus achieved through rational analysis.

Yet *Prospects* marks the point at which Russell's Millian ambitions are superseded by a Wellsian utopianism, and the transitional elite are depicted in a way which more closely approximates Wells's conception of the samurai than the purveyors of nineteenth-century positivist sociology. Like *Anticipations* (1901) and *A Modern Utopia* (1905), *Prospects* is based on extrapolations from current trends and presents a future in which a world state emerges as a logical end-product of rational analysis. Russell is of course less speculative than Wells as regards scientific innovation, his 'anticipations' are in this sense less inventive. On the other hand, he is more self-consciously objective in his approach, with the result that his elitism manifests itself only as a distaste for mass society whereas Wells's was expressive of his fear of the sub-human, subterranean, 'masses'.

In his impatience with democracy Russell overestimates the extent to which governments are constrained by the electorate, his whole argument being based on a conflation of the electoral process with the business of government. This impatience had been in evidence for a number of years, but it was exacerbated by a renewed faith in rational progress which can in turn be traced to the experience of middle-aged paternity, an experience which had for the first time given him an instinctive rather than a merely intellectual concern for posterity.[58] Having children of his own focused Russell's attention upon education, and he ransacked the subject with his customary energy, rapidly acquiring an authoritative tone in which he dismissed difficulties and proclaimed potentialities. In his essay 'Freedom in Society' (1926) he remarked: 'Miss McMillan at Deptford is training children who become capable of creating a free community. If her methods were applied to all children, rich and poor, one generation would suffice to solve all our social problems.'[59] To bring the millennium that much nearer, Russell in 1927 added his own establishment at Beacon Hill, an experiment sustained in its precarious existence by the proceeds from his popular books and American lecture tours.

Russell's own theory, first put forward in his book *On Education: Especially in Early Childhood*, is characteristically eclectic, drawing not only on the work of Margaret McMillan, but also Montessori, Pavlov, Freud, and perhaps most importantly, Watson. Children, in Russell's view, 'are born with only reflexes and a few instincts; out of these, by the action of the environment, habits are produced, which may be either healthy or morbid'.[60] Given Russell's intellectual background it is not surprising that he found Watson's ideas persuasive, for there are clear resemblances between behaviourism and associationism – the stimulus–response connection being in some respects little more than a transfer of the old associationist theory from mind to body, but with reinforcement rather than frequency the strengthening factor.[61]

Russell valued behaviourism as a method by which the cultivation of instincts and the inculcation of habit could be embarked upon at the earliest possible moment. 'It is clear', he remarks, 'that education of character must begin at birth, and requires a reversal of much of the practice of nurses and ignorant mothers.'[62] His residual Freudianism, however, led Russell to emphasise that correct habit formation must involve the sublimation rather than the repression of instinct: 'By creating the right habits and the right skill, we cause the child's instincts themselves to prompt desirable actions. There is no sense of strain, because there is no need to resist temptation. There is no thwarting and the child has a sense of unfettered spontaneity.'[63] By 'sense of spontaneity' Russell presumably means that the child enjoys the illusion of freedom as it undergoes the process of conditioning – a process designed to issue in the realisation of an 'ideal' character, having as its main components 'vitality, courage, sensitiveness and intelligence'.[64] Arguing in this instance from an environmentalist position Russell took the view that conditioning was inevitable, and therefore it was no curtailment of liberty to deny to someone the opportunity of becoming lethargic, timid, insensitive, and stupid – as the individual concerned could have no choice in the matter it was as well that the choices made for him were at least guided by common sense. As a basis for either utopian or dystopian thinking, behaviourist technique has much to recommend it, and Russell, always prone to oscillate between unrestrained optimism and bleak pessimism, neglected no part of its potential – initially it offered a promise, later it suggested a threat.

Although his utopian aspirations issued in no single product which could be counted as an addition to the genre, Russell's contribution certainly amounts to something more substantial than the occasional reiteration of Wellsian speculation. That the more pessimistic sections of *The Scientific Outlook* (1931) provided the groundwork for Aldous Huxley's *Brave New World* (1932) is well established, but what has attracted less attention is the extent to which his work of this period anticipates B.F. Skinner's *Walden Two*. Neither Russell nor Skinner had any interest in the notion of a static, 'perfect' utopia; their imagined societies are inherently progressive rather than being the culmination of progress, therefore their arguments for the scientific organisation of current knowledge and resources are not intended to be proof against future development and innovation. Both advocate an enhanced role for the 'expert' or 'planner'; a reduction to a minimum of what they describe as 'dreary' political activity; the conditioning of children in order to produce certain desirable character traits; the elimination of unnecessary labour; the establishment of creative leisure; and a rational approach towards sex including the introduction of a programme of eugenics (a subject which Russell raises again in *Marriage and Morals*).

Skinner's behaviourism was much more sophisticated than anything available to Russell; nevertheless, on most important points their views are similar in substance, and even at times similarly expressed – the Skinner character, Frazier, in *Walden Two*, for example, echoes Russell's apparent satisfaction with the notion of a merely subjective freedom during the process of conditioning: 'by using the principle of positive reinforcement – carefully avoiding force or the threat of force – we can preserve a personal sense of freedom'.[65] Both are sharply critical of majoritarian government, yet the conventions of the utopian novel allow Skinner to be unequivocal as regards the role of the 'planner', whereas Russell is compelled to manoeuvre within the parameters of Liberal discourse, and this results in some ambiguity on questions relating to deference and authority: 'The average man's opinions are much less foolish than they would be if he thought for himself: in science at least, his respect for authority is on the whole beneficial.'[66] In most respects, democracy and equality remain for Russell problematic ideals forever at odds with his concern for the progress of civilisation. To be conceived otherwise, such ideals require the support of an extreme environmentalism, and on this question Russell was never extreme in the manner of James Mill or J.B. Watson; for, although he thought it possible to 'cultivate intelligence'[67] as part of a desirable character, he also recognised 'innate' differences.

On Education brought about the second significant expansion in Russell's readership (the first was initiated by *Principles* in 1916 and the third by *History of Western Philosophy* in 1946). It was conceived as a popular work, employing a personal style of address and making extensive use of the parental anecdote; yet it was obviously the choice of subject matter, not the change of style, which occasioned the success. While aimed at those of the middle class who shared his distaste for the public school ethos, it functioned not as a prospectus for the 'progressive' alternative but rather as a manual offering guidance in the treatment of the recalcitrant infant. Of Russell's theory and practice his daughter later remarked: 'At the time, under the spell of scientific optimism, he accepted, applied and expounded an unpleasantly crude kind of conditioning process.'[68] Certainly, there was nothing indulgent about Russell's attitude; indeed, the stance taken in the book is – despite concessions made to Freud – curiously Victorian in its emphasis upon character-building. However, while Russell's belief in the stern conditioning of the demanding child might ultimately be traced to a residual Victorianism, it also has clear links with his utopianism.

In the late twenties, Russell, in the furtherance of his utopian ambitions, was compelled to make some accommodation with the mass market. Having to subsidise his school he was driven to cultivate a wider American audience, and in consequence his public image became that of a popular moralist. As he still regarded himself as a Cambridge intellectual with an international reputation, he was never entirely happy with the transformation in his perceived status, and the work he produced was to some extent written against the grain, with a diminishing sense of purpose and a gradual loss of self-esteem.

The tension between Russell's essentially elitist aims and his 'popular' entanglements emerges in a letter to H.G. Wells in which he broaches the possibility of obtaining financial support. Russell doubtless found this form of correspondence uncongenial, and his approach lacks something in subtlety in that he opens with a rather fulsome appreciation of the latest Wellsian project, *The Open Conspiracy*: 'Thank you very much for sending me your book on "The Open Conspiracy". I have read it with the most complete sympathy, and do not know of anything with which I agree more entirely.'[69] Yet though Russell's tone in the letter is uncharacteristically ingratiating, there seems no reason to suppose that his enthusiasm was entirely conditioned by financial considerations. Their aims were, after all, similar and Wells's book differs from *Prospects* only in as much as it proposes a peculiarly incoherent and unrealistic method of achieving them.

'The Open Conspiracy' was conceived as a secular 'religion' that would eventually issue in a world state: 'This candid attempt to take possession of the whole world must be made in the name and for the sake of science and creative activity.'[70] As an interim 'bible' Wells offers his own 'work in progress', the trilogy comprising *The Outline of History*, *The Science of Life* (which was then in preparation), and the promised sociological treatise (given the provisional and oddly Russellian title of 'The Conquest of Power') which was published in 1932 as *The Work, Wealth and Happiness of Mankind*. Wells initially envisaged the open conspirators expanding gradually through relatively unorganised activity, their main purpose being that of providing a progressive example in important functional groups. He thought it evident that in all such groups it was possible to distinguish 'a base and harmful section, a mediocre section following established usage and an active, progressive section to whom we turn naturally for developments leading towards the progressive world commonweal of our desires'.[71] There were, however, to be groups made up exclusively of the young and the like-minded 'arranged upon lines not unlike those of the Bohemian Sokols or the Italian Fasci'.[72] As Wells's argument proceeds, it becomes less nebulous and more elitist – the dream of an unorganised absorption of world power by the right-thinking, giving way to an increasing emphasis upon the training of the elect:

> There lies a great work for various groups of the Open Conspiracy. Successful schools would become laboratories of educational methods and patterns for state schools. Necessarily for a time, the Open Conspiracy children would become a social elite; from their first conscious moment they would begin to think and talk among clear-headed people speaking distinctly and behaving

frankly, and it would be a waste and loss to put them back for the scholastic stage among their mentally indistinct and morally muddled contemporaries.[73]

It was this part of the book to which Russell responded, offering evidence that there was a connection between his determination to ensure the survival of his school and his utopianism. His letter continues as follows:

I am every day more convinced that people who have the sort of ideas that we have ought not to expose their children to obscurantist influence, more especially during their early years when these influences can operate upon what will be their unconscious in adult life ... I believe profoundly in the importance of what we are doing here ... What we are doing is of course only an experiment on a small scale, but I confidently expect its results to be very important indeed.[74]

It is clear that Russell's ambitions for his own venture were, at the very least, unrealistic and as such entirely in keeping with his energetic pursuit throughout this period of a rationalism which was often either utopian or anachronistic. With regard to his near obsessive attacks on Christianity it tended to be the latter, causing him to maintain that the possibility of progress was largely dependent on the final victory of science over religion. In consequence, the discovery that a severely secular education did not necessarily produce reasonable children was for Russell both surprising and discouraging.

Because of his peculiarly dated rationalism, his 'popular' books of the twenties are not 'of the period' as are, say, the novels of Huxley – for all their lightness of touch they remain the unmistakable products of an Edwardian intellectual aristocrat with pronounced Wellsian leanings. *Marriage and Morals*, for example, is in substance a reiteration of the argument first put forward almost a quarter of a century earlier by Wells in *A Modern Utopia*. Yet Russell, in assuming that Edwardian utopianism could now be promulgated as mere common sense, misjudged the times and achieved a new notoriety – the reaction in America being particularly violent. Although Russell's text is enlivened by a sustained and witty attack on St Paul and the inclusion of passages from Lecky's account of the Rabelaisian medieval monasteries, his sardonic tone is combined with a high-minded 'moralising' explicitly at odds with Huxleyan hedonism: 'His [Huxley's] characters, like St Paul, view sexual intercourse merely as a physiological outlet; the higher values with which it is capable of being associated appear to be unknown to them.'[75] Russell's views were, however, open to misinterpretation and could, perhaps with some justification, be seen as self-serving.

His attitude towards sexual matters was identical with that of Wells who was of the opinion that in a 'modern' society the 'control of private morality, beyond the protection of the immature from corruption and evil example, will be no concern of the State's'.[76] The purpose of marriage as an institution was to provide an orderly arrangement for the production and care of children and should cease to be looked on after the manner of St Paul as a necessary curb on immoral behaviour. To this end, Wells proposed that a childless 'marriage' should 'expire at the end of three or four or five unfruitful years',[77] while Russell held that 'no marriage should be legally binding until the wife's first pregnancy'.[78] Both saw the state gradually taking on the role of the father in the care of offspring and actual fathers being chosen on strictly eugenic grounds. Russell, naturally enough, contemplates the possibility with an air of complacent anticipation: 'the men with the best heredity may come to be eagerly sought after as fathers, while other men, though they may be acceptable as lovers, may find themselves rejected when they aim at paternity'.[79]

On the question of eugenics, Russell maintained the position he had first established in 'The Politics of a Biologist' (1907), with the important difference that he no longer automatically assumed that the 'unfit' could be located in the 'lower classes': 'A great deal of fuss is made about the fact that the poor breed more than the rich. I cannot bring myself to regard this fact as very regrettable, since I see no evidence whatever that the rich are in any way superior to the poor.'[80] As with Wells, Russell's belief in eugenics had been inspired originally by a fear of 'race degeneration', and the change in his views was brought about by recent evidence of a falling birth-rate among the poor, causing them to appear less of a threat to civilisation.

Nevertheless, it is difficult to see how, on Russell's terms, a working-class man with aspirations towards paternity could offer convincing evidence of superior heredity. The problem would, of course, only arise if a programme of positive eugenics were implemented, and Russell thought this unlikely because

> The ideas of eugenics are based on the assumption that men are unequal, while democracy is based on the assumption that they are equal. It is, therefore, politically very difficult to carry out eugenic ideas in a democratic community when those ideas take the form, not of suggesting that there is a minority of *inferior* people such as imbeciles, but of admitting that there is a

minority of *superior* people. The former is pleasing to the majority, the latter unpleasing. Measures embodying the former fact can therefore win the support of the majority, while measures embodying the latter cannot.[81]

As he indicates, he was more hopeful as regards negative eugenics, and argued that the mentally deficient should be sterilised: 'Feeble-minded women, as everyone knows, are apt to have enormous numbers of illegitimate children, all, as a rule, wholly worthless to the community. These women would themselves be happier if they were sterilised, since it is not from any philoprogenitive impulse that they become pregnant.'[82] Whilst not endorsing the sterilisation programmes then current in some American states, thinking they were 'unscientific', he did consider that when categories of the 'unfit' other than the obviously mentally deficient could be accurately identified then the practice might be extended.

Despite now thinking the 'unfit' to be a relatively small minority of individuals, Russell's central aim in the field of eugenics remained that of devising some means of encouraging 'professional men to breed large families'.[83]

The expense of education is a grave burden in the professional classes, and therefore causes them to limit their families very severely. Probably their intellectual average is somewhat higher than that of most other classes, so that this limitation is regrettable. The simplest measure for dealing with their case would be to grant free education up to and including university to their children. That is to say, broadly speaking, that scholarships should be awarded on the merits of the parents rather than of the children.[84]

His argument had not changed in twenty years, but its reiteration by an avowed 'Socialist' only emphasised the idiosyncratic nature of his political stance.

Marriage and Morals is a 'progressive' text, but only on questions of sex; in regard to other matters Russell often merely gives an airing to long-standing prejudices. Not only did he remain convinced that 'women are on the average stupider than men' and negroes 'on the average inferior to white men', but also 'that one can generally tell whether a man is a clever man or a fool by the shape of his head'.[85] On another level the book is a theoretical elaboration and justification of his own practice, containing several reflections on the reasons why his type of individual experienced such difficulties with the married state: 'In general, marriage is easiest where people are least differentiated. When a man differs little from other men, and a woman differs little from other women, there is no particular reason to regret not having married someone else.'[86]

The Russells had never considered themselves to be 'married' in the conventional sense, and when Dora became pregnant by an American journalist in 1929 Russell initially reacted in a manner entirely becoming the author of the recently published *Marriage and Morals*.[87] Yet both his marital arrangements and his educational establishment were experiments in practical utopianism and could be sustained only so long as he remained an optimistic rationalist. By the late twenties there are signs that Russell's post-war burst of optimism was almost exhausted and that he was becoming disillusioned with both his marriage and his school. Neither 'failed' in terms of their original conception, it was merely the case that his mood began to change, and this change of mood is reflected in his general projections for the future; for while these remained consistent as regards detail, they began to include consideration of dystopian possibilities. Even as early as 1928, in his essay 'Some Prospects', he remarks:

> If wars are eliminated and production is organized scientifically, it is probable that four hours' work a day will suffice to keep everybody in comfort. It will be an open question whether to work that amount and enjoy leisure, or to work more and enjoy luxury; presumably some will choose one course, some the other. The hours of leisure will no doubt be spent by most people in dancing, watching football, and going to the movies. Children will be no anxiety, since the State will care for them; illness will be very rare; old age will be postponed by rejuvenation till a short time before death. It will be a hedonist's paradise, in which almost everyone will find life so tedious as to be scarcely endurable.[88]

And the following year in *Marriage and Morals* he concludes his chapter on eugenics with an equivocal prophecy which anticipates his position in *The Scientific Outlook*: 'I foresee the time when all who care for the freedom of the human spirit will have to rebel against a scientific tyranny. Nevertheless, if there is to be a tyranny, it is better that it should be scientific.'[89]

CHAPTER 9

Ideologies and dystopias

In June 1930, Russell, in a letter to an old Cambridge acquaintance, Maurice Amos, comments as follows on his current lack of political enthusiasm: 'I think you are entirely right in what you say about the Labour Party. I do not like them, but an Englishman has to have a Party just as he has to have trousers, and of the three Parties I find them the least painful.'[1] A little over a year later, the 'least painful' Party was in disarray, Oswald Mosley's 'New Party' had been formed, and the National Government entrenched in office. By 1932 Mosley's former parliamentary private secretary and one-time New Party member, John Strachey, had published *The Coming Struggle for Power* and the political formations of a peculiarly political decade began to take shape. Yet in a period which saw a dramatic politicisation of English intellectual life, Russell displayed a certain indifference even to those issues with which he might have been expected to engage passionately; indeed, it seems undeniable that he is strangely absent as an intellectual and political influence in the 1930s.

Russell was later to indicate that his political inactivity, and by extension his intellectual isolation, resulted from his being distanced from the prevailing radicalism on the question of the Soviet Union: 'What is true is that, after the Russian Revolution, my dislike of the Russian regime made it difficult for me to cooperate with those Western Radicals who were, as I thought, being misled into support of totalitarianism.'[2] However, while there was never a danger of his joining Shaw and the Webbs in their uncritical fellow-travelling, he was far from being a notably vocal anti-Communist during the inter-war period – his antipathy towards the Soviet Union (although certainly in evidence) was, like his distaste for Fascism, given only sporadic expression.

In his 1935 essay 'Scylla and Charybdis, or Communism and Fascism', he sums up his position as follows:

> It is said by many in the present day that Communism and Fascism are the only practical alternatives in politics, and that whoever does not support the one in effect supports the other. I find myself in opposition to both, and I can no more accept either alternative than, if I had lived in the sixteenth century, I could have been either a Protestant or a Catholic.[3]

While this makes it clear why he evinced so little interest in, say, the Spanish Civil War or the Popular Front, it offers no explanation of his lack of involvement in positive politics – Communism and Fascism did not, after all, exhaust the possibilities. That he conceived his political stance in entirely negative terms indicates a certain loss of confidence, a lack of political direction, but it is also true that the available issues were either unappealing or of a kind which necessitated some redefinement of his own beliefs.

Unemployment, for example, was a central problem of the period with which Russell was, on past performance, unlikely to be much concerned – his interest in welfare programmes had always been minimal and he was temperamentally incapable of anything resembling a sentimental attachment to the working class. His pacifism on the other hand was (so he was to claim later) becoming increasingly equivocal, and despite producing in *Which Way to Peace?* (1936) an argument for non-resistance, he was scarcely prominent in either Lansbury's Labour Party or Sheppard's Peace Pledge Union. Even in opposing Communism and Fascism he at first experienced difficulty, possibly because he detected affinities not only between the competing forms of totalitarianism but also between these and his own views, particularly as regards scientific organisation, race, and eugenics; and until he had curbed the excesses in his own thinking he was unable to inhabit the political centre with any sense of intellectual security. Russell's style of politics was in most respects simply unsuited to the thirties; his enthusiasm for organised political activity had never been intense and had further diminished after 1914; as such he was perhaps always unlikely to flourish in a period of movements and parties. His passionate opposition to the First World War had been sustained by personal political influence, whereas now he had drifted far from the centre of power; therefore, to have become politically effective, he would have had to overcome his distaste for membership.

Russell's feeling of isolation was, however, not entirely due to the fact that his Edwardian radicalism had been superseded – it resulted in part simply from the manner in which he chose to make his living. Of the major figures he was linked with before 1920, Whitehead and

Moore continued in the conventional role of professional philosopher, while Wittgenstein and Keynes pursued unconventional and starkly contrasting post-war careers. Bereft of an academic position and having neither Wittgenstein's disregard for wealth nor Keynes's ability to generate it, Russell had taken on the moderately lucrative role of non-academic intellectual. In the twentieth century, most non-academic intellectuals from Shaw and Wells to Orwell and Koestler made their name with works of literature. Russell is unique in that his early reputation was made with highly technical work accessible only to a tiny minority. Of necessity, his non-professional work took a form which caused him to be linked more often in the second half of his life with Shaw and Wells than with Keynes, Moore, and Wittgenstein. Yet Russell pursued this essentially literary career without the compensation of a literary, artistic, or journalistic environment. Once his Cambridge connections were weakened there are few instances of major new friendships or influences, and Russell's later writing often gives the impression of being impervious even to such contemporary opinion it takes note of. His main problem though was that his ideas – at least in their positive form – were singularly inappropriate to the 1930s and his absence as a significant political and intellectual figure in this period is reflected in his *Autobiography*, where these ten years are dismissed in four pages of text. His biographer, Clark, likewise devotes only twenty-eight pages to the thirties in a book of over seven hundred – these mainly to do with the problems Russell encountered in his private life.

In 1931 Russell succeeded to the earldom on the death of his brother Frank. Along with the title he acquired Frank's debts and dependants – new responsibilities which inclined him to connect his marital problems more closely with the financial burden of the school. It is also clear that the unexpected inheritance reactivated Russell's aristocratic pride, causing him to recoil from the 'progressive' semi-bohemian atmosphere in which he had been living, and to regard his current personal arrangements and intellectual activity as being somewhat ignominious. He was already conducting an affair with Patricia Spence, who eventually became his third wife, and her influence cannot be ignored, for it seems no coincidence that it was with her collaboration Russell carried out his act of filial piety in editing *The Amberley Papers*. By replacing a Cambridge idealist like Dora with a sophisticated Oxford graduate, Russell gave every indication that he was intent upon improving the tone of his existence. In the following year he obtained a legal separation from Dora and at the same time abandoned the school. The Russells divorced in 1935, the proceedings having been lengthy and acrimonious. His own children became Wards in Chancery and were removed to Dartington Hall. As regards Dora's initial non-Russellian offspring, his main concern was that its name should be expunged from his column in Debretts.

Due to these personal difficulties, the early thirties proved to be another unhappy period in Russell's life, and Beatrice Webb was again on hand to analyse his misery; indeed, as she was by now assiduously chronicling the demise of her generation, she was hardly likely to overlook someone whose career had declined entirely in accord with her predictions. On 21 April 1931 she reported in her diary that 'Bertrand Russell, now an Earl, lunched here on Sunday to talk over his new role as a Labour peer ... Poor Bertie; he has made a miserable mess of his life and he knows it. He said drearily, when I asked him if he was going back to his old love – mathematical metaphysics – "I am too old to write anything but pot-boilers".'[4] Two months later, Russell finished dictating a fragment of autobiography, the epilogue of which expands upon Mrs Webb's text:

> When I survey my life, it seems to me to be a useless one, devoted to impossible ideals. I have not found in the post-war world any attainable ideals to replace those which I have come to think unattainable. So far as the things I have cared for are concerned, the world seems to me to be entering upon a period of darkness ... My activities continue from force of habit, and in the company of others I forget the despair which underlies my daily pursuits and pleasures. But when I am alone and idle, I cannot conceal from myself that my life has had no purpose, and that I know of no new purpose to which to devote my remaining years. I find myself involved in a vast mist of solitude both emotional and metaphysical, from which I can find no issue.[5]

At this stage, Russell feared that he was on the brink of finding himself an elderly manufacturer of pot-boilers – the sort of writer who becomes (as Wells himself was shortly to become) an embarrassment to his publisher.[6] In 1930, Russell had written *The Conquest of Happiness*, while Wells was busy rounding off his trilogy with *The Work, Wealth and Happiness of Mankind* – the former was an entirely commercial exercise, the latter sustained a serious purpose. Both books convey a sense of political unreality, yet there are clear signs that in Russell's case the optimism had finally expired. Not only is there an implicit recognition that the gospel of leisure was plainly utopian, 'To be able to fill leisure intelligently is the last product of civilization, and at present very few people have reached this level',[7] but he concludes on a note which anticipates the 'epilogue' to his fragment of autobiography: 'Nothing is more fatiguing nor, in the long run, more exasperating than the daily effort to believe things which daily become more incredible.'[8]

This is not to say that Russell's central ideas underwent radical alteration during the early thirties, they were often just reworked from a more pessimistic standpoint as he experienced an increasing sense of futility and a growing feeling of intellectual isolation. What emerges is a new division in his work, in that he began producing genuinely popular journalism, writing from 1931 to 1935 some 150 articles for the Hearst newspapers with such titles as 'Who May Use Lipstick?' and 'Should Socialists Smoke Good Cigars?', and at the same time indulging his underlying mood – particularly in *The Scientific Outlook*, a book which provided the intellectual basis for later dystopian novels such as *Brave New World* and *Nineteen Eighty-Four*.

As an indication of what Russell's preferred future would look like, *The Scientific Outlook* is a profoundly ambiguous text: it is at once a culmination of those arguments he had been advancing since the early twenties for a rational, scientifically organised society, and a seeming rejection of at least some of their perceived implications. The 'scientific society' Russell depicts in Part Three of the book was not intended as a 'serious prophecy',[9] rather,

> It is an attempt to depict the world which would result if scientific technique were to rule unchecked ... There is, I think, a real danger lest the world should become subject to a tyranny of this sort, and it is on this account that I have not shrunk from depicting the darker features of the world that scientific manipulation unchecked might wish to create.[10]

Far from shrinking from the task, Russell pursues his speculations with a certain misanthropic relish, and although he states that 'The reader will have observed that features that everyone would consider desirable are almost inextricably mingled with features that are repulsive',[11] it remains an open question as to the point at which his own approval terminates.

During his 'utopian' phase, Russell had seen the possibility of scientific organisation providing the material conditions necessary to freedom. Similarly, the 'expert' was considered to be central to society's needs but marginal with regard to the business of living – guidance as to the 'true ends of life' being provided by a 'cultural' elite. Russell's administrative class bears a fairly close resemblance to the Wellsian samurai while his 'intelligentsia' were intended to function on the lines of an Arnoldian clerisy. In *The Scientific Outlook* he envisages the purely instrumental reasoning peculiar to the 'expert' remorselessly encroaching upon the traditional province of the clerisy, and those 'human' values which are thought inimical to efficient organisation being gradually extirpated. He is, in short, concerned with the likelihood of political procedures validated by science expanding 'unchecked' by a Liberal culture.

Yet it is not simply a question of Russell – after making a revised estimate of the future – returning to familiar Liberal formulations, for he retains the stance taken in *Prospects* to the effect that Liberalism was 'utterly inapplicable to the modern world as it has become'.[12] In *Prospects* he had argued that while an 'organic' society reduced actual freedom, it increased potential freedom. At that stage his optimism with regard to Liberal values had been high, for he saw the possibility that rather than being relegated to the uncontrolled interstices between self-concerned groups, they might perhaps expand into that arena of freedom provided by a benevolent, but suitably distant, 'Socialist' organisation. His later position – reflective of a diminished confidence in human nature – omits the optimistic speculations.

His attitude towards Liberalism is characterised by a belief that its political theory had become increasingly at odds with its economic practice – the latter creating the sort of society which could find no possible use for the former. In making his point, he cites Mill's *On Liberty*, a text which, having maintained a rather ghostly presence in his social writing, is finally acknowledged only to be declared redundant:

> Take, for example, such a book as Mill on Liberty. Mill maintains that while the State has a right to interfere with those of my actions that have serious consequences to others, it should leave me free where the effects of my actions are mainly confined to myself. Such a principle, however, in the modern world, leaves hardly any scope for individual freedom. As society becomes more organic, the effects of men upon each other become more and more numerous and important, so that there remains hardly anything in regard to which Mill's defence of liberty is applicable ... If we are to justify any particular form of individual liberty in the scientific society of the future, we shall have to do it on the ground that that form of liberty is for the good of society as a whole, but not in most cases on the ground that the acts concerned affect nobody but the agent.[13]

Russell is intent on taking a somewhat bleak view of things, and in listing those 'traditional principles which appear no longer defensible'[14] he includes both examples which he would undoubtedly defend, such as freedom of speech and of the press, and examples he would probably consider indefensible, such as the freedom to invest one's capital in a manner which disregarded the needs of the community.

Of more interest, however, are those examples which display the tension between his residual rationalist utopianism and his urge to push this sort of thinking towards 'logical' conclusions which he found in some sense satisfyingly repugnant. In fact, on most of the issues discussed, Russell's arguments are, up to a certain point, seriously intended, and some, such as those relating to housing, can, because they resurface unchanged in later essays, be accepted as entirely serious.[15] Like other intellectuals of the period, Russell had barely ceased issuing warnings as to the dysgenic effects of the 'teeming slums' when he began complaining that the suburban sprawl was aesthetically offensive, and here he claims that a few immense apartment blocks were, on grounds of health and efficiency, decidedly preferable to innumerable minute and unattractive units. Russell would, without doubt, have found life in a Le Corbusierian complex distinctly lacking in appeal, yet the stance taken here is entirely in line with his propensity to consider the individualistic demands of the vast majority of the population as being obviously frivolous and to some extent irrational.

This was particularly so with regard to the question of propagation. On this issue, Mill himself – being a good Malthusian – had (at least for some sections of the population) drawn the circle of individual liberty fairly tight; but Russell, while applying the principle on standard lines, 'Those who cause over-population are therefore doing an injury not only to their own children, but to the community',[16] anticipates the need for much stricter control than any envisaged by his godfather. Assuming an optimum level of population to have been established, he predicts that 'in the future there will be a quota of national immigrants into the world. Children in excess of the licensed figure will presumably be subjected to infanticide. This will be less cruel than the present method, which is to kill them by war or starvation.'[17] Russell had previously expressed 'enthusiasm' for infanticide in an equally equivocal text of 1897;[18] here, he is merely prophesying, but there seems no doubt that when (as now) he was in a stoical frame of mind, the grim Swiftian logic of the argument held a certain attraction.

What Russell is intent on demonstrating is not only that Mill's principle has no application to an 'organic' scientific society, but that such a society (which would, it is implied, also deal with any notion of natural rights with Bentham-like briskness) was likely to pursue the kind of policies he had broached in *Marriage and Morals* unrestrained by anything resembling his own 'Liberal' scruples. The modest sterilisation programme he had advocated would, for example, be seen as merely a 'first step': 'As time goes on we may expect a greater and greater percentage of the population to be regarded as mentally defective from the point of view of parenthood.'[19] Again, it is not at all clear whether Russell has any principled objection to this, as his main worry seems to be whether such justifiable curtailments of liberty will be carried out entirely in line with the public interest.

Currently unconvinced that there existed political strategies capable of preserving traditional values against the process of rationalisation, Russell felt forced to conclude that while the forms of democracy might survive, these would be increasingly bereft of meaning, real power passing into the hands of a scientifically trained oligarchy. Rather like Wells in *The Open Conspiracy*, Russell is drawn towards the conclusion that a 'samurai' class – after selflessly taking on the burdens of power – could be expected to develop into a largely hereditary oligarchy, as it was inevitable that they would appear to themselves as the most eugenically desirable members of a society in which strict eugenic controls were enforced.

On eugenics in general, Russell was of the opinion that

> there is hardly any limit to the departures from traditional sentiment which science may introduce into the question of reproduction. If the simultaneous regulation of quantity and quality is taken seriously in the future, we may expect that in each generation some 25 per cent. of women and some 5 per cent. of men will be selected to be the parents of the next generation, while the remainder of the population will be sterilized, which will in no way interfere with their sexual pleasures, but will merely render these pleasures destitute of social importance.[20]

It is at this point that the speculations begin to anticipate the dystopian novel. In fact, *Brave New World*, published in the following year, is so faithful an adaptation of Russell's scientific projection that he was tempted to sue Huxley for plagiarism.[21] Like Huxley, Russell envisaged a benevolent elite governing a contented population which spent most of its leisure time absorbed in trivia. Individuals would be bred so as to produce the characteristics appropriate to their social function, though 'For entirely inferior work negroes will be employed wherever possible.'[22] Not only is the racism in *The Scientific Outlook* 'innocent', but the depiction of the junior members of the elite as a proto-Hitler Youth appears disturbing only with hindsight, and while the social divide is often suggestive of relations between the Party and the proles in *Nineteen Eighty-Four*, it remains the case that Russell, like Huxley, was still too close to nineteenth-century political traditions to be able to conjure up anything resembling the atmosphere of totalitarianism to be found in Orwell.

Yet for our immediate purposes, Russell's dystopian excesses – the Shavian 'lethal chamber', the Huxleyan 'soma', the Orwellian 'Thought Police'[23] – are of less importance than are those more prosaic deliverances which are illustrative of his underlying beliefs. For example, his view that 'the most intelligent classes in the most scientific nations are dying out, and the Western nations as a whole do not do much more than reproduce their own numbers. Unless very radical measures are adopted, the white population of the globe will soon begin to diminish'[24] is put in the form of a statement rather than a prophecy, and one, moreover, which had, with slight variations, consistently found a place in his writing since the turn of the century. As a late-Victorian/Edwardian intellectual, Russell experienced few difficulties in combining a belief in Liberal values with a rationalist elitism. To this extent, *The Scientific Outlook* is best understood as a product of the Edwardian mind, and, as such, not a text in which Russell confronts the consequences of his own scientific utopianism and finds them finally at odds with his Liberal principles, but one which reflects his fear that power in a scientific society was likely to be misplaced. In other words, he would much prefer to offer guidance as a member of a clerisy than be controlled by an uncultured class of samurai. What he rejects at this stage is not necessarily the conditioning of the mediocre, but power without culture.

In his defence of cultural values Russell was always prepared to be flexible with regard to political principle, and at one time declared that if the cultural questions could be solved he would 'accept with more or less equanimity, any political or economic system which ministered to that end'.[25] His political strategies had in the main been calculated to protect 'civilised' values rather than advance Liberal principles, and on those questions where the two were potentially in conflict (such as eugenics), all considerations of democracy and equality were brushed aside in his desire to preserve the achievements of 'civilisation'. In his Wellsian phase, Liberal principles had been invoked only where expedient, and in general were taken to be anachronistic. By the time he came to write *The Scientific Outlook* he was obviously beginning to feel the loss, but once having dismissed Mill as irrelevant, he is reduced to exhortation: 'Science as the pursuit of power must not obtrude upon the sphere of values, and scientific technique, if it is to enrich human life, must not outweigh the ends which it should serve.'[26]

His only recourse is to suggest that those individuals who dominate their times be equipped with an acceptable education: 'The number of men who determine the character of an age is small ... The important men in the age that is just ended are Edison, Rockefeller, Lenin, and Sun Yat-sen. With the exception of Sun Yat-sen these were men devoid of culture, contemptuous of the past, self-confident, and ruthless.'[27] It is very much a case of 'educating our masters', though the threat is not in this instance of the 'tyranny of the majority', but of a superior minority who are presumably educable and can thus be taught to utilise technological innovation in the service of 'civilised' values. In his desire to civilise the 'scientific manipulator',[28] Russell displays his elitist preferences, yet it is not this aspect of his residual Edwardianism which is most striking. What dates the book is his restricted notion of the 'ruthless', for by singling out Edison and Rockefeller he reveals that intellectually he still inhabited a world in which the later careers of Hitler and Stalin were as yet unimaginable, even to the pessimistically inclined.

In that they did not emanate from a benevolent (though uncultured) scientific elite, the excesses of the thirties were not entirely of the kind Russell anticipated; yet with regard to substance, there were sufficient resemblances to have caused him some embarrassment had he not made a timely decision to prune the excesses of his own rationalist elitism. Thus by moderating his rationalism Russell also (and in some ways inadvertently) distanced himself from the incipient irrationalism. Later, as he became aware of the nature of power in the period, he abandoned his hopes that it could be civilised by an admixture of humanist culture and returned to the strategy of containing it by the development of an effective democracy.

This, however, was a gradual process of adaptation to political development, and in *Education and the Social Order* (1932) he retains the view that 'To educate rightly those who are going to be officials is ... very important in a scientific state.'[29] Russell had already adopted an altered stance in *The Scientific Outlook*; indeed, when engaged in writing the book he had felt obliged to warn his American publisher that any expectations based on previous pronouncements were likely to be unfulfilled:

I am afraid you may be disappointed that I am not more of an apostle of science but, as I grow older, and no doubt as a result of the decay of my tissues, I begin to see the good life more and more as a matter of balance and to dread all over-emphasis upon any one ingredient. This has always been the view of elderly men and must therefore have a physiological source, but one cannot escape from one's physiology by being aware of it.[30]

This letter offers some insight into how Russell conceived of his radicalism, for the moderation of his views, which he attributes to the ageing process, had the paradoxical effect of allowing his political stance to appear more consistently radical. Yet, whereas in *The Scientific Outlook* Russell's positivistic aspirations become more circumspect, it was only in *Education and the Social Order* that he began to make significant new adjustments in his arguments relating to race and heredity.

In *Marriage and Morals* he had tentatively considered the possibility that the 'lower classes' might not after all be inherently inferior, and by 1932 the non-white races were also given the benefit of the doubt, pending further progress in the science of eugenics: 'although the importance of congenital differences among human beings cannot be denied, the practical inferences drawn by eugenists are for the most part quite unscientific. No one knows what factors making for socially desirable qualities are hereditary, nor which of such factors are respectively dominant and recessive. There is not even any agreement as to what is socially desirable.'[31] The prevailing tension between Russell's eugenic beliefs and his behaviourism now finally issued in a compromise, and he became sharply critical of any extreme claims for either nature or nurture. He had always argued that there existed undeniable differences in natural ability, and the experience he had gained from his school only served to reinforce this conviction, therefore he regarded Watson's assertion that any child 'by a suitable education, can be turned into a Mozart or a Newton'[32] as untenable. On the other hand, he was no longer convinced that inherited abilities could be predicted with any acceptable degree of accuracy – a complete reversal of the position he had held consistently for some thirty years. He now concluded that 'nothing whatever should be presumed either for or against the intelligence of a pupil or group of pupils on account of the race or social status or personal achievements of their parents'.[33]

Russell's stance on the nature/nurture question was one which made an advocacy of a (non-Webbian) 'meritocracy' inevitable and this he saw as avoiding the errors of both 'aristocracy' and 'democracy': 'The error of aristocracy lay, not in thinking that some men are superior to others, but in supposing superiority to be hereditary. The error of democracy lies in regarding all claims to superiority as just grounds for the resentment of the herd.' [34] What he is opposing is not democratic forms of government but a militant egalitarianism, 'The democratic spirit run wild'. What he desired had, in most respects, remained unaltered since *German Social Democracy*, namely, that the average individual be brought to acknowledge – without resentment – that the qualities possessed by the superior individual were the most important natural resource of any society. However, while previously the exceptional individual was to be charged with the task of preserving 'civilised' values by maintaining intellectual traditions and adding to existing stocks of cultural achievement, he was now to be engaged in the business of establishing a secure framework for international co-operation.

Education and the Social Order is organised around the concepts of individualism and citizenship, and Russell somewhat reluctantly concedes the need to moderate the demands of individualism in accordance with the requirements of organisation. The book is in essence an essay in moderation and compromise; Russell gives way on his ideal of individualism so as to ensure that it possesses a future, and he asserts that 'the most vital need of the near future will be the cultivation of a vivid sense of citizenship of the world. When once the world as a single economic and political unit has become secure, it will be possible for individual culture to revive.'[35] There is a suggestion here that he regarded the period in historical terms, as a Dark Age awaiting a Renaissance, and he later remarked that 'most men feel more hopeless and impotent than they have felt since the Middle Ages'.[36]

Russell was always prone to universalise his own perceptions without making due allowance for his current mental state, yet in the early thirties his depression was in accord with the times and his pessimistic utterances begin to look like objective commentary:

> Our world is a mad world. Ever since 1914 it has ceased to be constructive, because men will not follow their intelligence in creating international cooperation, but persist in retaining the division of mankind into hostile groups. This collective failure to use the intelligence that men possess for purposes of self-preservation is due, in the main, to the insane and destructive impulses which lurk in the unconscious of those who have been unwisely handled in infancy, childhood, and adolescence ... The world has become so

intolerably tense, so charged with hatred, so filled with misfortune and pain that men have lost the power of balanced judgement which is needed for emergence from the slough in which man is staggering. Our age is so painful that many of the best men have been seized with despair.[37]

Whether individuals were more wisely handled in infancy before 1914 is debatable, but the date is significant and tends to indicate that the rather Yeatsian phrase 'many of the best men have been seized with despair' is self-revealing, and that it was this combination of despair and nostalgia which lay behind Russell's political absence in the 1930s.

In February 1932 Russell informed his publisher, Unwin, that he was anxious 'to write a book which will sell well and not involve too much research'.[38] *Education and the Social Order* was written during the summer and was the last of that series of books about which Russell is so defensive in his *Autobiography*. 'After this', he remarked, 'I gave up writing pot-boilers. And having failed as a parent, I found that my ambition to write books that might be important revived.'[39] At several points in his published writings, Russell singles out the year 1932 as marking the beginning of a new period in his career, yet like many other attempts at periodisation, it is useful without being exact; for although he produced in *Freedom and Organization 1814–1914* (1934) and *Power: A New Social Analysis* (1938) two substantial works, he also continued writing for the Hearst newspapers and in 1936 published *Which Way to Peace?*, a book he later considered 'insincere' and refused to have reprinted. What seems clear is that the end of Russell's phase as a 'popular' writer had as much to do with the state of the American economy as with his own decision on the matter. What is not in dispute is that 1932 signalled the end of the 'successful years' after which his income 'diminished catastrophically' – this was, in his view, 'due partly to the depression, which caused people to buy much fewer books, partly to the fact that I was no longer writing popular books, and partly to my having refused to stay with Hearst in 1931 at his castle in California'.[40] With regard to his social thought, the mid-thirties were characterised by a sense of uncertainty, a lack of political direction, and that he was drawn to the study of intellectual history at this time suggests an attempt at reorientation by someone acutely aware of having become adrift from his own intellectual tradition.

In contrast to the precise analytical nature of much of his philosophy, Russell in his social writing tended to favour a more discursive style, preferring to establish a context for his argument in historical terms rather than engaging in conflict with contemporary opinion. This is especially true of those books he produced in the 1920s, in which the opening historical survey often accounts for half the text. Russell was in fact becoming more of a historian than an analyst and this tendency combined with political dissatisfaction to produce in 1934 his solitary work of 'history'.

In *Freedom and Organization* Russell traces the interaction between political theory, scientific technique, and 'important individuals' in Europe and America from 1814 to 1914. Writing as a member of a generation that had been profoundly disturbed by the work of the Hammonds but was now equally disturbed by the way industrialism had begun to impinge on its own existence, it is not surprising that Russell was at this time prone to consider the nineteenth century selectively and charitably. Eschewing the approach of either the Hammonds or Strachey, he clearly chose his subject with a mind to disinter an image of 'the Golden Age'. In 'Western Civilization', an essay published the following year, Russell commented, 'I am afraid Europe, however intelligent, has always been rather horrid, except in the brief period between 1848 and 1914. Now, unfortunately, Europeans are reverting to type.'[41] Later, in a piece entitled 'Symptoms of Orwell's 1984', he was to take up the theme again, though by now the exposure of Stalinism had allowed him to abandon the somewhat petulant tone of the elderly Liberal and to take a more authoritative stance:

> Only those who remember the world before 1914 can adequately realise how much has already been lost. In that happy age, one could travel without a passport, everywhere except in Russia. One could freely express any political opinion, except in Russia. Press censorship was unknown, except in Russia. Any white man could emigrate to any part of the world ... Russia is still worse than the rest of the Western world, not because the Western world has preserved its liberties, but because, while it has been losing them, Russia has marched farther in the direction of tyranny than any Czar ever thought of going.[42]

Whatever its claims to disinterested scholarship, *Freedom and Organization* also represents an attempt by Russell to examine his own intellectual roots, and in surveying the 'brief period' of Liberal ascendancy he succumbed to a nostalgia for past politics – being particularly drawn towards the philosophic radicals. He was attracted by what he termed their 'intellectual sobriety',[43] which he saw as descending to them from Locke: 'They reasoned carefully on every subject of which they treated; they never imagined that they knew things by the light of nature; they were seldom misled by emotion; and although they were systematic, love of system hardly ever led them into errors which they would not have committed in any case.'[44] Engaged in a long withdrawal from his romanticism of the war years, Russell was not only painfully conscious of the regularity with which he himself had been 'misled by emotion', but was at the same time somewhat envious of the pre-Freudian 'happy innocence' of early nineteenth-century rationalism. Referring to James Mill's confidence in the pursuit of reason, he remarks:

it belongs to the age before Freud and before the growth of the art of propaganda. Oddly enough, in Mill's day his confidence was justified by the event. The Benthamites, who were learned men and authors of difficult books, aimed solely at appealing to men's reason, and yet they were successful; in almost all important respects, the course of British politics down to 1874 was such as they advocated. In the Victorian era, this victory of reason surprised no one; in our more lunatic period, it reads like the myth of a Golden Age.[45]

There is no doubt that Russell found the robust uncomplicated rationalism of the elder Mill extremely refreshing and decidedly preferable to the hesitant and introspective Liberalism of the younger.

Russell's current impatience with John Stuart Mill (which was perhaps merely an extension of an impatience with himself) finds expression in *Freedom and Organization* to the extent that he is seen primarily as 'victim' of his father's educational theories – a somewhat ineffectual intellectual who was prone to be 'poetic' and 'slightly sentimental'.[46] Whereas Malthus, Bentham, Ricardo, and James Mill are each accorded a separate chapter in the book, Russell reduces John Stuart Mill to the status of epigone – treating him as a faintly risible figure whose very attributes are to be considered somehow questionable: 'John Stuart Mill, their last representative, had less brains than Bentham or Malthus or Ricardo, but surpassed them in imagination and sympathy with the result that he failed to remain orthodox and even allowed himself to coquette with Socialism.'[47] The words 'failed' and 'coquette' are clearly selected with care and intended by Russell to convey the impression (subsequently reinforced by dismissive asides) that the temperament of the younger Mill was perhaps symptomatic of a fatal decline in a promising political culture.

The Philosophical Radicals, as a school, had certain important merits which, in our day, are apt to be overlooked. They applied to all existing institutions the test of utility, and accepted nothing on the mere ground of historical prescription. By this test, they found no justification for monarchy, aristocracy, religion, war, or empire. Liberals had a rhetorical and sentimental objection to some of these, but the objections of the Philosophical Radicals were argumentative, calm, and apparently derived from the inexorable voice of Reason.[48]

Once more, 'sentiment' is the key word and one which Russell picks up again in his concluding sentence, and in so doing indicates that he now considered that the contemporary world would be better served by Benthamite rationalism than by Millian 'Romanticism': 'It is not by pacifist sentiment, but by world-wide economic organisation, that civilized mankind is to be saved from collective suicide.'[49]

Russell during this period was making a conscious effort to eradicate those Millian traits in his own thinking which had found their clearest expression in *Principles* with his advocacy of 'The Principle of Growth'. He was now of the opinion that international organisation was of more immediate importance than self-culture; hence his determination to celebrate the Benthamite tradition as one which followed a line of intellectual descent down through Ricardo and Marx to modern Socialism, bypassing on the way that brand of Liberalism most closely associated with his godfather. Mill's Coleridgean sympathies, his friendship with Carlyle, his 'sentiment', are seemingly taken by Russell to suggest the 'taint' of Romanticism in his Liberalism, which is therefore deemed to be suspect.

A feature of Russell's engagement with ideas was his tendency to ignore complexity and ambiguity in an urge to polarise intellectual positions in a dramatic fashion, and in a decade in which irrationalism had invaded political life to an unprecedented degree, this tendency was, perhaps inevitably, exacerbated. In his essay, 'The Revolt Against Reason' (1935), Russell sought to clarify the intellectual battle-lines of the period by establishing the genealogy of a comparatively new type of irrationalist thought – one originating with the Romantic movement and characterised by a 'will-to-power'. In a sense, this essay of Russell's can be seen as a further (albeit implicit) criticism of Mill's attempt at synthesis in his essays on Bentham and Coleridge – an attempt which in retrospect could be condemned for muddying the clear waters of Benthamite rationalism.

In Russell's view, 'The belief in reason reached its maximum in the [eighteen] sixties; since then, it has gradually diminished, and it is still diminishing.'[50] As an alternative to the irrationalist 'movement' – which included among others Fichte, Carlyle, and Nietzsche – Russell cites the 'Benthamites and Socialists' who 'may be viewed as two wings of one party: both are cosmopolitan, both are democratic, both appeal to economic self-interest. Their differences *inter se* are as to means, not ends, whereas the new movement, which culminates (as yet) in Hitler, differs from both as to ends, and differs even from the whole tradition of Christian civilization.'[51] Not surprisingly, Russell found the 'ends' of the irrationalists as being most forcibly and 'openly' expressed by Nietzsche, and these he sees as being centred on 'the greatness of exceptional individuals'.[52] Yet he also insists that Fichte 'has received less than his due share of credit for inaugurating this great movement',[53] and goes on to argue that 'this [Fichte's] doctrine that the "noble" man is the purpose of humanity, and that the "ignoble" man has no claims on his own account, is of the essence of the modern attack on democracy'.[54] If we recall Russell's comment in 1894 to the effect that 'one Darwin is more important than 30 million working men and women'[55] and his subsequent less stark but similarly elitist deliberations, the sense of moral indignation which pervades this essay might be thought somewhat overdone. While it must be allowed that Russell had always opposed the 'Carlyle/Nietzsche' tradition and had vigorously attacked its social Darwinist manifestation in the early years of the century, there remained too close a correspondence between his own belief in individualism and eugenics and certain aspects of Nietzsche's thought for him to be able to distance himself from the latter in such a decisive manner: 'he [Nietzsche] wishes the unfit to be prevented from breeding, and he hopes, by the methods of the dog-fancier to produce a race of supermen, who shall have all the power, and for whose benefit alone the rest of mankind shall exist'.[56]

As already mentioned, the paradox in Russell's thinking was that what brought him closest to the irrationalist camp was his tendency towards an overweening rationalism, rather than the mild Millian Romanticism of which he was now so suspicious. It is ironic, therefore, that it is precisely the romantic element in Russell's early work which, because it anticipated the Socialist humanism of the 1950s and 60s, allowed him to transcend his largely Edwardian frame of reference and extend his intellectual 'life' beyond its natural term. However, while Tawney, for example, had in *Equality* (1931) only recently demonstrated that this kind of political 'romanticism' was entirely compatible with a belief in democracy, Russell, driven by an urge to establish a totally unambiguous central position, was increasingly forced back towards an undiluted rationalist Liberalism – a process which resulted in his unequivocally Popperian 'Philosophy and Politics' (1947).

This is not to say that what Russell alludes to as 'the slow abandonment of many of the beliefs that had come to me in the moment of "conversion" in 1901'[57] was in any way a consistent process. He had published 'In Praise of Idleness' in 1932 and its companion piece 'Useless Knowledge' in 1935, a year in which he also wrote 'The Case for Socialism'. Yet what is notable about all three essays is that Russell is no longer interested even in speculating on the essential creativity of an untrammelled human nature. In the earlier essay, he follows Clive Bell in declaring that 'without the leisure class, mankind would never have emerged from barbarism',[58] and while he maintains his belief that increased leisure for all would be a more efficient way of producing the occasional Darwin, he considered that the number of the creative would remain extremely small.

Almost as if to preserve his individuality, his intellectual isolation, Russell throughout the thirties progressively distanced himself from political extremes by curbing any perceived excesses in his own thinking. This steady moderation of his views on both the romantic/creative side and the scientific/rational side, coupled with a greater tolerance of the faults of democratic government, recall his reaction to the threat of Bolshevism in 1920 and, to some extent, his response to German Socialism in 1896. His essay, 'The Case for Socialism', for example, is remarkably similar in tone to *German Social Democracy*; indeed, the tactics he advocates for contemporary 'Socialists' are identical to those he had suggested to the German Social Democrats in the 1890s. 'I am', he declares,

> as convinced a Socialist as the most ardent Marxian, I do not regard Socialism as a gospel of proletarian revenge, nor even, *primarily* as a means of securing economic justice. I regard it primarily as an adjustment to machine production demanded by considerations of common sense, and calculated to increase the happiness, not only of proletarians, but of all except a tiny minority of the human race. If it cannot now be realised without a violent upheaval, this is to be attributed largely to the violence of its advocates. But I still have some hope that a saner advocacy may soften the opposition, and make a less catastrophic transition possible . . . I am persuaded that, if Socialist propaganda were conducted with less hate and bitterness, appealing not to envy but to the obvious need of economic organization, the task of persuasion would be enormously facilitated, and the need for force correspondingly diminished.[59]

Such views, when considered within the prevailing political context, appear to have lost nothing of their original naïvety.

His faith in rational self-interest and the democratic process, revived by his reacquaintance with the philosophic radicals, now serve to support a conviction that it is better to risk the 'tyranny of the majority' than to allow power to be possessed by a small minority – no matter how attractively exceptional their qualities or benevolent their intentions. It would seem that a benign oligarchy was excluded from consideration because he feared the alternative to democracy was now Fascism, for he concludes with the remark that 'Whoever weakens the respect for democratic government is, intentionally or unintentionally, increasing the likelihood, not of Socialism or Communism, but of Fascism.'[60] Yet the uncertainties of Russell's political stance, so much in evidence throughout this period, are highlighted by the fact that the following year he was advocating a policy of non-resistance against any future German aggression.

Given his pacifist principles, it might seem inevitable that he should, in the late thirties, emerge as a supporter of Chamberlain's policy of appeasement; but the position taken up in *Which Way to Peace?* goes far beyond this, and suggests that by interpreting the Nazi movement in terms of its genealogy he failed to perceive its true nature, merely regarding it as yet another manifestation of that peculiarly German weakness for philosophical nationalism – a temporary aberration of a 'truly civilized nation'. In his own view Russell was being entirely consistent, as he had preached non-resistance in 1915 when German aggression was not just a matter of rhetoric; thus the defence he offers of *Which Way to Peace?* in his *Autobiography* – that it was 'unconsciously insincere'[61] – appears on the one hand unnecessary, and on the other disingenuous. Although his pacifism was central to those beliefs associated with his conversion of 1901 and which he was now slowly modifying, there is no concrete evidence of a change in his position until 1940, when Russell (by then working in America) let it be known through Kingsley Martin and the *New Statesman* that he was now a supporter of the war against Hitler. That Russell's anti-Communism was more in evidence than his anti-Fascism was because he retained a conviction that Germany, being a genuinely civilised nation, was less of a long-term threat than was a still largely 'uncivilised' Russia. This, however, did not alter his view that active politics in the thirties meant a loss of integrity, an implied alignment with one of two unacceptable ideologies, and as the political atmosphere became more charged, so his withdrawal became more noticeable.

Russell's increasing indifference to politics coincided with a growing need for a more secure income, and in 1937 he approached Moore as to the possibility of returning to Cambridge. Moore was unable – or perhaps because of his distaste for Russell's company, unwilling – to help, therefore he (Russell) began to sound out American universities and had hopes of taking over from Whitehead at Harvard. In the mean time, he retreated into his own history, devoting eighteen months to editing (with the new Lady Russell) his parents' papers. There was, as he later admitted, 'something of the ivory tower in this work': 'My parents had not been faced with our modern problems; their radicalism was confident, and throughout their lives the world was moving in directions that to them seemed good.'[62] Russell's nostalgia for the nineteenth century can be seen as a central feature of his work in the 1930s, and what is lacking in his writing of this period is precisely that which he envied his Liberal predecessors, namely a 'confident radicalism'.

His own radicalism, previously confident often to the point of excess, was now confronted with the realisation of its extremes, both in terms of irrationalist romanticism and 'Socialist' organisation, yet he was uncomfortable with a hesitant moderation which might appear to link him with an anachronistic Liberalism. Thus, when commenting on his stance in *Power* (1938) – his first exclusively political text since *Prospects* – he remarks: 'I maintained that a sphere for freedom is still desirable even in a socialist state, but this sphere has to be defined afresh and not in liberal terms.'[63] His efforts to avoid being characterised as an elderly, somewhat outmoded, Liberal were, however, generally unsuccessful, and Orwell, reviewing *Power* in the *Adelphi*, complained of Russell's unsatisfactory treatment of the 'contemporary situation', maintaining that 'like all liberals he is better at pointing out what is desirable than at explaining how to achieve it'.[64] For Orwell, Russell's was 'an essentially *decent* intellect',[65] yet the emphasis he gives to this, one of his favourite adjectives, serves to point up limitations as well as qualities, and suggests what was undoubtedly true, that despite his brilliance and occasional cynicism, Russell retained some of the psychological innocence of the nineteenth century, and as a result lacked imaginative insight into the possible consequences of totalitarianism – intellectually at ease with Marx and Freud, he was uncomprehending of Stalin and Hitler.

For the purposes of the present study, it is altogether appropriate that *Power*, like *German Social Democracy*, should emerge from a series of lectures given at the London School of Economics; for in it Russell returns to a wholehearted belief in democratic solutions, and thus in some sense completes a forty-two-year cycle of development in his thinking. Not that he retreats to an 'innocent' Liberalism, for his purpose in *Power* is to confront the psychological realities of modern politics. Yet, while he gives every indication of being alert to the weaknesses in Liberal theory, he also offers evidence of being unable to grasp the concept of the irrational in other than intellectual terms; therefore *Power* remains, for all his efforts to 'distance' himself from the tradition, a recognisably Liberal text.

Since *Principles* Russell had thought Liberal theory to be psychologically inadequate, and although he is now intent on pressing the claims of a single dominant instinct rather than a pair of opposites, that which he rejects remains the same – that is, the notion that 'economic self-interest could be taken as the fundamental motive in the social sciences'.[66] Certain human desires are, in Russell's view, 'insatiable and infinite',[67] but a 'desire for commodities ... is finite, and can be fully satisfied by a moderate competence'.[68] Power, on the other hand, is one of the 'infinite desires of man',[69] and Russell is concerned to prove that 'The laws of social dynamics are laws which can be stated in terms of power, not in terms of this or that form of power ... power, like energy, must be regarded as continually passing from any one of its forms into any other, and it should be the business of social science to seek the laws of such transformations.'[70] On first sight this looks like an attempt to marry a Nietzschean reductionist psychology with Victorian social theory; yet despite sometimes being interpreted in this manner,[71] the psychology is not reductionist in any general sense and the 'laws of social dynamics' are not revealed – Russell's aims are more modest, namely, to 'classify the forms of power'[72] as a necessary first step to the discovery of these laws.

As such, Russell is only tentatively a 'Nietzschean' sociologist, and his claim that 'Love of power ... is disguised, among the more timid, as an impulse of submission to leadership'[73] is effectively negated by the preceding statement that it is 'very unevenly distributed'.[74] Indeed, it would seem that from Russell's point of view the average man has only a negligible desire for power, but this does not affect his argument as 'Love of power ... is a characteristic of the men who are causally important.'[75] As always with Russell, it is the exceptional individual who effects change – the only difference being that he now sees the need for the collective to restrain the exceptional, rather than, as was previously the case, regarding the main priority as being the freeing of the exceptional from constraints imposed by the uncomprehending and mediocre. Now of a pessimistic persuasion, Russell is no longer celebrating the creative impulse in man, but warning of the will-to-power.

Not surprisingly, he does not interpret his altered stance in quite these terms; rather, he sees himself as examining human nature in its current historical manifestation and by so doing 'making the present and the probable near future more intelligible than it can be to those whose imaginations are dominated by the eighteenth and nineteenth centuries. Those centuries were in many ways exceptional, and we seem to be now returning, in a number of respects, to forms of life and thought which were prevalent in earlier ages.'[76] The nineteenth century retains its status as a Golden Age of rationalism, though it is not clear from this whether the philosophic radicals are to be seen as the creators or the beneficiaries of an atypical period in European history. There is, in fact, every indication that Russell was unimpressed with the achievements of the thirties' intelligentsia, and had, as a consequence, rather lost faith in the intellectuals as a class.

In all his previous books, the intellectual is seen as being, without question, the most important figure in society, as both a preserver of the past and as a creator of the future. Whether as a 'clerisy' preserving traditional values, or as a body of 'experts' concerned with the scientific organisation of society, the intellectuals' role was seen as central, and, in *The Scientific Outlook*, mutually reinforcing – the 'clerisy' imparting respect for cultural values which restrain the tendencies towards rationalist excess characteristic of the 'expert'. Yet the 'scientific' oligarchy he had prophesied in *The Scientific Outlook* had not materialised, and the apparent 'failure' of the intellectuals is something Russell explains as being the result of their decline as a 'priestly' class:

> Science, in giving some real acquaintance with natural processes, has destroyed the belief in magic, and therefore the respect for the intellectual ... The intellectuals, finding their prestige slipping from them as a result of their own activities, become dissatisfied with the modern world. Those in whom the dissatisfaction is least take to Communism; those in whom it goes deeper shut themselves up in their ivory tower.[77]

There is an element of self-justification in these somewhat Weberian reflections, a suggestion that – despite having prepared a retreat to the philosophy department of the University of Chicago – his profound discontent signified in some sense a more 'radical' stance than did the mere possession of a Party card. Furthermore, from Russell's point of view the intellectual in the 'ivory tower' had not 'abrogated the use of his reason' and was to this extent still qualified to offer 'rational' solutions.

Russell's attempt to analyse the nature of power by means of exhaustive classification carries certain Benthamite overtones, and his intellectual affinities with the philosophic radicals are also evident in that his aim of containing power in all its multifarious manifestations is intended to restore democracy to its previously healthy condition. In his view, 'The most successful democratic politicians are those who succeed in abolishing democracy and becoming dictators. This, of course, is only possible in certain circumstances; no one could have achieved it in nineteenth-century England.'[78] *Power*, clearly, represents something of a recantation on Russell's part, particularly with regard to his elitist aspirations, as any argument to the effect that 'an oligarchy is admirable if it consists of "good" men'[79] is now firmly rejected, for 'the arguments from history and psychology ... have shown how rash it is to expect irresponsible power to be benevolent'.[80] He is now preoccupied with the 'taming of power' in the areas of politics, economics, propaganda, and psychology by means of, and for the sake of, democracy.

Russell had produced arguments for a more 'effective' democracy in previous books, but his commitment had usually been to democracy as a means to securing essentially elitist ends and this tendency increased as the electorate expanded and his distaste for majoritarian rule became more pronounced. Here, while still protective of the rights of minorities, he is more suspicious of interest groups and argues that 'the only practicable form of impartiality ... is the rule of the majority'.[81] For Russell, 'Bentham's political doctrines, and the whole of nineteenth-century liberalism, were designed to prevent the arbitrary exercise of power. But such methods have come to be considered incompatible with efficiency',[82] and the main thrust of his argument is aimed at updating Bentham in designing a 'democracy more thorough-going, more carefully safeguarded against official tyranny, and with more deliberate provision for freedom of propaganda, than any purely political democracy that has ever existed'.[83]

On the political side, he suggests a combination of federalism, devolution, and pluralism, with interest groups playing a largely defensive role. In economics, he reiterates his arguments for industrial democracy, emphasising that public 'ownership' must be united with public 'control'. Propaganda, he feels, can be contained by ensuring that all sides of an issue are given expression, and he suggests the novel device of a single newspaper 'with different pages allocated to different parties'.[84] On this question he remained something of a Millian, in that there is an implicit assumption that by these means reason will inevitably prevail. Yet it is on the question of psychology that Russell is driven back to a reliance on the 'Liberal educator' and a 'diffused liberal sentiment',[85] and he outlines 'the task of a liberal education' as follows: 'to give a sense of the value of things other than domination, to help to create wise citizens of a free community, and through the combination of citizenship with liberty in individual creativeness to enable men to give human life that splendour which some few have shown that it can achieve'.[86] These final sentiments are quintessentially Russellian and were, with slight variations, to become familiar in allied propaganda material, but the current market for Liberal idealism was a poor one, and the book, as he himself conceded, 'fell rather flat'.[87] Russell was not on hand to witness the relative failure of *Power*, for by the time it was published in October he was already in Chicago, restored – for a brief and hectic period – to academic life after a gap of over twenty years.

Compared with someone like Auden, Russell had slipped through the 1930s practically unnoticed – thus when Auden sailed for America in January 1939, his leaving was seen to have political or at least symbolic significance, whereas Russell's departure a few months earlier produced little comment.[88] Although both were drawn to America by the promise of financial security, Auden was intent on escaping the burden of politics, while Russell was seeking refuge from a peculiarly inimical political atmosphere. He was not, however, entirely confident that America would prove noticeably more congenial, for, whereas he had – unlike Auden – actually *experienced* the thirties as a 'low dishonest decade', he viewed it in terms of general trends rather than as a self-contained 'period' and was resigned to becoming increasingly adrift from modern political culture. In his 'auto' obituary, published in *The Listener* in 1936, he had – somewhat underestimating his own endurance – fixed his death for June 1961, and concludes the piece as follows: 'He had many friends, but had survived almost all of them. Nevertheless, to those who remained he appeared, in extreme old age, full of enjoyment, no doubt owing, in large measure, to his invariable health, for politically, during his last years, he was as isolated as Milton after the Restoration. He was the last survivor of a dead epoch.'[89] Yet while he was, in one respect, the 'last survivor', in 1961 he was far from being isolated, politically or otherwise; indeed, the world had never been more attentive.

Epilogue: Russell and the idea of the clerisy

Bertrand Russell, though an aristocratic Liberal who was impatient of politics, suspicious of the state, indifferent to production, and whose central theme was the importance of a natural elite (or more particularly the exceptional individual), sustained a reputation as a radical intellectual for most of a long career. In a sense this is not the paradox it seems as Russell's impatience with parliamentary politics must be set alongside his extra-parliamentary activity culminating in his involvement with CND – an involvement which demonstrated that his Gladstonian passion for the 'single great issue' was undiminished. His suspicion of the state, though illustrative of a residual Whiggism which made for an uneasy relationship with Socialism, also allowed for the incorporation of Pluralist and even Anarchist elements into his thinking. The indifference to production, which could be construed as an indifference to working-class aspiration, stemmed from a belief that in the West at least the technology was already available to meet existing needs. For Russell, a rational society would be one in which progress was measured, not by increased consumption, but by an increase in the number of those with sufficient leisure to realise the 'true ends of life'. The radical implications of a 'natural' elite are less clear, though as Russell saw one of its functions to be that of maintaining a vital culture while embodying the aristocratic ideals of civility, spontaneity, individuality, and creativity, it could be said to provide a model for a burgeoning meritocracy. There is, though, a tension between the idea of a clerisy and the idea of a meritocracy, one which I think can best be brought out by examining Russell's intellectual elitism against the background of changing cultural values.

As a philosopher Russell was an academic figure and his fame is largely distinct from his reputation in this area – unlike Sartre, for example, who acquired fame as an existentialist, Russell was never in this sense famous for his logical atomism. Yet his work as a non-academic intellectual derives some of its authority from its being produced by a major philosopher – for the general reader could not help but feel that he was being granted crumbs from a table (albeit one with which he was probably fairly familiar) and that Russell lived on much more intimate terms with the truth than he did or was ever likely to. Although Russell could scarcely deny that this was the case, he refused to admit any connection between his technical philosophy and the views he expressed in his other books. In the passage previously referred to in the Schilpp volume (see p. 93), for example, he complains,

With regard to *Social Reconstruction*, and to some extent with my other popular books, philosophic readers, knowing that I am classified as a 'philosopher', are apt to be led astray. I did not write *Social Reconstruction* in my capacity as a 'philosopher'. I wrote it as a human being who suffered from the state of the world, wished to find some way of improving it, and was anxious to speak in plain terms to others who had similar feelings. If I had never written technical books, this would be obvious to everyone; and if the book is to be understood, my technical activities must be forgotten.[1]

Russell has a point, and for someone who had done so much to establish the boundaries of philosophy's legitimate province, the conflation was doubtless irritating. It was, however, not only 'philosophic' readers who were led astray, and his 'plain man' stance here is disingenuous since the 'others who had similar feelings' were in the first instance members of the intelligentsia well aware of his reputation as a mathematician and technical philosopher, whereas the wider audience the book eventually reached was informed of the author's status as a Fellow of the Royal Society. Russell was, in short, exercising intellectual authority. Moreover, by employing the word 'Principles' in the title, he was not only beginning to make a habit of drawing on its Newtonian connotations, but keeping company with every major Victorian social theorist from Mill to Marshall who had similarly gestured towards 'science' by way of Bentham. *Principles of Social Reconstruction* was intended to be 'popular' only in the sense that Benjamin Kidd's *Principles of Western Civilization* or Herbert Spencer's *Principles of Sociology* had been popular.

The book was not offered as a necessarily hospitable text, and the middle-class general reader – especially one who had dipped into the English Idealists – might be forgiven for believing that in certain passages he was encountering a species of 'philosophy'; for example:

Reverence and worship, the sense of an obligation to mankind, the feeling of imperativeness and acting under orders which traditional religion has interpreted as Divine inspiration, all belong to the life of the spirit. And deeper than all these lies the sense of a mystery half revealed, of a hidden wisdom and glory, of a transfiguring vision in which common things lose their solid importance and become a thin veil behind which the ultimate truth of the world is dimly seen. It is such feelings that are the source of religion, and if they were to die most of what is best would vanish out of life.[2]

What we have here is not philosophy – not at least in Russell's sense of the term – but the traditional rhetorical discourse of the secular clerisy. Though written by an analytical philosopher, *Principles* was using essentially Benthamite means towards largely Coleridgean ends, and Russell was merely unfortunate in that as a social thinker he inhabited a tradition which had recourse to a vocabulary he had rejected so forcefully as a professional philosopher. Coleridge, Carlyle, Arnold, and to some extent Mill, all drew freely on German Idealism in an attempt to invest Art, Culture, and the Pursuit of Knowledge with transcendental attributes.[3] When Russell – also inspired by an aspect of German culture – employed the remnants of his Idealist vocabulary he naturally caused confusion amongst his philosophic readers.

Given his aims it is difficult to see how he could have done otherwise, for defending and promoting the life of the mind was a task which – while not exactly outside the scope of analytical philosophy – would hardly be accomplished by restricting one's audience to the admirers of G.E. Moore's *Principia Ethica*. On the other hand, Russell could ill afford to disguise his credentials no matter how inappropriate they might seem. As with all advocates of a clerisy his authority stemmed from his offering evidence of a superior education, exceptional ability, even 'genius'. Like the higher clergy a clerisy was given a hearing on matters outside the professional competence of its members precisely because of its presumed access to the arcane and the sacred.

The problem for Russell, as for all those who were convinced that the intellectuals were a distinct class of peculiar importance to society, was how to maintain this unassuming, inoffensive, but ultimately Platonic relationship with society (or at least some sections of it). Believing themselves to form a 'natural' yet (depending on views of heredity) 'open' aristocracy, they shared a sense of vocation and a profound anxiety lest their separateness should issue in isolation and respect turn to indifference, even hostility. Selflessly obsessed with their self-preservation they sought to retain and in some cases advance their role in society by inculcating the notion of their indispensability – hence their conspicuous engagement in cultural and scientific education. To some extent, therefore, their educational activities were spurious in that what they were intent upon was preserving the 'life of the mind' as an option for a gifted minority. Their main aim, then, was not the improvement of taste or the dissemination of knowledge – though they would claim success in both areas – but to establish conditions in which tolerant appreciation of their arcane activities was assured. On this view Russell's technical philosophy *is* linked to his social thought in the sense that the former endowed him with a priestly authority while the latter drew on this authority to argue for the kind of society that would value obscure pursuits which appeared to lack any utility.

The activities of the clerisy were therefore circular and the circle could in theory be broken by either too little or too much success in mediation and education. In the passage from *Power* quoted in the last chapter, Russell expresses the view that the spread of education had already robbed the intellectual of his priestly power: 'The reason for this is that scientific knowledge though difficult is not mysterious but open to all who take the trouble.' As such, 'The modern intellectual inspires no awe.'[4] The notion that the intellectual class was peculiarly vulnerable to the dissemination of knowledge, that the rise of the meritocracy signalled the decline of the clerisy, is in a sense the reverse of the old fear of the 'tyranny of the majority' – knowledge is not threatened by a philistine democracy, it is itself democratised – the clerisy has performed the function of transitional elite and is now redundant. Russell's tone suggests that this outcome held as little appeal as did the alternative – in either case the intellectual's role was diminished, his importance discounted, reverence withheld.

Despite a pervasive pessimism, however, the clerisy in general maintained its traditional discourse, the anxious note being struck by Julian Huxley,

> Whenever the lag in communication between science and general thought grows considerable, whenever science, through laziness, pride, or pedantry, fails to make herself understood, and whenever the public, through laziness, stupidity, or prejudice, fails to understand, then we shall proceed to a lamentable divorce. It will not be merely the results of science which will not be assimilated, but science herself and the spirit of science will not be understood; and scientists will become an isolated caste in a half hostile environment.[5]

the transcendental by J.B.S. Haldane, 'The scientific point of view is lofty enough to satisfy any of the aspirations of the human spirit. I believe that the future of Western civilization depends upon whether or not it can assimilate that scientific point of view.'[6] Like Russell in *The Scientific Outlook*, Huxley and Haldane were 'popularisers' of science; they were not, though, merely mediating between their professional work and the public – the nearest Russell himself came to doing this was in *The Problems of Philosophy* – rather they were working to ensure the preservation of a benevolent elite in a democratic state.

The point about intellectuals – one Russell never tired of reiterating – was not what they knew, but what they could discover or create; hence, his real concern was not that of too many people 'taking the necessary trouble' to learn all that he knew (an unlikely eventuality in any case) but that a combination of democracy and scepticism would inhibit innovation and issue in mediocrity; in short, a move away from the expensive uncertainties of pure science towards the more predictable gratifications of technology. In fact, though scientific knowledge might lend itself more readily to dissemination than did high culture, it was the latter which seemed more immediately under threat in the post-war world precisely because the technical advances in mass communication pointed towards a market-based common culture inimical to clerisy values.[7]

It was a problem addressed by I.A. Richards in *Principles of Literary Criticism* (1924), the final attempt to provide Coleridgean aesthetics and the clerisy tradition with Benthamite support:

> What is needed is a defensible position for those who believe that the arts are of value. Only a general theory of value which will show the place and function of the arts in the whole system of values will provide such a stronghold. At the same time we need weapons with which to repel and overthrow misconceptions. With the increase of population the problem presented by the gulf between what is preferred by the majority and what is accepted as excellent by the most qualified opinion has become infinitely more serious and appears likely to become threatening in the near future. For many reasons standards are much more in need of defence than they used to be. It is perhaps premature to envisage a collapse of values, a trans-valuation by which popular taste replaces trained discrimination. Yet commercialism has done stranger things: we have not yet fathomed the more sinister potentialities of the cinema and the loudspeaker, and there is some evidence, uncertain and slight no doubt, that such things as 'best-sellers' (compare *Tarzan* with *She*), magazine verses, mantelpiece pottery, Academy pictures, Music Hall songs, County Council buildings, War Memorials ... are

decreasing in merit. Notable exceptions, in which the multitude are better advised than the experts, of course occur sometimes, but not often.[8]

In Richards's *Principles* and Russell's *Principles*, the 'poet' or the 'highly civilized individual' is not just the product of a dominant culture, he is, because of innate qualities – his possession of nicely balanced impulses – of great benefit to society as a whole. Therefore it is for Richards not true that 'criticism is a luxury trade': 'The rear-guard of society cannot be extricated until the vanguard has gone further. Goodwill and intelligence are still too little available. The critic, we have said, is as much concerned with the health of the mind as any doctor with the health of the body. To set up as a critic is to set up as a judge of values.'[9]

From the point of view of the vanguard (which for Russell, Richards, and later, Leavis, tended to centre on Cambridge) the secondary educational activities of the clerisy had their own importance and required abilities which were rare. As such it is hardly surprising that the public activities of the clerisy have been carried on in the main not by philosophers and scientists but by writers and literary critics. Indeed, in the procession from Coleridge to Eliot, Mill and Russell are the only notable philosophers to pursue the idea of the clerisy in their work. The reason for this is not hard to find, for among the many attributes they shared was a fluency and clarity of style which enabled them to sustain lengthy careers as non-academic intellectuals. Of the two, Russell's is the more notable achievement as the professionalisation of philosophy progressed at a more rapid rate than did that of English studies, therefore the distance between the professional extremes of Mill and Arnold were much less great than those which obtained between Russell and Leavis.

The work of the clerisy required some subtlety, its central aims were rarely stated overtly, the 'idea' itself remained nebulous, the notion of 'endowment' scarcely raised after Coleridge. In consequence, Russell was extremely irritated when his country house conversations provided material for Aldous Huxley's *Crome Yellow* (1921). In the novel he is caricatured as Mr Scogan, an elderly intellectual whose elitist pronouncements such as the following anticipate both in content and subtlety of expression Clive Bell's *Civilization: An Essay* (1928):

'Eccentricity ... It's the justification of all aristocracies. It justifies leisured classes and inherited wealth and privilege and endowment and all the other injustices of that sort. If you are to do anything reasonable in this world, you must have a class of people who are secure, safe from public opinion, safe from poverty, leisured, not compelled to waste their time in the imbecile routines that go by the name of Honest Work. You must have a class of which the members can think and, within the obvious limits, do what they please. You must have a class in which people who have eccentricities can indulge them and in which eccentricity in general will be tolerated and understood. That's the important thing about an aristocracy. Not only is it eccentric itself – often grandiosely so; it also tolerates and even encourages eccentricity in others.'[10]

Yet Russell was always drawn to the Platonic idea of aristocratic rule – even in the generally hostile account of Plato offered in *History of Western Philosophy* he cannot resist inserting the opinion that:

If there were a more exact science of government, and more certainty of men following its precepts, there would be much to be said for Plato's system. No-one thinks it unjust to put the best men into a football team, although they acquire thereby a great superiority. If football were managed as democratically as the Athenian government the students to play for their university would be chosen by lot.[11]

At Garsington Russell doubtless felt free to speculate openly on the subject of a 'rational' society, but in his books such ideas form a subtext. Thus, *Principles* is notable for its radical zeal, expressing the conviction that the growth in state power, the obsession with property, and the onset of war were a consequence of an undue dominance of the possessive impulse, and that 'Liberation of creativeness ought to be the principle of reform both in politics and in economics.'[12] It nonetheless remains an example of traditional clerisy literature, for by stressing creativity over possession Russell was well placed to argue that the artist, the intellectual, and especially the genius were society's most valuable natural resource and therefore conditions should obtain in which they could flourish. Not only were they the creators of all that was worth preserving, they were the only individuals capable of sustaining that restless discontent which prevented stagnation. Russell's rather self-serving concern for the exceptional, his belief that they should be encouraged and enabled to act as a clerisy, has its counterpart in his relative indifference to the concerns of the ordinary such as social justice, security, material well-being, work, and the problems of industrial production. It was not simply a question of his aestheticism being elitist, it was also ascetic and marked by a distaste for the vulgar materialistic demands of mass society.

As a cultural critic Russell was scarcely unique in being unable to empathise with the desires of the ordinary man; from Arnold to Hoggart the suggestion was always that with a modicum of effort he could occupy himself in less disagreeable ways. Fastidious, and averse to sentimentality, Russell promoted a demanding conception of the good life. For most, however, the Cambridge/Bloomsbury ideal was not only unrealisable, it was not even an ideal. Russell recognised this yet he found it difficult to accord value to ways of living which differed markedly from his own.

In 1932 he published 'In Praise of Idleness', an essay which though not as tactless as its title suggests, is more attentive to the problems of 'civilization' than the condition of the unemployed. In it the four-hour day is once more offered as a panacea, and Russell, who experienced no difficulty with leisure himself, hints at ways in which others could use theirs to his satisfaction:

> It is an essential part of any such social system that education should be carried further than it usually is at present, and should aim, in part, at providing tastes which would enable a man to use leisure intelligently. I am not thinking mainly of the sort of things that would be considered 'highbrow'. Peasant dances have died out except in remote rural areas, but the impulses which caused them to be cultivated must still exist in human nature. The pleasures of urban populations have become mainly passive: seeing cinemas, watching football matches, listening to the radio, and so on. This results from the fact that their active energies are fully taken up with work; if they had more leisure, they would again enjoy pleasures in which they took an active part.[13]

Aside from gesturing towards a 'folk' culture even more nebulous than the one to which Leavis was so attached, Russell provides few clues as to the form these pleasures will take, though we can assume that he was not intending to drum up business for the local dance-halls.

He has, in fact, little to offer a working-class audience with no cultural aspirations and moves on quickly to suggest that a more leisured professional class would have the energy to follow those traditional utopian part-time pursuits of writing, painting, and pottering about in the shed. The ideal remains that of the intellectual aristocracy, the image indulged that of the Stephen sisters sharing a house with Darwin; yet with the genetic material being dispersed as a democracy rapidly transformed itself into a meritocracy, Russell has recourse to his alternative explanation of the origins of excellence, namely the Romantic notion of genius. The professional classes will thus be prepared for visitation by the transcendent while acting as a supplement to the universities which 'useful as they are, are not adequate guardians of the interests of civilization in a world where everyone outside their walls is too busy for unutilitarian pursuits'.[14]

Russell's conception of genius, his belief that most things of enduring value are produced by exceptional, unencumbered, preferably unappreciated individuals – even in science he suspected that the necessary organisation of ability curtailed creativity – meant that the idea of a meritocracy made him uneasy. In Russell's view, a meritocracy threatened to be little more than a climbing frame for the likes of Sidney Webb who was – not surprisingly – one of its great advocates, rather than providing opportunities for the likes of D.H. Lawrence who – equally unsurprisingly – was not. The clerisy tradition may have leaned towards Bentham to bolster its authority, but it did, after all, originate with Coleridge.

Although Russell did lean increasingly towards Bentham in the 1930s, what he then demanded of an aesthetic clerisy was not so much works of art as the maintenance and elaboration of values – as such he considered it dangerous for its members to be recruited into a state-run meritocracy. As I suggested earlier, his ideal was a bifurcation of society in which mundane matters such as the organisation of the economy could be left in the hands of 'scientific' meritocrats while innovation in both pure science and the arts was entrusted to an independent clerisy.

Yet the alternative to a meritocracy was not a society guided by a clerisy (itself perpetuated by the provision of conditions suitable for the random appearance of the exceptional), but the kind of society which – in theory at least – admitted of no exceptions. A Marxist such as Christopher Caudwell had no doubts as to the suitability of 'highbrow' culture for everyone, though its availability was dependent on the complete reorganisation of society. In the mean time he lectured Russell on the 'bestiality' of his idea of Liberty and compares the relative freedom enjoyed by 'A' (Russell in the guise of an Oxford don), 'B' a worker, and 'C' an unemployed man; he writes:

> It is not because B and C are unenlightened that they are members of the working class, but because they are members of the working class, they are unenlightened. And Russell, who writes 'In Praise of Idleness', praises rightly, for he is clever because he is idle and bourgeois, not idle and bourgeois because he is clever.[15]

It is debatable as to which part of this Russell would have found most offensive, though the odds must be on 'bourgeois'.

Caudwell does, however, point up with vigorous incoherence the fact that clerisy culture, despite its supposed value to 'society', was never available or intended to be available for working-class consumption. The question then arises as to the outer limits of its influence. As we have seen, the clerisy was thought even by its members to be engaged in educational pursuits, and the Cambridge Apostles who represented the most distinct community of intellectuals to which Russell belonged had from the days of F.D. Maurice close connections with the Working Men's Colleges. Aside from a brief period during the First World War Russell himself rarely had contact with the working class, but E.M. Forster, a fellow Apostle, taught at the Workers' Educational Association for twenty years and created in Leonard Bast probably the best-known lower-class cultural aspirant of the twentieth century.

Howard's End is a 'clerisy' book and Bast represents the 'extreme verge' of its audience: 'We are not concerned with the very poor. They are unthinkable, and only to be approached by the statistician or the poet', but he is not the preferred audience, this is represented by the Schlegel sisters. Bast is depicted in his 'not unpleasant little hole' reverently reading Ruskin, hoping to 'come to Culture suddenly, much as the Revivalist hopes to come to Jesus'.[16] Despite his reverence, Bast cannot shed the vulgarities of his class, and his aspirations are seen to be intrusive and disagreeable. Forster's attitude towards class was equivocal for both Liberal and sexual reasons, and his own notion of the clerisy: 'The aristocrats, the elect, the chosen, the "Best People" – all the words that describe them are false, and all attempts to organise them fail'[17] – is notable for being defined in self-consciously colloquial terms. Yet Forster's pious belief that the 'creative and sensitive' were scattered sparingly throughout society is scarcely convincing, for as with all members of the clerisy from Arnold on, his chief hope was for a tolerant cultured middle class to act as a buffer between his ideals and a wider democracy. Although he desired a 'non-ascetic' aristocracy this was merely expressing a preference for 'Bloomsbury' rather than 'Scrutiny' values, and did not signify an identification with those whose lives were dominated by the urgency of their physical needs. Bast represents the point at which cultural ambitions exist but are seen to be futile, he is the kind of person who, as the opportunities for education expanded, was characterised by Hoggart as the 'not quite bright' and by Amis as 'tapped untalent'.

If we take the substance of what the clerisy had to offer as being most succinctly expressed by Matthew Arnold – 'the best that has been thought and said' – Bast is important in being the first of those fictional staging posts which, appearing at around twenty-year intervals and in strict alphabetical order, marked the retreat from Arnold's ideal and gave clear indication of the clerisy's decline in influence. While Bast is an unemployed clerk killed by too much culture, his successors, Orwell's Gordon Comstock and Amis's Jim Dixon, are respectively a failed poet defeated by culture and a failing academic rescued from culture. All are brought to realise the intimate relationship between class and high culture, yet, paradoxically, the progress from clerk to provincial academic is accompanied by a waning of culture's attraction.

Forster, Orwell, and Amis were all in their early thirties when they published these novels: as writers they represent the span from upper to lower middle class and their successive careers are also indicative of a broadening of the concept of 'culture' together with a diminution of deference – the movement from 'sublime Beethoven' to 'filthy Mozart'.[18] What is common to all three novels, though, is the depiction of a peculiarly etiolated version of high culture (foreign composers aside) which nonetheless demanded of its aspirants social qualification. In Bast, such a culture inspired reverence, in Comstock, bitterness, in Dixon, mockery, and it is only the last response which at all questions the authority or the necessity of what is on offer. Indeed, Dixon represents the antithesis of the clerisy, someone who values the lower pleasures over the higher, the material over the spiritual; moreover, he could not, like Bast and Comstock, be dismissed in biological terms as an example of 'poor stock' – he was offensively healthy.

In all this Dixon resembles that more substantial representative of the ordinary and the fleshly, the rather Wellsian figure of Leopold Bloom who because neither ascetic nor aesthetic provoked the hostility of both the Scrutiny and Bloomsbury groups. Bloomsbury's attitude towards Joyce – naturally Modernism's sole non-elitist – is well illustrated by Forster's discussion in *Aspects of the Novel.* Here the Joycean vision is contrasted explicitly with the Arnoldian – *Ulysses* is 'a dogged attempt to cover the universe with mud, an inverted Victorianism, an attempt to make crossness and dirt succeed where sweetness and light failed':

> The action of those 400,000 words occupies a single day, the scene is Dublin, the theme is a journey – the modern man's journey from morn to midnight, from bed to the squalid tasks of mediocrity, to a funeral, newspaper office, library, pub, lavatory, lying-in hospital, a saunter by the beach, brothel, coffee stall, and so back to bed. And it coheres because it depends from the journey of a hero through the seas of Greece, like a bat hanging to a cornice. Ulysses himself is Mr Leopold Bloom – a converted Jew – greedy, lascivious, timid, undignified, desultory, superficial, kindly, and always at his lowest when he pretends to aspire. He tries to explore life through the body.[19]

Joyce's Bast-like improprieties are set against the 'exquisite' offerings of Goldsworthy Lowes Dickinson, yet the tone is peevish rather than authoritative, and in this somewhat mean-spirited defence of the 'life of the mind' Forster even succeeds in making the word 'kindly' appear peculiarly applicable to the ill-bred.

With regard to matters of aesthetics Russell, where he was not uncertain, was often indifferent, and one of the main weaknesses of his cultural criticism lay precisely in this – that on questions of taste he attended too much to the ways of Bloomsbury and so disregarded areas of life best illustrated by what one critic refers to as 'Leopold Bloom's endearing little ways'.[20] It was not until the time of Jim Dixon's ascendancy in the 1950s that Russell could remark of the working class: 'a great number of those workers who ought to have known better ... have failed to appreciate the importance of a scientific education and have preferred an education which apes the classical education of their erstwhile masters. This preoccupation with what they call culture is most depressing.'[21]

As a parallel to the above we might look at how Russell himself progressed from being portrayed in the products of high culture during and after the First World War to being a 'participant' in popular culture after the Second. His great period as a 'character' was in the early twenties when, aside from being maligned as Bertie Reid in Lawrence's short story 'The Blind Man', he appeared as Sir Joshua Mattheson in *Women in Love*, Mr Scogan in *Crome Yellow*, and the eponymous Mr Appolinax in Eliot's poem. There is little that is subtle in any of these characterisations, all merely confirm Mary Agnes Hamilton's remark that at Garsington his was 'the dominant mind', and Russell is displayed as an oppressive fixture in aristocratic country-house culture. Depicted variously as a Saurian, Classical, and Eighteenth-century figure, he is seen as possessing an antique potency, representing something which though ancient was intellectually impregnable, compelling and rapacious:

> He talked with an ever-increasing energy, his hands moved in sharp, quick, precise gestures, his eyes shone. Hard, dry, and continuous, his voice went on sounding and sounding ... with the insistence of a mechanical noise.[22]

> his [Mr Appolinax] dry and passionate talk devoured the afternoon.[23]

> the talk going on, ceaselessly, Joshua's voice dominating.[24]

Although Russell appeared to be at the centre of a homogeneous elite culture, there is a sense that even here he was regarded as an alien presence – that like Lawrence, but for opposite social and intellectual reasons, he was seen as being out of place, 'brilliant' but nonetheless faintly risible. T.S. Eliot reporting home from Cambridge in 1915 had already assumed the slightly condescending air which Bloomsbury, from Virginia Woolf down, habitually adopted in its dealings with Russell:

> I met several very agreeable men this term, too. Two Irishmen, who have rather raised my opinion of that race, one or two new Englishmen, and several Indians (whom on the whole I find more congenial than the English – but Bertie Russell says they give him the creeps). As I have said already, I don't think there is any more *brains* here than at Harvard, but the average of culture is far higher. A cultivated aristocracy is sadly to seek even in England, but God knows it is (far) better here than in our Slater-ised society ... Not that Bertie Russell is not an aristocrat, but not quite in that sense; he has a sensitive, but hardly a cultivated mind, and I begin to realise how unbalanced he is. I do enjoy him quite as much as any man I know; we had breakfast with him, and stayed talking with him one night till one o'clock; he talked very well about the war, and is wonderfully perceptive, but in some ways an immature mind: wonderfully set off in contrast by Santayana (who was in Cambridge too).[25]

For Eliot, Russell's lack of culture, balance, and maturity make him a distinctly un-Arnoldian figure – an advocate of the clerisy perhaps but certainly not equipped to be one of its number.

In 1915 Russell was about to become estranged from Cambridge, and by the 1920s there was little of substance connecting him to Bloomsbury. He was not exactly an isolated figure, but his Wellsian activities reduced his status in what remained of the pre-war elite culture. This itself became less homogeneous and its cultural authority much reduced as the intelligentsia expanded in the wake of a rapidly developing mass media which provided opportunities for many more writers and journalists.[26] As a journalist Russell profited, yet though by now also distanced from Eliot, he shared his distaste for mass enthusiasms. Although the majority had not yet grown tyrannical, Russell, a middle-aged man restored to rationalist beliefs, was in intellectual reaction against the 'idea' of a mass society. This, however, involved certain hypocrisies, for like many of his contemporaries he adapted remarkably well to the mass media and to the end of his life read popular novels. His defence of this practice amounted to a confirmation of the 'two cultures' – William Gerhardi on a weekend visit to H.G. Wells met Russell and recorded the following exchange: 'On the railway platform Bertrand Russell bought himself a detective novel to read in the train. When I expressed mild amazement that he should not want to read anything better, he said: "You a novelist, read popular science. I, a scientist, read popular fiction." '[27]

That Russell valued – in theory at least – the existence of high culture does not necessarily mean that he was obliged to keep abreast of its products. As I suggested earlier the major works of Modernism held little appeal, and there are indications that for Russell some offered evidence of cultural decline. His references to such matters were rarely specific and became increasingly vague – in his preferred society there is usually a great deal of painting and writing going on (music tends to get short shrift) but the pursuit of excellence in the arts seems peculiarly divorced from any notion of an avant-garde. Being on firmer ground with scientific innovation, Russell's later versions of the idealised intellectual tended – like Wells's – to have a scientific bent, and his comments on the aesthetic side of life amount to little more than exercises in exhortation and uplift. Even as early as 1931 Russell would seem to have had nothing to offer the young aesthetic intellectuals apart from uplift, a point Anthony Powell makes by implication in *Afternoon Men*:

'Do you read Bertrand Russell?'
'Why?'
'When I feel hopeless,' she said, 'I read Bertrand Russell.'
'My dear.'
'You know, when he talks about mental adventure. Then I feel reinspired.'
'Reinspired to what?'
'Just reinspired.'[28]

As an intellectual Russell's experience of the thirties was bleaker than most – his income declined steadily after 1932 and those who might have been expected to replenish the ranks of the clerisy began to identify with the material aims of the working class, becoming 'political' in ways he found unappealing. The same year also marked the beginning of 'Scrutiny', a 'clerisy' by other means – a product of the 'Cambridge milieu', it offered a professional and ascetic opposition to Bloomsbury values, but more importantly it was, though equally elitist, better suited to the requirements of a meritocracy.[29] Russell, for his part, was always wary of the universities becoming the sole cultural authority and his doubts were reinforced by his experience of American institutions during the war. In his essay, 'British and American Nationalism', printed in *Horizon* January 1945, he writes,

> The educational effect of 'Democracy', as understood in America, is curious. Every taxpayer feels that he has a right to object if, in any State-supported institution, anything is taught of which he personally disapproves. If, in a State university, a biology teacher ventures to express a belief in evolution, or a teacher of ancient history throws doubt on the complete historicity of the Pentateuch, or a teacher of astronomy mentions that the Inquisition opposed Galileo, the President of the university in question is inundated with indignant letters from uneducated farmers or fanatical Irishmen, saying that their hard-earned money ought not to be spent on the dissemination of such pestiferous falsehoods ... 'Democracy' is interpreted as meaning that the majority knows best about everything.[30]

Although he thought Britain was currently better served because of the financial independence of Oxford and Cambridge, he took the view that in provincial universities academic freedom existed only as a 'survival'.

On his return to England after the war, he became once again an 'establishment' figure – Earl Russell OM, Nobel Prize Winner and Reith Lecturer. Courtesy of the BBC his 'dry and passionate talk' could dominate the airwaves and Russell rapidly became a skilled performer on radio and later television – as he had less and less to say that was new, so he was in the happy position of having more and more new people to say it to.

In 1959 he participated with Woodrow Wyatt in a series of television 'dialogues' later published as *Bertrand Russell Speaks His Mind.* Lest the reader be in any doubt as to what Russell was best noted for, the word MIND occupies a third of the dustjacket and the impression given is that something previously inaccessible was now open to the public. If the cover packaged him as the embodiment of a stately home, the blurb inside promoted him as a kind of 'coming attraction':

> The brilliance of Bertrand Russell needs no introduction, for he is one of the greatest philosophers, scientists and social critics of our time. The contents of this book, however, are of particular significance, for here we see Lord Russell's personality and mind captured at the moment of spontaneous inspiration ... Only the freshness of recorded speech can bring alive the philosopher's true character as he discourses on such matters as fanaticism, birth control, the H-bomb and the future of mankind ... This pungent book is essential reading for every person interested in observing the mind of a great humanist and scientist as it deals with great ideas.[31]

Yet, while Russell's fluency was certainly impressive, it derived from long practice rather than spontaneity, and the discussions mainly demonstrated that at eighty-seven his memory remained remarkable.

What the general public was offered in the fifties and sixties was a semi-retired secular clerisy as a diversion – above all it was the presence and the performance which fascinated.[32] Seen on television Russell inevitably appeared even more of an alien figure than he had done at Garsington, particularly as he continued to be so impervious to the aspirations of that 'common humanity' which now comprised his audience. When prompted by Wyatt to speculate on what man will do in a leisured future – the four-hour day being reduced to a ten-hour week – Russell's thoughts turned contentedly towards the past:

> Well, he'll do – if the sort of world that I imagine when I'm feeling happy can exist – he will do what well-to-do, cultivated people have done in the past. Consider, for instance, the eighteenth-century aristocrat, who quite often was a very cultivated man. He had a great deal of leisure and he knew what to do with his leisure, although many of them did things they'd better not have done. Quite a lot of them did very good things, encouraging art, and making beautiful parks and beautiful houses, and altogether things that are desirable. And I foresee when I am feeling cheerful a world in which that sort of use of leisure will be possible for everybody, because everybody will have reached a sufficient level of culture.[33]

Given that the possessive impulses were being feverishly encouraged by every post-war Western government, even the suggestion that all life could tend towards the condition of the old aristocracy and that the clerisy, rather than being embattled, would hold sway over a 'cultured' population, appears perverse. Yet his speculations were perhaps less idiosyncratic than they seem, for in some respects they merely confirm Wiener's thesis which in essence was that 'British political opinion bore the imprint of the aristocracy long after the demise of the aristocracy's power.'[34] The direction a democracy takes, however, tends to be determined in the last instance by Benthamite rather than Coleridgean preoccupations, and although the clerisy was (with the aid of technology) given access to previously ignored social territory, its point of view had no real influence.

In his 'auto' obituary Russell had predicted he would die in the summer of 1961, the precise moment when he could be said to have reached his widest British audience. On 26 May of that year he was central to BBC Television's most popular programme, *Hancock's Half Hour*, then reaching a third of the nation. Like a latter day Leonard Bast Hancock is alone in his room equipped with books by Marx, Spengler, and of course Russell. He remarks,

> Too much going on in my mind, you see. Nuclear disarmament, the future of mankind, China, Spurs, oh it's very hard to be an intellectual these days. Let's have a go at old Bertie Russell ... Now then, let's have a good look at this. *Human Knowledge – Its Limit and Scope* by Bertrand Russell. Introduction.[35]

Several hours, several attempts, and much dictionary-thumbing later, he has reached the end of page 1 of the Introduction:

> Well, well, well, isn't that remarkable. A man of eighty-eight, writing this. It's amazing. I'll just about have finished it by the time I'm eighty-eight. Oh well, seven o'clock, first things first. Time the peacock showed his feathers, I fancy.[36]

The curiously dispiriting spectacle of futile persistence, of the 'half-baked mind ... being done good to'[37] is lightened by the familiarity with which Russell is approached – Hancock is astonished rather than dismayed and scarcely humbled by his inadequacy. The culture Russell represents is seen as being obscurely desirable but its possession is not really high on the list of priorities. It was, of course, Russell's abiding concern that his conception of 'first things' was not widely shared – from his perspective ordinary life appeared arid when it did not appear pathological.

Hancock was perhaps the last example of the Bast literary tradition, for by the early sixties a major expansion of the universities was taking place; and this decade, which saw the clerisy's role almost completely institutionalised, also saw the culture of which they were so protective increasingly discounted as values rapidly changed.[38] Russell, however, remained fortunate to the extent that the publication of his *Autobiography* coincided with Michael Holroyd's biography of Lytton Strachey and the beginning of the Bloomsbury 'industry'. The interest aroused had of course less to do with a resurrection of clerisy values than with the disclosure of a style of living so well suited to the times, and Russell doubtless shared Hancock's view that it was 'very hard to be an intellectual these days' at least in the sense he understood the term. In 1958 he had expressed admiration for the manner in which Keynes carried out his role as a public intellectual:

> Keynes was venturesome. The people who teach at universities are on the whole fearful men; that is why they are in universities and not outside. Their teachings, on the whole, are the teachings of fearful men, and this is one of the reasons why they are not very effective and why one should not take too much notice of them. All intellectuals should suffer a certain amount of persecution, as early in life as possible. Not too much. That is bad for them. But a certain amount.[39]

Like Keynes, Russell was a remarkably venturesome non-academic intellectual; thus to see him merely as an embattled aristocrat whose concern for the preservation of Liberal values tended increasingly to focus on the 'cultural' questions rather than the political, would be to disregard the breadth of his interests (equally, references to his 'breadth and variety' can be overdone, as his very 'Englishness' began to restrict his cultural range especially after the First World War). Yet if we are to make any judgements as to the kind of intellectual Russell was, emphasis must be placed somewhere, and the 'idea of the clerisy' accounts for much in his thinking that would otherwise seem idiosyncratic. Not only does his preoccupation with the 'priestly' role of the intellectuals help to explain his lack of enthusiasm for the state, for politics, and production, it is also related to the way in which his radicalism and his rationalism so often form a paradoxical alliance. Even his views on sexual freedom, which brought notoriety and helped to sustain his reputation as an 'advanced' thinker, fit all too neatly with a sporadic advocacy of positive eugenics in that the encouragement of increased sexual activity amongst the middle classes appeared necessary if they were to compete with the lower orders who required (and received) no such encouragement.

Russell, in his sexual proclivities much as in his political activities, seemed, like Sartre, the very model of a modern intellectual. In most important respects, however, he more closely resembled Keynes, and his modernity was distinctly questionable. In fact, Russell's claim in his 'obituary' that 'His life, for all its waywardness, had a certain anachronistic consistency, reminiscent of that of the aristocratic rebels of the early nineteenth century',[40] proved even in the long term to be justified. With regard to his social and political thought it too had a certain consistency of purpose because its central themes were all to a greater or lesser extent related to the clerisy tradition which itself was rooted in nineteenth-century values. In this area at least, Russell's achievement was to remain obdurately anachronistic without seeming so; yet there is no doubt that his beliefs were essentially at odds with the times into which he survived. The reason for this is hardly obscure, as his intellectual stance was based on a refusal to accept that there was safety in numbers, and in arguing from this position he was often 'incorrect', but rarely wrong.

Notes

INTRODUCTION

1 Alan Ryan, *Bertrand Russell: A Political Life* (1988) p. 72.

2 'In or about December 1910 human character changed.' Virginia Woolf, 'Mr Bennett and Mrs Brown', *Collected Essays* vol. 1 p. 320.

3 Russell's *Autobiography* is seductive in the sense indicated by Alan Ryan when he remarks, 'I have thought long and hard about background reading, but have come to the conclusion that Russell's life straddled so many years and so many issues that a list would be almost endless. Mine, therefore, begins and ends with Russell's *Autobiography*.' Ryan, *Bertrand Russell*, p. 218.

The problem with the *Autobiography* is that Russell (naturally enough) reveals himself entirely on his own terms and sees no need to provide his own ideas with much in the way of an intellectual setting. This essentially Russellian perspective is not much altered by the invaluable work being done in the Russell archive at McMaster University, for although his background is currently receiving greater attention in the various volumes of the *Collected Papers*, the *Autobiography* (the first, the most substantial, and most widely available product of the archive) still tends to shape the discussion of Russell's writing.

4 Alan S. Kahan in his recent study, *Aristocratic Liberalism: The Social and Political Thought of Jacob Burckhardt, John Stuart Mill, and Alexis de Tocqueville* (1992), attempts to define the concept by analysing the views of a selection of nineteenth-century Liberal intellectuals.

5 I was mildly surprised that Russell was not included among the numerous elitist intellectuals condemned by means of selective quotation in John Carey, *The Intellectuals and the Masses: Pride and Prejudice among the Literary Intelligentsia 1880–1939* (1992). For a more balanced view of the role of the public intellectual in the twentieth century see D.L. LeMahieu, *A Culture for Democracy: Mass Communication and the Cultivated Mind in Britain Between the Wars* (1988) and Stefan Collini, 'Intellectuals in Britain and France in the Twentieth Century: Confusions, Contrasts and Convergence' in Jeremy Jennings (ed.) *Intellectuals in Twentieth-Century France: Mandarins and Samurais* (1993).

1 A YOUNG MAN OF CHARACTER

1 Michael Bentley, *Politics Without Democracy 1815–1914* (1984) p. 204.
2 Russell, *Autobiography* vol. 1 (1967) p. 15.
3 George Santayana, *My Host the World* (1953) p. 36.
4 Noel Annan, 'The Intellectual Aristocracy', in J.H. Plumb (ed.), *Studies in Social History* (1955) p. 281.
5 Russell, *Collected Papers* vol. 1: *Cambridge Essays 1888–99* (1983) p. 5.
6 *Ibid.* p. 13.
7 *Ibid.* p. 14.
8 See Dora Russell, *The Tamarisk Tree*, vol. 1 *My Quest for Liberty and Love* (1975) p. 160.
9 Russell, *Cambridge Essays* p. 53.
10 Russell, 'State-Socialism' (1889), *Cambridge Essays* pp. 28–9.
11 *Ibid.* p. 29.
12 Russell, 'Evolution as Affecting Modern Political Science' (1889), *Cambridge Essays* p. 27.
13 Russell, *Autobiography* vol. 1 p. 36.
14 *Ibid.* p. 100.
15 *Ibid.* pp. 68–9.
16 Russell, *My Philosophical Development* (1959) p. 38.
17 *Ibid.* p. 37.
18 Russell, *Autobiography* vol. 1 p. 63.
19 For an account of Russell's abandonment of Idealism see Russell, *My Philosophical Development* ch. 5.
20 According to Peter Hylton, *Russell, Idealism and the Emergence of Analytic Philosophy* (1990), Russell adhered to 'idealist doctrine ... not as a brief aberration but genuinely and profoundly' (p. 105), yet his discussion centres on 'An Essay on the Foundations of Geometry' which was Russell's Fellowship Dissertation and as such an 'intellectual exercise' of a kind.
21 Russell, *Selected Letters* (ed. Nicholas Griffin, 1992) p. 23.
22 Russell, *Cambridge Essays* p. 93.
23 *Ibid.* p. 95.
24 Russell, *Selected Letters* p. 119.
25 Stefan Collini stresses 'the very considerable distance between the dominant Victorian ideal of character and any ideal of *Bildung* which it may at first sight seem to resemble. *Bildung*, at least in its purest Romantic form, suggests an openness to experience, a cultivation of the subjective response, an elevation of the aesthetic, and an exploratory attitude towards one's own individuality and potential, all of which carry a different, perhaps more self-indulgent, certainly more private, message and political bearing. Dilettantism may, it has been suggested, be "a possible parody of *Bildung*," but it is clearly the very antithesis of character.' Stefan Collini, 'The Idea of "Character" in Victorian

Political Thought', *Transactions of the Royal Historical Society* 5th series, 35 (1985) 38.

For other discussions of 'character' see Richard Bellamy, *Liberalism and Modern Society* (1990) and J.A. Mangan and James Walvin (eds.), *Manliness and Morality* (1987).

2 FELLOW-TRAVELLING WITH THE FABIANS

1 Russell, *Autobiography* vol. I (1967) p. 130.
2 *Ibid.* p. 125.
3 Russell, 'Sidney and Beatrice Webb', *Portraits from Memory and other Essays* (1956) p. 98.
4 Beatrice Webb, *Our Partnership* (1948) p. 215.
5 According to Alan Wood, *Bertrand Russell: The Passionate Sceptic* (1957) p. 40, Russell's separate lecture to the Fabian Society had not been particularly well received by his audience: 'It was his first big public speech, and he was very nervous. ("I dreaded it, and wished I could break my leg before it.") He did not make much of a success of handling questions and criticisms, and Graham Wallas took him aside afterwards and gave him some hints on this.'
6 Russell, 'German Social Democracy as a Lesson in Political Tactics' (1896), *Cambridge Essays* p. 310.
7 Sidney and Beatrice Webb, *The Letters* (ed. Norman Mackenzie) vol. II (1978) p. 39.
8 Russell, *German Social Democracy* (1896; 2nd edn 1965) p. 1.
9 *Ibid.* p. 24.
10 *Ibid.* pp. 25–6.
11 *Ibid.* p. 27.
12 *Ibid.* p. 40.
13 Louis Greenspan, *The Incompatible Prophecies: Bertrand Russell on Science and Liberty* (1978) p. 55.
14 Quoted in Ronald Clark, *The Life of Bertrand Russell* (1975) p. 51.
15 Russell, *German Social Democracy* p. 163.
16 *Ibid.* p. 92.
17 *Ibid.* p. 145.
18 *Ibid.* p. 162.
19 *Ibid.* p. 170.
20 *Ibid.* p. 160.
21 *Ibid.* p. 162.
22 *Ibid.* p. 165.
23 *Ibid.* p. 164.
24 *Ibid.* p. 164.
25 *Ibid.* p. 142.
26 *Ibid.* p. 170.
27 *Ibid.* p. 171.

28 Willard Wolfe, *From Radicalism to Socialism* (1975) p. 147.
29 Norman St John Stevas, *Walter Bagehot* (1959) p. 201.
30 Wolfe, *Radicalism to Socialism* p. 295.
31 Quoted in Barry Feinberg and Ronald Kasrils, *Bertrand Russell's America* (1973) p. 24.
32 Russell, 'Self-Appreciation' (1897), *Cambridge Essays* p. 72.

3 OUT OF THE MORAL GYMNASIUM

1 Russell, *Collected Papers* vol. XII: *Contemplation and Action 1902–14* (ed. Richard A. Rempel et al., 1985) p. 56 .
2 Russell, *Principles of Social Reconstruction* (1916; 1971 edn) p. 147.
3 Russell, *Autobiography* vol I pp. 145–6.
4 *Ibid.* p. 147.
5 Katharine Tait, *My Father Bertrand Russell* (1975) p. 42.
6 Russell, *Autobiography* vol. I p. 164.
7 Russell, 'Journal' (9 March 1905), *Contemplation and Action* p. 27.
8 Ronald W. Clark, *The Life of Bertrand Russell* (1975) p. 84.
9 Russell, *Autobiography* vol. I p. 166.
10 *Ibid.* p. 187.
11 F.R. Leavis, *The Common Pursuit* (1952) p. 128.
12 Alan Donagan, 'Victorian Philosophical Prose: J.S. Mill and F.H. Bradley' in George Levine and William Madden (eds.), *The Art of Victorian Prose* (1968) p. 57.
13 Russell, *Autobiography* vol. I p. 150.
14 Russell, 'A Free Man's Worship' (1903) reprinted in *Mysticism and Logic and Other Essays* (1917; 1963 edn) p. 51.
15 *Ibid.* p. 28.
16 Russell, *Autobiography* vol. I p. 86.
17 *Ibid.* p. 148.
18 Sidney and Beatrice Webb, *The Letters* vol. II p. 163.
19 Russell, *Autobiography* vol. I p. 188.
20 Quoted in David S. Thatcher, *Nietzsche in England 1890–1914: The Growth of a Reputation* (1970) p. 154.
21 J.M. Keynes, 'My Early Beliefs' in S.P. Rosenbaum (ed.), *The Bloomsbury Group: A Collection of Memoirs, Commentary and Criticism* (1975) p. 63.
22 Michael Holroyd, *Lytton Strachey: The Unknown Years 1880–1910* (1967) p. 211.
23 *Ibid.* p. 127.
24 R.F. Harrod, *The Life of John Maynard Keynes* (1951) p. 89.
25 *Ibid.*, p. 90.
26 Russell, *Autobiography* vol. I p. 74.
27 *Ibid.* p. 166.
28 See in particular Karl Miller, *Doubles: Studies in Literary History* (1985) and Elaine Showalter, *Sexual Anarchy: Gender and Culture at the Fin de Siècle* (1991).

29 Leonard Woolf, *Sowing: An Autobiography of the Years 1880–1904* p. 114.

30 This aspect of the Moore/Russell relationship is brought out in Paul Levy's biography of Moore, a book which presents a rather jaundiced and at times inaccurate picture of Russell. According to Levy, 'The objects of Moore's bad temper – which it must be admitted sometimes amounted to rage – were, in a single notable instance, Graham Wallas, and, almost regularly, Bertrand Russell. Moore loathed Wallas, and, on balance, disliked Russell.' Paul Levy, *Moore: G.E. Moore and the Cambridge Apostles* (1979) p. 12.

31 Levy's argument that Moore found Russell in some sense 'intellectually unclean' would be convincing only if he had demanded intellectual purity from his friends. It was, in fact, Russell rather than Moore who was outraged by the manner in which *Principia Ethica* was utilised by the original members of the Bloomsbury group. By exaggerating Russell's faults, Levy endeavours to erase the odd blot on Moore's record, particularly in regard to the tactics he employed in order to edge Russell out of the Apostles' inner circle.

32 In his 'Journal' (April 1903), *Contemplation and Action* p. 21, Russell records his disappointment at being prevented by Moore from escaping his depressing home life into the company of the Apostles: 'My three weeks' holiday was reduced to a week with George Trevy in Devonshire, because Moore, to whose reading party I was going, wrote curtly to say he didn't want me.'

33 Leonard Woolf, *Sowing*, p. 134.

34 See Russell, *Autobiography* vol. 1 p. 70.

35 In Russell's view, Wittgenstein's state of mind was such that involvement with the Society at that time would have been hazardous. As in Whitehead's case, Russell probably exaggerated the dangers, yet even so, his prediction that Wittgenstein would 'retire in disgust' proved correct; a fact which Paul Levy, *Moore* p. 270, grudgingly acknowledges: 'Though Russell may have had his own reasons for warning the Society against Wittgenstein, he was perfectly correct about what Wittgenstein's reaction to the Society would be.' For a discussion of Apostle politics from Wittgenstein's perspective see Brian McGuinness, *Wittgenstein A Life: Young Ludwig (1889–1921)* (1988) and Ray Monk, *Ludwig Wittgenstein: The Duty of Genius* (1990).

36 Clark, *The Life* p. 193.

37 Quoted in Ottoline Morrell, *Ottoline at Garsington: Memoirs 1915–1918* (ed. Robert Gathorne-Hardy, 1974) p. 56.

38 Russell, *Autobiography* vol. 1 p. 70.

39 Paul Delany, *D.H. Lawrence's Nightmare: The Writer and his Circle in the Years of the Great War* (1979) p. 68.

40 Russell, *Autobiography* vol. 1 p. 209.

41 Oscar Wilde, *The Picture of Dorian Gray* (1891; 1950 edn) p. 13.

42 Both Lawrence and Conrad have been interpreted as offering hints of

suppressed homosexuality in their writing and this might suggest that it was not entirely coincidental that Russell should have been struck by the peculiarly intense nature of his relationship with both these writers. For a discussion of Conrad's 'homosexuality', see Jeffrey Meyers, *Homosexuality and Literature 1890–1930* (1977).

43 Sidney and Beatrice Webb, *The Letters* vol. II p. 372.
44 Clark, *The Life* p. 178.
45 Anthony Storr, *Jung* (1973) pp. 81–2.
46 Francis Fergusson quoted in David S. Thatcher, *Nietzsche in England* p. 211.
47 Ronald Bagg, *Hippolytos* (1974) p. 6.
48 Russell, *Autobiography* vol. I p. 205.
49 Ottoline Morrell, *Ottoline: The Early Memoirs* (ed. Robert Gathorne-Hardy, 1963) p. 256.
50 Morrell, *Ottoline at Garsington* p. 45.
51 Russell, *Autobiography* vol. II p. 23.
52 Russell, 'Mysticism and Logic' in *Mysticism and Logic* p. 23.
53 *Ibid.* pp. 19–20.
54 *Ibid.* p. 23.
55 *Ibid.* p. 22.
56 D.H. Lawrence, *Letters to Bertrand Russell* (ed. Harry T. Moore, 1948) p. 34.
57 *Ibid.* p. 63.

4 POLITICAL SCIENCE

1 Russell, *Autobiography* vol. II pp. 19–20.
2 D.H. Lawrence, *Letters to Bertrand Russell* (ed. Harry T. Moore, 1948) p. 77.
3 Ronald W. Clark, *The Life of Bertrand Russell* (1975) p. 206.
4 See Jo Vellacott, *Bertrand Russell and the Pacifists in the First World War* (1980) pp. 25–6.
5 Russell, *Principles* p. 9.
6 Russell, *Autobiography* vol. I p. 127.
7 D.A. Hamer, *Liberal Politics in the Age of Gladstone and Rosebery* (1972) p. 236.
8 See Russell, *German Social Democracy*, especially ch. 6.
9 Hamer, *Liberal Politics* p. 267.
10 See Richard A. Rempel, 'From Imperialism to Free Trade: Couturat, Halevy and Russell's First Crusade', *Journal of the History of Ideas* 40 (1979) 425–6.
11 Russell, *Autobiography* vol. I p. 146.
12 G.R. Searle, *The Quest for National Efficiency* (1971).
13 H.G. Wells, *Experiment in Autobiography: Discoveries and Conclusions of a Very Ordinary Brain (Since 1866)* (1934) vol. II p. 765.
14 In his 'Journal' (1902–5) Russell refers to some of his meetings with the Co-efficients, making clear that while he was sympathetic with their

overall aims, he was not drawn to his fellow members. *Contemplation and Action* pp. 15–18.

15 Russell, *Autobiography* vol. 1 p. 167.

16 *Ibid.* p. 170.

17 Russell, 'The Tariff Controversy', *Edinburgh Review* 199 (January 1904) 192.

18 *Ibid.* p. 169.

19 *Ibid.* p. 195.

20 Russell, *Autobiography* vol. 1 p. 182.

21 G.R. Searle, *Eugenics and Politics in Britain, 1900–1914* (1976) p. 4.

22 Russell, 'The Politics of a Biologist', *Albany Review* no. 11 (1907) 92.

23 Russell, *Our Knowledge of the External World as a Field for Scientific Method in Philosophy* (1980 edn) p. 14.

24 See Searle, *The Quest for National Efficiency*.

25 Greta Jones, *Social Darwinism and English Thought: The Interaction Between Biological and Social Theory* (1980) p. 113. On this question see also G.R. Searle, 'Eugenics and Class' in Charles Webster (ed.), *Biology, Medicine and Society 1840–1940* (1981). In this article Searle classifies Edwardian eugenists as follows: strong, weak, medical, career, and rhetorical. Searle places the Webbs amongst the merely rhetorical remarking, 'I doubt whether it is reasonable to call such people eugenists at all', and would probably regard Russell in much the same light. There is, however, a case for saying that for a time Russell numbered among the 'weak' eugenists, those who were 'attracted to eugenics, or to aspects of it, without feeling under any compulsion to abandon the political creed in which they had been brought up. "Weak eugenists" were content, in other words, to graft eugenics onto one or other of the traditional creeds.' Webster, pp. 239–40.

26 Russell, 'The Politics of a Biologist' p. 96.

27 *Ibid.* p. 91.

28 Russell, *Philosophical Essays* (1910; rev. edn 1966) p. 47.

29 Russell, 'The Politics of a Biologist' p. 91.

30 *Ibid.* p. 95.

31 *Ibid.* p. 97.

32 Searle, *Eugenics* p. 67.

33 Russell, 'The Politics of a Biologist' p. 98.

34 *Ibid.* p. 94.

35 *Ibid.* p. 94.

36 G.R. Searle quotes Pearson as follows: 'Eugenics will never come about by democratic means. We might as successfully ask the weeds in a garden to make way of their own accord for the flowering plants whose development they choke. Let my readers think what a gardener could achieve if his tenure of office depended on the consent of the weeds.' Searle, *Eugenics* p. 68.

37 Russell, *Principles* ch. 6 'Marriage and the Population Question'.

38 Alan Wood, *Bertrand Russell the Passionate Sceptic* (1957) p. 71.

39 Russell, 'Liberalism and Women's Suffrage', *Contemporary Review* 94 (July 1908) 15.
40 *Ibid.* p. 15.
41 *Ibid.* p. 16. Russell's commitment to democracy and equality (at least in abstract terms) is clear from his paper 'On the Democratic Ideal' (1906), where he states that, 'Equality, in some sense, is necessary to all the best human relationships. But it is necessary to define this sense very carefully. It is not necessary that there should be equality in virtue, in intellect, or in attainment; and it is not necessary that either side should be unconscious of the absence of such equality. The kind of equality which is essential is a circumscribed and special kind; it is that kind which was affirmed by advocates of the Rights of Man.' *Contemplation and Action* p. 250. Equally evident from his Journal of the period is what he himself terms his 'fastidiousness and undemocraticness'. 'Journal' (February 1903), *Contemplation and Action* p. 18.
42 *Ibid.* p. 16.
43 *Ibid.* p. 12.
44 *Ibid.* p. 13.
45 For an analysis of the work of Trotter and McDougall, see Reba N. Soffer, 'New Elitism: Social Psychology in Prewar England', *Journal of British Studies* 8 (1969) 111–40.
46 Sidney Webb, 'Physical Degeneracy or Race Suicide', *The Times* (11 and 16 October 1906).
47 Russell, *Autobiography* vol. I p. 201.
48 According to Richard Rempel, 'Russell's address to the Bedford Liberal Organisation reveals the degree to which he and other New Liberals recognised that the chief legislative measures of the future had to be directed towards solving economic problems in politics.' Rempel 'From Imperialism' 441.
49 There is also the likelihood that Russell was already something of a specialist on this topic as one of his closest friends, Crompton Davies, ran the Land Values Organisation of which Ottoline Morrell was a keen supporter.
50 Peter Clarke, *Liberals and Social Democrats* (1978) p. 195.
51 Russell, *Political Ideals* (1977 edn) p. 51.
52 Quoted in Rempel, 'From Imperialism' 442.
53 Beatrice Webb, *The Diaries* vol. III (1905–24) pp. 181–2.
54 Quoted in Clark, *The Life* p. 256.
55 Russell, 'The Entente Policy, 1904–1915: A Reply to Professor Gilbert Murray' reprinted in Russell, *Justice in War-Time* (1916) p. 188.
56 Russell, *Autobiography* vol. II p. 74.

5 THE SAGE OF CAXTON HALL

1 Russell, 'Memories and Studies', *The Cambridge Review* (16 November 1911).

2 Russell, *The Cambridge Review* (1911).
3 Russell, *Autobiography* vol. II p. 16.
4 Norman Angell, *The Great Illusion* (3rd edn 1911) p. 171.
5 Russell, *The Cambridge Review* (1911).
6 Russell, *Autobiography* vol. II p. 17.
7 *Ibid.* p. 17.
8 Marvin Swartz, 'A Study in Futility: The British Radicals at the Outbreak of the First World War' in A.J.A. Morris (ed.), *Edwardian Radicalism 1900–1914* (1974) p. 257.
9 Ronald W. Clark, *The Life of Bertrand Russell* (1975) p. 252.
10 Russell's research enterprise was transformed into a polemic against Gilbert Murray and was published as a pamphlet under the title of 'The Entente Policy 1904–1915' reprinted in Russell, *Justice in War-Time* (1916).
11 Reprinted in Russell, *Autobiography* vol. II p. 41.
12 Clark, *The Life* p. 246.
13 'The Place of Science in Liberal Education' reprinted in *Mysticism and Logic* (1976 edn) p. 34.
14 Russell, *Our Knowledge of the External World* (1980 edn) pp. 20–1.
15 According to one authority, 'The notion of a disposition, a "tendency to behave", is far less rigid, or deterministic, than the notion of an instinct. Dispositions are consistent with a much higher level of conscious activity than seems implicit in the common usage of the term "instinct". Dispositions do not totally determine behaviour, but are simply inclinations which can be modified by other forces. The change was vital to Wallas's theories, for he included among the dispositions, a disposition to conscious behaviour.' Terence J. Qualter, *Graham Wallas and the Great Society* (1980) p. 114.
16 Graham Wallas, *The Great Society* (1914) pp. 64–5.
17 Russell, 'Why Nations Love War' reprinted in *Justice in War-Time* p. 63.
18 Wallas, *The Great Society*, p. 66.
19 Russell, *Autobiography* vol. II p. 17.
20 Mary Agnes Hamilton, *Remembering My Good Friends* (1944) p. 75.
21 Russell's most direct link with Freudianism at the time was possibly through Frieda Lawrence – a woman he did not much care for but whom he apparently regarded as formidable. He remarks in his autobiography that 'Lawrence, though most people do not realise it, was his wife's mouthpiece. He had the eloquence, she had the ideas. She used to spend part of every summer in a colony of Austrian Freudians at a time when psychoanalysis was little known in England.' *Autobiography* vol. II p. 23. Frieda Lawrence's relations with the 'Left' Freudians are analysed in Martin Green's *The Von Richthofen Sisters* (1974).
22 Russell, 'War, the Offspring of Fear' (Union of Democratic Control Pamphlet No. 3, 1914) p. 3.
23 Russell, 'An Appeal to the Intellectuals of Europe', *Justice in War-Time* p. 11.

24 Russell, 'Is a Permanent Peace Possible?', *Justice in War-Time* pp. 99–100.
25 Russell, *Principles* p. 9.
26 *Ibid.* pp. 11–12.
27 J.S. Mill, 'Bentham' in *Collected Works* vol. x (ed. John M. Robson, 1969) p. 77.
28 Richard Wollheim, 'Bertrand Russell and the Liberal Tradition' in George Nakhnikian (ed.), *Bertrand Russell's Philosophy* (1974) p. 209.
29 Paul Arthur Schilpp (ed.), *The Philosophy of Bertrand Russell* (1944), p. 730.
30 See Qualter, *Wallas* pp. 113–17.
31 Russell, *Principles* p. 11.
32 *Ibid.* p. 11.
33 *Ibid.* p. 11.
34 Wollheim, 'Russell and the Liberal Tradition' p. 211.
35 Russell, *Principles* p. 9.
36 See in particular, P. Smart, 'Mill and Human Nature' in I. Forbes and S. Smith (eds.), *Politics and Human Nature* (1983) and Gerald F. Gaus, *The Modern Liberal Theory of Man* (1983), especially ch. 4.
37 J.S. Mill, *On Liberty* in *Collected Works* vol. XVIII (ed. John M. Robson, 1977) p. 264.
38 Russell, *Principles* pp. 15–16.
39 *Ibid.* p. 18.
40 *Ibid.* p. 18.
41 Ernest Jones, 'War and Sublimation' in Jones, *Essays in Applied Psycho-Analysis* (1923) pp. 389–90.
42 See in particular J.N. Figgis, *Churches in the Modern State* (1914).
43 Russell, *Principles* p. 25.
44 Bernard Bosanquet, *The Philosophical Theory of the State* (1965 edn) p. 57.
45 *Ibid.* p. 74.
46 D.H. Lawrence, *Letters to Bertrand Russell* (ed. Harry T. Moore, 1948) p. 89.
47 Russell, *Principles* pp. 19–20.
48 Lawrence, *Letters to Bertrand Russell* p. 82.
49 *Ibid.* p. 87.
50 Quoted in A.W. Wright, *G.D.H. Cole and Socialist Democracy* (1979) p. 32.
51 Ernest Barker, *Political Thought from Spencer to Today* (1915) p. 233.
52 G.D.H. Cole, *The World of Labour* (1913) p. 421.
53 On the Fabians as 'Pluralists' and 'Humanists' see Stanislaw Ehrlich, *Pluralism On and Off Course* (1982) p. 53, and Ian Britain, *Fabianism and Culture: A Study in British Socialism and the Arts 1884–1918* (1982) p. 271.

Russell, of course, acquired rather fixed ideas about the Webbs early on in his career, but was scarcely alone in identifying Fabianism with centralisation, nor in seeing the Webbs as being singularly deficient in aesthetic appreciation.

54 In cataloguing the attractions of Guild Socialism, A.W. Wright in *Cole* p. 100 remarks that 'For others, like Bertrand Russell, it seemed to offer simply the least harmful and dangerous of political doctrines.'

55 Harold J. Laski, *Studies in the Problems of Sovereignty* (1917; 1968 edn) p. 3.
56 This distinction was, of course, fairly well established, according to Andrew Vincent and Raymond Plant in *Philosophy, Politics and Citizenship: The Life and Thought of the British Idealists* (1984) p. 100: 'Bernard Bosanquet was at pains in many places to distinguish two distinct types of individualism, these were distinguished under the ideas of atomic individualism, or "theories of the first look", and ethical individualism, or "higher individualism".'
57 Russell, *Principles* p. 33.
58 *Ibid.* p. 18.
59 *Ibid.* p. 31.
60 Graham Wallas, *Human Nature in Politics* (1908) pp. xiii–xiv; 'When men become conscious of psychological processes of which they have been unconscious or half-conscious, not only are they put on their guard against the exploitation of those processes in themselves by others, but they become better able to control them from within.'
61 Russell, *Principles* p. 44.
62 *Ibid.* p. 44.
63 *Ibid.* p. 47.
64 *Ibid.* p. 149.
65 *Ibid.* p. 41.
66 Russell remarks in his *Autobiography* vol. II p. 38: 'Throughout my life I have longed to feel that oneness with large bodies of human beings that is experienced by the members of enthusiastic crowds. The longing has often been strong enough to lead me into self deception. I have imagined myself in turn a Liberal, a Socialist, or a Pacifist, but I have never been any of these things, in any profound sense. Always the sceptical intellect, when I have wished it most silent, has whispered doubts to me, has cut me off from the facile enthusiasms of others, and has transported me into a desolate solitude.'
67 Quoted in Russell, *Contemplation and Action* p. 384.
68 Russell, *Principles* p. 147.
69 *Ibid.* p. 51.
70 *Ibid.* p. 51.
71 *Ibid.* p. 49.
72 *Ibid.* p. 50.
73 *Ibid.* p. 50.
74 *Ibid.* pp. 63–4.
75 *Ibid.* p. 78.
76 The main source for this tradition of cultural criticism is Raymond Williams, *Culture and Society 1780–1950* (1958).
77 The thesis Freud developed in *Civilization and Its Discontents* was already implicit in his 1915 essay 'Thoughts for the Times on War and Death'. For a discussion of this, see Patrick Brantlinger, *Bread and Circuses: Theories of Mass Culture as Social Decay* (1983) ch. 5.

78 On the distribution of wealth in Edwardian society, see Paul Thompson, *The Edwardians: The Remaking of British Society* (1977).
79 Russell, *Principles* pp. 79–80.
80 *Ibid.* pp. 67–8.
81 See Isaiah Berlin, 'Two Concepts of Liberty' in Berlin, *Four Essays on Liberty* (1969).
82 Russell, *Principles* p. 68.
83 *Ibid.* p. 81.
84 See Russell, *Autobiography* vol. II p. 54.
85 Russell, *Principles* p. 123.
86 D.H. Lawrence, *The Letters of D.H. Lawrence* (ed. Aldous Huxley, 1932) p. 247.
87 Lawrence, *Letters to Bertrand Russell* p. 94.
88 Russell, *Principles* p. 84.
89 *Ibid.* p. 90.
90 *Ibid.* p. 92.
91 *Ibid.* p. 91.
92 *Ibid.* p. 91.
93 *Ibid.* pp. 93–4.
94 Wallas, *The Great Society* pp. 174–5.
95 Russell, *Principles* p. 141.
96 For the opposing view on this matter see Martin J. Wiener, *English Culture and the Decline of the Industrial Spirit 1850–1980* (1981) p. 24.
97 On the eugenics movement, see Greta Jones, *Social Darwinism and English Thought* (1980), G.R. Searle, *Eugenics*, and Charles Webster (ed.), *Biology, Medicine and Society 1840–1940* (1981).
98 Quoted in G.R. Searle, 'Eugenics and Class' in Webster, *Biology, Medicine and Society* p. 241.
99 Russell, *Principles* pp. 128–9.
100 G.R. Searle, 'Eugenics and Class' p. 235.
101 *Ibid.* p. 236.
102 Russell, *Principles* p. 125.
103 See Wiener, *English Culture.*
104 Russell, *Principles* p. 96.
105 According to A.J.M. Milne: 'One way of expressing the essence of Green's doctrine is to say that genuine human achievement is non-competitive in the sense that, to borrow Bosanquet's phrase, "it is not diminished by being shared".' *The Social Philosophy of English Idealism* (1962) p. 110.
106 Matthew Arnold, *Culture and Anarchy* (1969 edn) p. 69.
107 On this subject see Ben Knights, *The Idea of the Clerisy in the Nineteenth Century* (1978) and Anthony Arblaster, *The Rise and Decline of Western Liberalism* (1984) ch. 15.
108 Russell, *Autobiography* vol. II p. 59.
109 Russell, *Principles* p. 155.

110 Russell, *Principles* p. 158.
111 *Ibid.* pp. 169–70.
112 Quoted in Clark, *The Life* p. 268.
113 Virginia Woolf, *The Letters* (ed. Nigel Nicolson) vol. II (1976) p. 76.
114 *Ibid.* p. 78.
115 *Ibid.* p. 133.
116 Russell, *Autobiography* vol. I pp. 70–1.
117 Russell, *Principles* pp. 106–7.
118 W.H. Auden, *Forewords and Afterwords* (1973) p. 511. For a discussion of the Eton/Oxford generation of the 1920s see Martin Green, *Children of the Sun* (1977) and Humphrey Carpenter, *The Brideshead Generation: Evelyn Waugh and his Generation* (1989).

6 ANARCHIST TENDENCIES

1 Russell, *Autobiography* vol. II p. 2.
2 *Ibid.* p. 59.
3 Enumerating the duties of the 'authorities' in *Political Ideals* p. 54, Russell remarks: 'They will reflect that, though errors which are traditional are often widespread, new beliefs seldom win acceptance unless they are nearer to the truth than what they replace; and they will conclude that a new belief is probably either an advance, or so unlikely to become common as to be innocuous.'
4 Russell was prosecuted as the author of a leaflet criticising the treatment of a conscientious objector, Ernest F. Everett. For a full account of the case see Jo Vellacott, *Russell and the Pacifists in the First World War* (1980).
5 See Vellacott, *Russell and the Pacifists* p. 79.
6 *New Statesman* 23 December 1916.
7 Annan, *The Intellectual Aristocracy*, in J.H. Plumb (ed.), *Studies in Social History: A Tribute to G.M. Trevelyan* (1955) p. 249.
8 Russell, *Political Ideals* p. 51.
9 Russell, *Principles* p. 83.
10 Russell, *Political Ideals* p. 25.
11 *Ibid.* p. 16.
12 *Ibid.* p. 17.
13 *Ibid.* p. 29.
14 According to A.M. McBriar, *Fabian Socialism and English Politics 1884–1918* (1966) p. 268, 'In a sense, there was an element of "deterrence" even in the Minority Report, which agreed at least that habitual idleness, vagrancy, and mendacity should be suppressed with the full vigour of the law.'
15 Russell, *Political Ideals* p. 58.
16 Russell, *Principles* p. 95.
17 Russell, *Political Ideals* pp. 24–5.
18 G.D.H. Cole, *Self-Government in Industry* (1972 edn) p. 52.

19 *Ibid.* p. 169.
20 *Ibid.* p. 210.
21 Russell, *Political Ideals* p. 18.
22 Cole, *Self-Government* p. 231.
23 Russell, *Political Ideals* p. 10.
24 *Ibid.* p. 15.
25 *Ibid.* p. 15.
26 *Ibid.* pp. 63–4.
27 Quoted in Ronald W. Clark, *The Life of Bertrand Russell* p. 318.
28 Russell wrote a front page article for the organ of the No Conscription Fellowship, *The Tribune*, and in it asserted that, 'The American garrison which will by that time be occupying England and France, whether or not they will prove efficient against the Germans, will no doubt be capable of intimidating strikers, an occupation to which the American army is accustomed when at home.' Quoted in Vellacott, *Russell and the Pacifists* p. 224.
29 Benjamin R. Barber, *Superman and Common Men: Freedom, Anarchy and the Revolution* (1971) p. 31.
30 Russell, *Roads to Freedom* p. 57.
31 On this point, Thomas A. Spragens, Jr, *The Irony of Liberal Reason* (1981) p. 286, comments:

> The fact is that the relativist democrats draw liberal conclusions from their philosophical premises only because tacitly they trade on a tradition they in theory reject: the tradition of civility, as Ernest Barker and Walter Lipmann call it. Hume interpreted his scepticism as grounds for moderation and humanity not so much because of strictly logical reasons as because he was himself moderate and humane. Similarly, Russell, Smith, and Kelsen were all liberal and tolerant men of very real moral sensitivity. Any of these moral sceptics, Hume as well as the twentieth-century thinkers, might equally well have said what Leslie Stephen wrote: 'I now believe in nothing, but I do not the less believe in morality ... I mean to live and die like a gentleman if possible.'

32 Santayana, in the paper which was instrumental in converting Russell to relativism, had written:

> The twang of intolerance and of self-mutilation is not absent from the ethics of Mr Russell and Mr Moore, even as it stands; and one trembles to think what it may become in the mouths of their disciples. Intolerance itself is a form of egoism, and to condemn egoism intolerantly is to share it ... I cannot help thinking that a consciousness of the relativity of values, if it became prevalent, would tend to render people more truly social than would a belief that things have instrinsic and unchangeable values, no matter what the attitude of any one of them may be.

'The Philosophy of Bertrand Russell' in George Santayana, *Winds of Doctrine* (1913; 1940 edn) p. 151.
33 Russell, *Roads to Freedom* p. 108.
34 On this point K.C. Hsiao, *Political Pluralism* (1927) p. 127, writes: 'Whatever may be the avenue of approach – whether it be through law and legal theory, through the problem of representative government, or, lastly, through economic and social organisation – the final outcome of

the pluralistic argument is, in every instance, not multiplicity as such (as we naturally expect), but some unity that transcends and points beyond mere multiplicity.'

35 Russell, *Political Ideals* p. 42.
36 Peter Kropotkin, *The Essential Kropotkin* (eds. Emile Capouya and Keitha Tompkins, 1975) p. 86.
37 Peter Kropotkin, *The Conquest of Bread* (1906; 1972 edn) p. 124.
38 Russell, *Roads to Freedom* p. 81.
39 *Ibid.* p. 89.
40 *Ibid.* p. 133.
41 *Ibid.* p. 130.
42 *Ibid.* pp. 127–8.
43 *Ibid.* p. 143.
44 Clark, *The Life* p. 344.
45 Russell, *Autobiography* vol. II p. 38.
46 Russell, 'Democracy and Direct Action', *The English Review* 28 (May 1919) 398.
47 *Ibid.* p. 403.
48 Russell, *Autobiography* vol. II p. 113.
49 *Ibid.* p. 115.
50 *Ibid.* p.115.
51 Beatrice Webb, *The Diaries* vol. III (1905–24). Norman and Jeanne MacKenzie (eds.) pp. 396–7 excised extracts quoted from Clark, *The Life* p. 402.

7 RUSSIA, CHINA, AND THE WEST

1 Russell, *Practice and Theory of Bolshevism* (1920) p. 42.
2 Russell, *Practice and Theory of Bolshevism* (1949 edn) preface.
3 For a discussion of this, see L.P. Carpenter, *G.D.H. Cole: An Intellectual Biography* (1973) ch. 3.
4 *Ibid.* p. 93.
5 Ronald W. Clark, *The Life of Bertrand Russell* p. 384.
6 Quoted in Russell, *Autobiography* vol. II p. 122.
7 Quoted in Clark, *The Life* p. 382.
8 H.G. Wells, *Russia in the Shadows* (1920).
9 H.N. Brailsford, *The Russian Workers' Republic* (1921).
10 Russell, *Autobiography* vol. II p. 102.
11 Russell, *Practice and Theory of Bolshevism* (1920) p. 105.
12 *Ibid.* p. 72.
13 *Ibid.* p. 107.
14 In fact Russell's attitude towards Russia was noticeably less hostile in published statements as a candidate during the 1923 election. See Clark *The Life*, and Alan Wood, *Bertrand Russell: The Passionate Sceptic* (1957) ch. 15.

15 David Caute, *The Fellow-Travellers* (1973) p. 6.
16 Russell, *Autobiography* vol. II p. 107.
17 In reference to the 'theological' aspects of Marxism Russell states, 'Bolshevism is not merely a political doctrine; it is also a religion, with elaborate dogmas and inspired scriptures. When Lenin wishes to prove some proposition, he does so, if possible, by quoting texts from Marx and Engels.' *Practice and Theory of Bolshevism* (1920) p. 8.
18 *Ibid.* pp. 119–20.
19 *Ibid.* p. 127.
20 *Ibid.* p. 114.
21 *Ibid.* p. 8.
22 *Ibid.* p. 131.
23 *Ibid.* p. 134.
24 *Ibid.* p. 29.
25 *Ibid.* p. 29.
26 *The Problem of China* pp. 17–18.
27 Jerome Ch'en, *China and the West: Society and Culture 1815–1937* (1979) p. 1.
28 Russell, *The Problem of China* (1922) p. 10.
29 *Ibid.* p. 11.
30 *Ibid.* p. 12.
31 'There are three forces on the side of life which require no exceptional mental endowment, which are not very rare at present, and might be very common under better social institutions. They are love, the instinct of constructiveness, and the joy of life.' Russell, *Principles* (1916 edn) p. 23.
32 Russell, *The Problem of China* p. 12.
33 *Ibid.* p. 202.
34 *Ibid.* p. 70.
35 *Ibid.* p. 197.
36 *Ibid.* p. 201.
37 Quoted in Ross Harrison, *Bentham* (1983) p. 169.
38 Russell, *The Problem of China* p. 200.
39 *Ibid.* p. 209.
40 *Ibid.* p. 221.
41 *Ibid.* p. 221.
42 *Ibid.* p. 242.
43 Russell, *Practice and Theory of Bolshevism* p. 42.
44 Russell, *The Problem of China* p. 76.
45 J.S. Mill, *On Liberty* in *Collected Works* vol. XVIII (ed. John M. Robson, 1977) p. 273.
46 Russell, *The Problem of China* p. 9.
47 *Ibid.* p. 200.
48 *Ibid.* p. 204.
49 Russell, 'Eastern and Western Ideals of Happiness' in *Sceptical Essays* (1928).
50 Russell, 'Free Thought and Official Propaganda' in *Sceptical Essays* p. 103.

51 Russell, 'Joseph Conrad' in *Portraits from Memory* p. 85.
52 The breadth of Russell's culture in the 1890s, for example, can be judged by the 750 titles in his 'What Shall I Read?', *Cambridge Essays* pp. 347–65. In this list are included some twenty novels by Henry James as well as works by Meredith and Turgenev.
53 Russell, 'D.H. Lawrence' in *Portraits from Memory* p. 105.
54 *Ibid.* pp. 107–8.
55 Raymond Williams, *Culture and Society 1780–1950* (1958; 1971 edn) p. 209.
56 Russell, 'Joseph Conrad' in *Portraits from Memory* pp. 81–2.
57 See Russell, *Autobiography* vol. II p. 18.
58 Hugh Kenner, *The Invisible Poet: T.S. Eliot* (1959; 1965 edn) p. 125.
59 See Russell, *Autobiography* vol. II p. 173.
60 See Chris Baldick, *The Social Mission of English Criticism 1848–1932* (1983) and Roger Kojecky, *T.S. Eliot's Social Criticism* (1971).

8 THE WELLSIAN TRAJECTORY

1 On this topic see Peter Clarke, *Liberals and Social Democrats* (1978) chs. 7 and 8.
2 Russell, *Portraits from Memory* (1956) pp. 78–80.
3 For a discussion of this see Clarke, *Liberals and Social Democrats* ch. 7 pt 2.
4 Russell, 'Free Thought and Official Propaganda' (1922) in *Sceptical Essays* (1928) p. 168.
5 Russell, *Prospects of Industrial Civilization* (1923) p. 16.
6 *Ibid.* p. 16.
7 J.M. Keynes, 'My Early Beliefs' in Keynes, *Two Memoirs* (1949) p. 103.
8 Russell, 'Can Men Be Rational?' (1923) in *Sceptical Essays* p. 49.
9 *Ibid.* p. 49.
10 *Ibid.* p. 45.
11 *Ibid.* p. 51.
12 Russell, 'Free Thought' p. 151.
13 *Ibid.* p. 152.
14 Russell, 'Can Men Be Rational?' p. 51.
15 Russell, *Prospects* p. 19.
16 *Ibid.* p. 19.
17 *Ibid.* p. 33.
18 *Ibid.* p. 34.
19 *Ibid.* p. 38.
20 *Ibid.* p. 42.
21 *Ibid.* p. 43.
22 *Ibid.* p. 45.
23 *Ibid.* pp. 125–6.
24 *Ibid.* p. 57.
25 *Ibid.* p. 55.
26 *Ibid.* p. 95.

27 *Ibid.* p. 273.
28 *Ibid.* p. 134.
29 *Ibid.* p. 135.
30 *Ibid.* p. 135.
31 *Ibid.* p. 143.
32 *Ibid.* p. 144.
33 *Ibid.* p. 152.
34 *Ibid.* p. 228.
35 *Ibid.* p. 229.
36 *Ibid.* p. 230.
37 G.D.H. Cole, *Guild Socialism Restated* (1920) pp. 115–16.
38 Russell, *Prospects* p. 172.
39 *Ibid.* p. 181.
40 *Ibid.* p. 158.
41 *Ibid.* p. 158.
42 *Ibid.* pp. 219–20.
43 *Ibid.* p. 50.
44 *Ibid.* p. 165.
45 *Ibid.* p. 163.
46 Rather in the manner of Eliot's 'Tradition and the Individual Talent', Russell remarks at this juncture: 'It would seem, for the history of art, that nine-tenths of artistic capacity, at least, depends upon tradition, and one-tenth, at most, upon individual merit. All the great flowering periods of art have come at the end of a slowly maturing tradition.' *Prospects* p. 183.
47 See Francis Mulhern, *The Moment of 'Scrutiny'* (1979) pp. 117–18.
48 Russell, *Prospects* p. 186.
49 *Ibid.* p. 187.
50 *Ibid.* p. 212.
51 *Ibid.* p. 217.
52 *Ibid.* pp. 220–1.
53 Q.D. Leavis, *Fiction and the Reading Public* (1932; 1979 edn) p. 213.
54 Russell, 'The Need for Political Scepticism' (1924) in *Sceptical Essays* pp. 30 and 144.
55 *Ibid.* p. 130.
56 *Ibid.* pp. 144–5.
57 Maurice Cowling, *Mill and Liberalism* (1963) pp. 130–1.
58 See Russell, *Autobiography* vol. II p. 150.
59 Russell, 'Freedom in Society' (1926) in *Sceptical Essays* p. 182.
60 Russell, *On Education: Especially in Early Childhood* (1926; 1976 edn) p. 29.
61 In his discussion of Bentham in *Freedom and Organization 1814–1914* (1934) p. 112, Russell remarks, 'There is an important respect in which associationism and behaviourism have exactly similar consequences. Both are deterministic, that is to say, they think that what we do is governed by laws which are, at least in great part, ascertainable, so that our actions in given circumstances can be predicted by a good psychologist.'

62 Russell, *On Education* p. 32.
63 *Ibid.* p. 204.
64 *Ibid.* p. 41.
65 B.F. Skinner, *Walden Two* (1948; repr. 1962) p. 264.
66 Russell, *On Education* p. 54.
67 *Ibid.* p. 50.
68 Katharine Tait, *My Father Bertrand Russell* (1976) p. 59.
69 Russell, *Autobiography* vol. II p. 180.
70 H.G. Wells, *The Open Conspiracy: Blue Prints for a World Revolution* (1928) p. 36.
71 *Ibid.* p. 58.
72 *Ibid.* p. 106.
73 *Ibid.* pp. 140–1.
74 Russell, *Autobiography* vol. II pp. 180–1.
75 Russell, *Marriage and Morals* (1929) p. 103.
76 H.G. Wells, *A Modern Utopia* (1905) p. 191.
77 *Ibid.* p. 193.
78 Russell, *Marriage and Morals* p. 133.
79 *Ibid.* pp. 212–13.
80 *Ibid.* p. 212.
81 *Ibid.* p. 206.
82 *Ibid.* p. 203.
83 *Ibid.* p. 206.
84 *Ibid.* p. 205.
85 *Ibid.* pp. 83, 209, and 201.

In the first edition of *Marriage and Morals* Russell writes: 'It seems on the whole fair to regard negroes as on the average inferior to white men, although for work in the tropics they are indispensable, so that their extermination (apart from questions of humanity) would be highly undesirable.' In the 1963 edition he had this altered to read 'There is no sound reason to regard negroes . . .' p. 171.

86 *Ibid.* pp. 109 and 111–12.
87 For an account of this period in Russell's life see Dora Russell, *The Tamarisk Tree: My Quest for Liberty and Love* (1975) ch. 11.
88 Russell, 'Some Prospects' (1928) in *Sceptical Essays* p. 249.
89 Russell, *Marriage and Morals* p. 214.

9 IDEOLOGIES AND DYSTOPIAS

1 Russell, *Autobiography* vol. II p. 195.
2 Russell, 'Reply to Criticisms' in Paul Schilpp (ed.), *The Philosophy of Bertrand Russell* (1944) p. 729.
3 Russell, 'Scylla and Charybdis, or Communism and Fascism' (1935) in *In Praise of Idleness* (1935) p. 109.
4 Beatrice Webb, *The Diaries* vol. IV: *1924–43* (1985) p. 244.

5 Russell, *Autobiography* vol. II pp. 159–60.
6 See Norman and Jeanne MacKenzie, *The Time Traveller: The Life of H.G. Wells* (1973) p. 400.
7 Russell, *The Conquest of Happiness* (1930; pbk 1979) p. 160.
8 *Ibid.* p. 185.
9 Russell, *The Scientific Outlook* (1931) p. 269.
10 *Ibid.* p. 269.
11 *Ibid.* p. 269.
12 Russell, *Prospects* p. 55.
13 Russell, *The Scientific Outlook* pp. 224–5.
14 *Ibid.* p. 225.
15 See, for example, his essay 'Architecture and Social Questions' (1935) in *In Praise of Idleness.*
16 *Ibid.* p. 229.
17 *Ibid.* pp. 229–30.
18 See Russell, 'Self-Appreciation' (1897) in *Cambridge Essays.*
19 Russell, *The Scientific Outlook* p. 230.
20 *Ibid.* pp. 261–2.
21 Philip Thody, *Aldous Huxley* (1973) pp. 50–1, remarks: 'So much of *Brave New World* resembles *The Scientific Outlook* that one wonders at times if Huxley put any original ideas into his book.' Russell also took this view, and complained to Unwin that *Brave New World* was 'merely an expansion of the two penultimate chapters of *The Scientific Outlook* ... The only thing he has added is the Bokanovsky twins ... Otherwise the parallelism applies in great detail, e.g. the prohibition of Shakespeare and the intoxicant producing no headache.' Quoted in Ronald W. Clark, *The Life of Bertrand Russell* (1975) p. 454.
22 Russell, *The Scientific Outlook* p. 249.
23 *Ibid.* pp. 257, 189 and 265–6.
24 *Ibid.* p. 246.
25 Russell, *The Problem of China* p. 10.
26 Russell, *The Scientific Outlook* p. 275.
27 *Ibid.* pp. 275–6.
28 *Ibid.* p. 278.
29 Russell, *Education and the Social Order* (1932) p. 86.
30 Russell, *Autobiography* vol. II p. 200.
31 Russell, *Education and the Social Order* p. 51.
32 *Ibid.* p. 47.
33 *Ibid.* p. 55.
34 *Ibid.* p. 84.
35 *Ibid.* p. 27.
36 *Ibid.* p. 247.
37 *Ibid.* pp. 246–8.
38 Quoted in Clark, *The Life* p. 448.
39 Russell, *Autobiography* vol. II p. 190.

40 Russell, *Autobiography* vol. II p. 191.
41 Russell, 'Western Civilization' (1935) in *In Praise of Idleness* p. 175.
42 Russell, 'Symptoms of Orwell's 1984' in *Portraits from Memory* p. 203.
43 Russell, *Freedom and Organization 1814–1914* (1934; 1978 edn) p. 139.
44 *Ibid.* p. 139.
45 *Ibid.* pp. 120–1.
46 *Ibid.* p. 140.
47 *Ibid.* p. 93.
48 *Ibid.* p. 507.
49 *Ibid.* p. 510.
50 Russell, 'The Revolt Against Reason', *Political Quarterly* (January 1935) reprinted as 'The Ancestry of Fascism' in *In Praise of Idleness* p. 89.
51 *Ibid.* pp. 89–90.
52 *Ibid.* p. 90.
53 *Ibid.* p. 91.
54 *Ibid.* p. 93.
55 Quoted in Clark, *The Life* p. 51.
56 Russell, 'The Revolt Against Reason' in *In Praise of Idleness* p. 97.
57 Russell, *Autobiography* vol. II p. 191.
58 Russell, 'In Praise of Idleness' (1932) in *In Praise of Idleness* p. 26.
59 Russell, 'The Case for Socialism' (1935) in *In Praise of Idleness* pp. 121–2 and 125.
60 *Ibid.* p. 150.
61 Russell, *Autobiography* vol. II p. 191.
62 *Ibid.* p. 193.
63 *Ibid.* p. 193.
64 George Orwell, 'Review of *Power*', *Adelphi* (January 1939) reprinted in *Collected Essays, Journalism and Letters* (1970 edn) vol. II p. 413.
65 *Ibid.* p. 414.
66 Russell, *Power: A New Social Analysis* (1938) p. 10.
67 *Ibid.* p. 8.
68 *Ibid.* p. 10.
69 *Ibid.* p. 9.
70 *Ibid.* pp. 10–12.
71 V.J. McGill, 'Russell's Political and Economic Philosophy' in Schilpp (ed.), *The Philosophy of Bertrand Russell* p. 588, remarks: 'Russell, in 1938, following the fashion of Schopenhauer, Nietzsche, and other romantic philosophers, attempted to reduce all the instincts to one, the love of Power.'
72 Russell, *Power* p. 13.
73 *Ibid.* p. 13.
74 *Ibid.* p. 12.
75 *Ibid.* p. 13.
76 *Ibid.* pp. 13–14.
77 *Ibid.* pp. 44–6.

78 *Ibid.* pp. 47–8.
79 *Ibid.* p. 287.
80 *Ibid.* p. 304.
81 *Ibid.* p. 288.
82 *Ibid.* p. 294.
83 *Ibid.* p. 303.
84 *Ibid.* p. 307.
85 *Ibid.* p. 308.
86 *Ibid.* p. 319.
87 Russell, *Autobiography* vol. II p. 193.
88 For a discussion of Auden's 'political' career during the 1930s, see in particular, Samuel Hynes, *The Auden Generation: Literature and Politics in England in the 1930s* (1976) and Valentine Cunningham, *British Writers of the Thirties* (1988).
89 Russell, 'The Last Survivor of a Dead Epoch', *The Listener* 12 August 1936, reprinted as 'Obituary' in *Unpopular Essays* (1950) p. 223.

EPILOGUE: RUSSELL AND THE IDEA OF THE CLERISY

1 Paul Schilpp (ed.), *The Philosophy of Bertrand Russell* (1944) pp. 730–1.
2 Russell, *Principles* (1916 edn) pp. 207–8.
3 See Ben Knights, *The Idea of the Clerisy in the Nineteenth Century* (1978) Introduction.
4 Russell, *Power* pp. 44–5.
5 Julian Huxley, *Essays in Popular Science* (1926; 1937 edn) p. vi.
6 J.B.S. Haldane, *The Inequality of Man* (1932; 1937 edn) p. 139.
7 See Francis Mulhern, *The Moment of 'Scrutiny'* (1979) ch. 1 and D.L. LeMahieu, *A Culture for Democracy* (1988).
8 I.A. Richards, *Principles of Literary Criticism* (1924; 1967 edn) pp. 25–6.
9 *Ibid.* p. 46.
10 Aldous Huxley, *Crome Yellow* (1921; 1982 edn) p. 57.
11 Russell, *History of Western Philosophy* (1946; 1967 edn) p. 130.
12 Russell, *Principles* p. 6.
13 Russell, *In Praise of Idleness* pp. 25–6.
14 *Ibid.* p. 26.
15 Christopher Caudwell, *Studies in a Dying Culture* (1938) pp. 197–8.
16 E.M. Forster, *Howard's End* (1910; 1953 edn) p. 44.
17 E.M. Forster, 'What I Believe' (1939) in *Two Cheers for Democracy* (1951) p. 83.
18 Forster, *Howard's End* p. 31 and Kingsley Amis, *Lucky Jim* (1954; 1961 edn) p. 63.
19 E.M. Forster, *Aspects of the Novel* (1927; 1962 edn) pp. 125–6.
20 Richard Poirier, *The Renewal of Literature* (1987) p. 105.
21 Kenneth Harris, *Talking To ...* (1971) p. 118.
22 Huxley, *Crome Yellow* p. 128.

23 T.S. Eliot, *Collected Poems 1909–1962* (1963) p. 33.
24 D.H. Lawrence, *Women in Love* (1921; 1983 edn) p. 101.
25 Valerie Eliot (ed.), *The Letters of T.S. Eliot* vol. 1: *1898–1922* (1988) p. 92.
26 See Mulhern, '*Scrutiny*' and LeMahieu, *Democracy*.
27 William Gerhardi, *Memoirs of a Polyglot* (1931) p. 265.
28 Anthony Powell, *Afternoon Men* (1931; 1979 edn) p. 24.
29 See Malcolm Bradbury, 'A Matter for Serious Scrutiny! F.R. Leavis in the 1950s' in Bradbury, *No, Not Bloomsbury* (1987) and Mulhern, '*Scrutiny*'.
30 *Horizon* 11 (January 1945) 24–5.
31 *Bertrand Russell Speaks His Mind* (1960).
32 For example, A.J.P. Taylor in his television appearances often came perilously close to being more 'performer' than historian; indeed, his popular reputation was rather like that of a music-hall 'memory man'.
33 *Bertrand Russell Speaks His Mind* pp. 171–2.
34 Martin J. Wiener, *English Culture and the Decline of the Industrial Spirit 1850–1980* (1980) p. 159.
35 Ray Galton and Alan Simpson, *Hancock's Half Hour* (1974) p. 64.
36 *Ibid.* p. 69. The sketch issued out of Galton's, Simpson's, and Hancock's experiences as working-class autodidacts in the early 1950s.
37 Forster, *Howard's End* p. 35.
38 See Alan Sinfield, *Literature, Politics and Culture in Post-War Britain* (1989) ch. 13, and Robert Hewison, *Too Much* (1986).
39 Kenneth Harris, *Talking To* ... p. 115.
40 Russell, 'Obituary' in *Unpopular Essays* (1950) p. 223.

Bibliography

The place of publication is London, unless otherwise stated.

1 WORKS BY RUSSELL

MAJOR WORKS

1896 *German Social Democracy* (2nd edn 1965)
1910 *Philosophical Essays* (rev. edn 1966)
1910–13 *Principia Mathematica* (in collaboration with Alfred North Whitehead) 3 vols. (Cambridge)
1912 *The Problems of Philosophy* (pbk edn Oxford 1959)
1914 *Our Knowledge of the External World as a Field for Scientific Method in Philosophy* (repr. 1980)
1916 *Principles of Social Reconstruction* (pbk edn 1971)
Justice in War-Time (1st edn Chicago 1916; facsimile edn Nottingham)
1917 *Political Ideals* (1st edn New York 1917; 1st English edn 1963; pbk edn 1977)
Mysticism and Logic and Other Essays (1976 edn)
1918 *Roads to Freedom* (pbk edn 1977)
1920 *The Practice and Theory of Bolshevism* (2nd rev. edn 1949)
1922 *The Problem of China*
1923 *The Prospects of Industrial Civilization* (in collaboration with Dora Russell)
1924 *Icarus or the Future of Science*
1925 *What I Believe*
1926 *On Education: Especially in Early Childhood* (pbk edn 1976)
1927 *An Outline of Philosophy* (1951 edn)
1928 *Sceptical Essays* (pbk edn 1966)
1929 *Marriage and Morals* (pbk edn 1976)
1930 *The Conquest of Happiness* (pbk edn 1979)
1931 *The Scientific Outlook*
1932 *Education and the Social Order*
1934 *Freedom and Organization 1814–1914* (1978 edn)
1935 *In Praise of Idleness and Other Essays* (1948 edn)
1936 *Which Way to Peace?*

1937 *The Amberley Papers* (edited by B.R. and Patricia Russell) 2 vols. (1966 edn)
1938 *Power: A New Social Analysis*
1946 *History of Western Philosophy* (1967 edn)
1949 *Authority and the Individual*
1950 *Unpopular Essays*
1956 *Portraits from Memory and Other Essays*
1957 *Why I Am Not a Christian and Other Essays on Religion and Related Subjects* (edited with an appendix on the Bertrand Russell case by Paul Edwards)
1959 *My Philosophical Development*
1960 *Bertrand Russell Speaks His Mind*
1961 *The Basic Writings of Bertrand Russell 1903–1959* (edited by Robert E. Egner and Lester E. Denonn)
1967 *The Autobiography of Bertrand Russell* vol. I: *1872–1914*
1968 *The Autobiography of Bertrand Russell* vol. II: *1914–1944*
1969 *The Autobiography of Bertrand Russell* vol. III: *1944–1967*
1975 *Mortals and Others: American Essays 1931–1935* vol. I (edited by Harry Ruja)
1983 *The Collected Papers of Bertrand Russell* vol. I: *Cambridge Essays 1888–99* (ed. Kenneth Blackwell et al.)
1985 *The Collected Papers of Bertrand Russell* vol. XII: *Contemplation and Action 1902–14* (ed. Richard A. Rempel et al.)
1988 *The Collected Papers of Bertrand Russell* vol. XIII: *Prophecy and Dissent 1914–16* (ed. Richard A. Rempel et al.)
1992 *The Selected Letters of Bertrand Russell* vol. I: *The Private Years 1884–1914* (ed. Nicholas Griffin)

ARTICLES, SPEECHES, AND PAMPHLETS

Key to abbreviations: BRA *Bertrand Russell's America*; BW *Basic Writings*; CE *Cambridge Essays*; CA *Contemplation and Action*; IPI *In Praise of Idleness*; JWT *Justice in War-Time*; ML *Mysticism and Logic*; PD *Prophecy and Dissent*; PE *Philosophical Essays*; PM *Portraits from Memory*; SE *Sceptical Essays*; UE *Unpopular Essays*.

1896 'German Social Democracy, as a Lesson in Political Tactics', CE pp. 312–18
'The Uses of Luxury', CE pp. 320–3
'Mechanical Morals and the Moral of Machinery', CE pp. 347–65
1903 'The Free Man's Worship', *Independent Review* 1 415–24 (repr. ML)
1904 'On History', *Independent Review* 3 207–15 (repr. PE)
'Review of G.E. Moore's Principia Ethica', *Independent Review* 2 328–33
'Mr Charles Booth's Proposals for Fiscal Reform', *Contemporary Review* 85, 198–206 (repr. CA pp. 225–32)
'The Tariff Controversy', *Edinburgh Review* 199 (January) 149–96 (repr. CA pp. 193–215)

1906 'On the Democratic Ideal', CA pp. 248–56
'The Status of Women', CA pp. 258–65
1907 'The Development of Morals' (Review of Hobhouse), *Independent Review* 12, 204–10 (repr. CA pp. 336–40)
'The Politics of a Biologist' (Review of Chatterton-Hill), *Albany Review* no. 11 (October) 92 (repr. CA pp. 366–73)
1908 'Liberalism and Women's Suffrage', *Contemporary Review* 94 (July) 11–16 (repr. CA pp. 277–84)
'Biology and Politics' (review of Chatterton-Hill), *Nation* 3 (September) 918, 920 (repr. CA pp. 374–5)
'Transatlantic "truth"' (review of William James's *Pragmatism*), *Albany Review* 2 no. 10, 393–410 (repr. as 'William James's Conception of Truth', PE)
'Determinism and Morals', *Hibbert Journal* (October) 113–21
1909 'Pragmatism', *Edinburgh Review* 209, 363–88 (repr. PE)
1910 'Address to the Bedford Liberal Association', CA pp. 297–303
'Ethics', *New Quarterly* 3, 21–34 (repr. as 'The Elements of Ethics', PE)
'The Philosophy of William James', *Nation* 7 (October) 793–4
1911 'Memories and Studies' (review of William James), *Cambridge Review* (16 November; repr. CA p. 377)
1912 'The Philosophy of Bergson', *The Monist* 22, 321–47
'The Essence of Religion', *Hibbert Journal* (October; repr. CA pp. 112–22)
1913 'Science as an Element in Culture', *New Statesman* 1 (24 and 31 May) 202–4, 224–36 (repr. as 'The Place of Science in a Liberal Education', ML)
1914 'Mysticism and Logic', *Hibbert Journal* 12, 780–803 (repr. ML)
'On Scientific Method in Philosophy' (The Herbert Spencer lecture, Oxford; repr. ML)
'Why Nations Love War', *War and Peace* (November, repr. JWT)
'War, the Offspring of Fear', Union of Democratic Control Pamphlet No. 3 (repr. PD)
1915 'The Ethics of War', *International Journal of Ethics* 25, 127–42 (repr. JWT)
'Is a Permanent Peace Possible?', *Atlantic Monthly* 115, 127–41 (repr. JWT)
'The Future of Anglo-German Rivalry', *Atlantic Monthly* 116, 127–33 (repr. JWT)
'War and Non-Resistance', *Atlantic Monthly* 116, 266–74 (repr. PD)
'An Appeal to the Intellectuals of Europe', *International Review* 1 nos. 4 and 5, 145–51, 223–30 (repr. JWT)
'The State and Its External Relations', *Proceedings of the Aristotelian Society* 16, 301–10
1916 'The Danger to Civilization', *Open Court* 30, 170–80 (repr. JWT)
'The Entente Policy, 1904–1915: A Reply to Professor Gilbert Murray', National Labour Press pamphlet (repr. JWT)
1917 'Idealism on the Defensive', *Nation* 21
1919 'Democracy and Direct Action', *English Review* 28 (May) 396–403
'Democracy and Efficiency', *Athenaeum* 270
'Economic Unity and Political Division', *The Dial* 66, 629–31

1920 'Dreams and Facts', *The Dial* 68, 214–20 (repr. SE)
'Socialism and Liberal Ideals', *English Review* 30 (May and June) 449–55 and 499–508
1921 'The Happiness of China', *Nation* 28, 505–6
'Industry in Undeveloped Countries', *Atlantic Monthly* 127, 787–95
'Some Traits in Chinese Character', *Atlantic Monthly* 128, 771–7
1922 'Hopes and Fears as Regards America', *The New Republic* 30 (15 and 22 March) 70–2 and 99–101 (repr. BRA)
'Instinct and the Unconscious', *The New Leader* 1, 12
'Free Thought and Official Propaganda' (Conway Memorial Lecture: repr. SE)
1923 'The Recrudescence of Puritanism', *Outlook* 52, 300–2 (repr. SE)
'Can Men Be Rational?', *Rationalist Annual* (repr. SE)
1924 'New Morals for Old: Styles in Ethics', *Nation* 118, 479–99 (repr. BW)
'The Need for Political Scepticism', *Freeman* 8, 124–6 (repr. SE)
'Psychology and Politics', *The Dial* 80, 179–88 (repr. SE)
'Machines and Emotions', *Outlook* 53 (repr. SE)
'The American Intelligentsia', *Nation and Athenaeum* 36, 50–61 (repr. BRA)
'Philosophy in the Twentieth Century', *The Dial* 77, 271–90 (repr. SE)
1925 'Materialism: Past and Present', Intro. to F.A. Lange, *The History of Materialism* (repr. BW)
1926 'Freedom in Society', *Harper's Monthly Magazine* 152 (March) 438–41 (repr. SE)
'Is Science Superstitious?' *The Dial* 81, 179–86 (repr. SE)
'The Harm That Good Men Do', *Harper's* 153, 529–34 (repr. SE)
1928 'The New Philosophy of America', *Fortnightly Review* 129, 618–23 (repr. BRA)
'The Value of Scepticism', *Plain Talk* 13, 423–30 (repr. SE)
1930 'Homogeneous America', *The Outlook and Independent* 154 (February) 285–7 (repr. BRA)
'China's Philosophy of Happiness', *The Thinker* (February) 16–23
'Politics and Theology', *Political Quarterly* 1, 179–85
1931 'Modern Tendencies in Education', *Spectator* 146, 926–7
'Free Speech in Childhood', *New Statesman and Nation* 1, 486–8
1932 'In Praise of Idleness', *Harper's* (October) 552–9 (repr. IPI)
1933 'The Modern Midas', *Harper's* 166, 327–34 (repr. IPI)
1934 'Man versus Insects', *Scribner's Magazine* 96 (December) 380 (repr. IPI)
'Why I Am Not a Communist', *Modern Monthly* 8 (April) 133–4
1935 'The Revolt Against Reason', *Political Quarterly* 6, 1–19 (repr. as 'The Ancestry of Fascism' in IPI)
'"Useless" Knowledge' in IPI
'The Case for Socialism' in IPI
1936 'The Last Survivor of a Dead Epoch', *The Listener* 16 (12 August) 289 (repr. UE)

1937 'On Being Modern-Minded', *Nation* 144, 47–8
'Philosophy's Ulterior Motives', *Atlantic Monthly* 159, 149–55 (repr. UE)
'Power – Ancient and Modern', *Political Quarterly* 8, 155–64
'The Future of Democracy', *The New Republic* 80, 381–2
'The Superior Virtue of the Oppressed', *Nation* 144, 731–2 (repr. UE)
'Two Prophets' (review of R. Osborne's *Freud and Marx*) *New Statesman and Nation* 13, 416
1945 'American and British Nationalism', *Horizon* 11 (January) 17–30
1947 'Philosophy and Politics' (National Book League Lecture; repr. UE)

2 WORKS BY OTHER AUTHORS

Abrams, Philip. *The Origins of British Sociology 1834–1914* (Chicago 1968)
Ackroyd, Peter. *T.S. Eliot* (1984)
Adams, Ian. *The Logic of Political Belief: A Philosophical Analysis of Ideology* (Md. 1989)
Aiken, Lillian W. *Bertrand Russell's Philosophy of Morals* (New York 1963)
Alexander, Edward. *Matthew Arnold and John Stuart Mill* (1965)
Allen, Peter. *The Cambridge Apostles: The Early Years* (Cambridge 1978)
Allett, John. *New Liberalism: The Political Economy of J.A. Hobson* (Toronto 1981)
Angell, Norman. *The Great Illusion* (3rd edn 1911)
Annan, Noel. *Leslie Stephen: His Thoughts and Character in Relation to his Time* (1951)
The Curious Strength of Positivism in English Political Thought (1959)
Our Age: Portrait of a Generation (1990)
Anschutz, R.P. *The Philosophy of J.S. Mill* (Oxford 1953)
Arblaster, Anthony. *The Rise and Decline of Western Liberalism* (Oxford 1984)
Arnold, Matthew. *Culture and Anarchy* (1869; 1969 edn)
Literature and Dogma (1873; 1904 edn)
Auden, W.H. *Forewords and Afterwords* (1973)
Ayer, A.J. 'Obituary of Russell', *New Statesman* (6 February 1970)
Russell (1972)
Bagehot, Walter. *Physics and Politics* (1872)
Bagg, Ronald. *Hippolytos* (Oxford 1974)
Baldick, Chris. *The Social Mission of English Criticism 1848–1932* (Oxford 1983)
Barber, Benjamin R. *Superman and Common Men: Freedom, Anarchy and the Revolution* (Harmondsworth 1971)
'Solipsistic Politics: Russell's Empiricist Liberalism', *Political Studies* 23 no. 1 (1975) 12–28
Barker, Ernest. *Political Thought from Spencer to Today* (1915)
'The Discredited State', *Political Science Quarterly* 2 (1915)
Barker, Michael. *Gladstone and Radicalism: The Reconstruction of Liberal Policy in Britain 1885–1894* (Brighton 1975)
Barker, Rodney. *Political Ideas in Modern Britain* (1978)
Batchelor, John. *The Edwardian Novelists* (1982)

Bedford, Sybil. *Aldous Huxley* 2 vols. (1973–4)
Beetham, David. *Max Weber and the Theory of Modern Politics* (1974)
Bell, Clive. *Art* (1914)
Civilization: An Essay (1928; repr. Harmondsworth 1938)
Bell, Michael (ed.). *The Context of English Literature 1900–1930* (1980)
Bell, Quentin. *Bloomsbury* (1968; repr. 1974)
Virginia Woolf 1882–1912 (1972)
Virginia Woolf 1912–1941 (1972)
Bellamy, Richard. *Liberalism and Modern Society* (Oxford 1992)
Bellamy, Richard (ed.). *Victorian Liberalism* (1990)
Belloc, Hilaire. *The Servile State* (1914)
Benda, Julien. *The Treason of the Intellectuals* (1928; repr. New York 1969)
Benewick, Robert, R.N. Berki and Bhikhu Parekh (eds.). *Knowledge and Belief in Politics: The Problems of Ideology* (1973)
Bennett, Arnold. *The Journals* 2 vols. (1932)
Bentley, Michael. *Politics Without Democracy 1815–1914* (1984)
The Climax of Liberal Politics: British Liberalism in Theory and Practice 1868–1918 (1987)
Bergonzi, Bernard. *The Turn of the Century: Essays on Victorian and Modern English Literature* (1973)
Reading the Thirties (1978)
Exploding English: Criticism, Theory, Culture (Oxford 1990)
Bergson, Henri. *Creative Evolution* (English trans. 1911)
Berlin, Isaiah. *Four Essays on Liberty* (Oxford 1969)
Berman, Marshall. *All That Is Solid Melts Into Air: The Experience of Modernity* (1982)
Bernstein, Edouard. *Evolutionary Socialism* (1889; repr. New York 1961)
Biddiss, Michael D. *The Age of the Masses* (Harmondsworth 1977)
Bock, Kenneth. *Human Nature and History: A Response to Sociobiology* (Columbia 1980)
Bosanquet, Bernard. *The Philosophical Theory of the State* (1899; repr. 1965)
Bottomore, T.B. *Elites and Society* (Harmondsworth 1976)
Bowler, Peter J. *The Invention of Progress: The Victorians and the Past* (Oxford 1989)
Bracher, Karl Dietrich. *The Age of Ideologies: A History of Political Thought in the Twentieth Century* (1984)
Bradbury, Malcolm. *The Social Context of Modern English Literature* (Oxford 1971)
No, Not Bloomsbury (1987)
Bradley, F.H. *Ethical Studies* (Oxford 1876; 1959 edn)
Appearance and Reality (1893; 1978 edn)
Essays on Truth and Reality (1914; 1968 edn)
Bradley, Ian. *The Call to Seriousness: The Evangelical Impact on the Victorians* (1976)
The Optimists: Themes and Personalities in Victorian Liberalism (1980)
Brailsford, H.N. *The Russian Workers' Republic* (1921)
Branson, Noreen. *Britain in the Nineteen Twenties* (1975)
Branson, Noreen, and Margot Heinemann. *Britain in the Nineteen Thirties* (1971)

Brantlinger, Patrick. *Bread and Circuses: Theories of Mass Culture as Social Decay* (New York 1983)
Crusoe's Footprints: Cultural Studies in Britain and America (1990)
Breuer, Georg. *Sociobiology and the Human Dimension* (Cambridge 1982)
Briggs, Asa, and John Saville (eds.). *Essays in Labour History 1886–1923* (1971)
Brinton, Crane. *English Political Thought in the 19th Century* (New York 1962)
Britain, Ian. *Fabianism and Culture: A Study in British Socialism and the Arts 1884–1918* (Cambridge 1982)
Brockway, Fenner. *Inside the Left: Thirty Years of Platform, Press, Prison and Parliament* (1942)
Brown, Kenneth D. (ed.). *Essays in Anti-Labour History: Responses to the Rise of Labour in Britain* (1974)
Bullock, A., and M. Shock (eds.). *The Liberal Tradition* (Oxford 1956)
Burke, John P., et al. *Marxism and the Good Society* (Cambridge 1981)
Burrow, J.W. *Evolution and Society: A Study in Victorian Social Theory* (Cambridge 1966)
A Liberal Descent: Victorian Historians and the English Past (Cambridge 1981)
Whigs and Liberals: Continuity and Change in English Political Thought (Oxford 1988)
Butt, J., and I.F. Clarke (eds.). *The Victorians and Social Protest: A Symposium* (1973)
Cacoullos, Ann R. *Thomas Hill Green: Philosopher of Rights* (New York 1974)
Campbell, Tom. *Seven Theories of Human Society* (Oxford 1981)
Carey, John. *The Intellectuals and the Masses: Pride and Prejudice among the Literary Intelligentsia 1880–1939* (1992)
Carpenter, Humphrey. *The Brideshead Generation: Evelyn Waugh and his Generation* (1989)
Carpenter, L.P. *G.D.H. Cole: An Intellectual Biography* (Cambridge 1973)
Carr, E.H. *The Russian Revolution from Lenin to Stalin 1917–1929* (1979)
Caudwell, Christopher. *Studies in a Dying Culture* (1938)
Caute, David. *The Fellow-Travellers* (1973)
Chadwick, Owen. *The Secularization of the European Mind in the Nineteenth Century* (Cambridge 1975)
Chapman, Raymond. *The Victorian Debate: English Literature 1832–1901* (1968)
Chatterton-Hill, George. *Heredity and Selection in Sociology* (1907)
Ch'en, Jerome. *China and the West: Society and Culture 1815–1937* (1979)
Chesterton, G.K. *Autobiography* (1936)
Clark, Jon, et al. (eds.). *Culture and Crisis in the 30s* (1979)
Clark, Ronald W. *The Life of Bertrand Russell* (1975)
Clarke, I.F. *Voices Prophesying War* (Oxford 1976)
Clarke, Peter. 'The Progressive Movement in England', *Transactions of the Royal Historical Society* 5th series, 24 (1974) 151–81
Liberals and Social Democrats (Cambridge 1978)
'Bertrand Russell and the Dimensions of Victorian Liberalism', *Russell* ns 4 (Summer 1984) 207–21

A Question of Leadership: Gladstone to Thatcher (1991)
Clayre, Alasdair. *Work and Play: Ideas and Experience of Work and Leisure* (1974)
Cockshut, A.O.J. *The Art of Autobiography* (New Haven, Conn. 1984)
Cohen, David. *J.B. Watson: The Founder of Behaviourism* (1979)
Cohen, G.A. *Karl Marx's Theory of History: A Defence* (Oxford 1978)
Cole, G.D.H. *The World of Labour* (1913; repr. 1915)
'Freedom in the Guild', *New Age* (5 November – 31 December 1914)
Labour in War Time (1915)
'Democracy and the Guilds' *New Age* (4 February 1915)
'Conflicting Social Obligations', *Proceedings of the Aristotelian Society* 15 (1915–16)
'The Nature of the State in View of its External Relations', *Proceedings of the Aristotelian Society* 16 (1915–16)
Self-Government in Industry (1917; repr. with an introduction by J.G. Corina, 1972)
'The Guilds, the State, the Consumer: Mr S.G. Hobson and Others', *New Age* (6 December 1917)
Guild Socialism Re-stated (1920; repr. with an introduction by Richard Vernon, NJ 1980)
Social Theory (1920)
Cole, Margaret. *The Story of Fabian Socialism* (1961)
The Life of G.D.H. Cole (1971)
The Webbs and Their Work (1949; 1974 edn)
Collini, Stefan. 'Idealism and Cambridge Idealism', *Historical Journal* 18 no. 1 (1975) 171–7
'Hobhouse, Bosanquet and the State: Philosophical Idealism and Political Argument in England 1880–1980', *Past and Present* 72 (1976) 86–111
'Liberalism and the Legacy of Mill', *Historical Journal*, 20 (1977) 237–54
Liberalism and Sociology: L.T. Hobhouse and Political Argument in England 1880–1914 (Cambridge 1979)
'Political Theory and the "Science of Society" in Victorian Britain', *Historical Journal* 23 no. 1 (1980) 203–31
'The Idea of "Character" in Victorian Political Thought', *Transactions of the Royal Historical Society* 5th series, 35 (1985) 38
Public Moralists: Political Thought and Intellectual Life in Britain 1850–1930 (Oxford 1991)
Matthew Arnold: A Critical Portrait (Oxford 1994)
Collini, Stefan, Donald Winch, and John Burrow. *That Noble Science of Politics: A Study of Nineteenth-Century Intellectual History* (Cambridge 1983)
Colls, Robert, and Philip Dodd (eds.). *Englishness: Politics and Culture 1880–1920* (1986)
Cooke, Alistair. *Six Men* (1977)
Cowling, Maurice. *Mill and Liberalism* (Cambridge 1963)
Religion and Public Doctrine in Modern England (Cambridge 1980)

Cox, C.B., and A.E. Dyson (eds.). *The Twentieth Century Mind: History, Ideas and Literature in Britain* vol. I: *1900–1918*; vol. II: *1918–1945* (Oxford 1972)
Cranston, Maurice. 'Bertrand Russell: Towards a Complete Portrait', *Encounter* (April 1976) 65–70
Crawshaw-Williams, Rupert. *Russell Remembered* (Oxford 1970)
Crick, Bernard. *George Orwell: A Life* (1980)
Crook, Paul. *Darwinism, War and History* (Cambridge 1994)
Crowder, George. *Classical Anarchism: Political Thought of Godwin, Proudhon, Bakunin, and Kropotkin* (Oxford 1991)
Cunningham, Valentine. *British Writers of the Thirties* (Oxford 1988)
Currie, Robert. *Genius: An Ideology in Literature* (1974)
Dale, Peter. *The Victorian Critic and the Idea of History: Carlyle, Arnold, and Pater* (1977)
Dangerfield, George. *The Strange Death of Liberal England* (1936)
Dauenhauer, Bernard P. (ed.). *At the Nexus of Philosophy and History* (Georgia 1987)
Day, Gary. *The British Critical Tradition: A Re-evaluation* (1993)
Deane, Herbert A. *The Political Ideas of H.J. Laski* (New York 1955)
Delany, Paul. *D.H. Lawrence's Nightmare: The Writer and his Circle in the Years of the Great War* (Brighton 1979)
Delavenay, Emile. *D.H. Lawrence and Edward Carpenter: A Study in Edwardian Transition* (1971)
Dennis, Norman, and A.H. Halsey. *English Ethical Socialism: Thomas More to R.H. Tawney* (Oxford 1988)
Dickinson, G. Lowes. *The Autobiography and Other Unpublished Writings* (ed. Dennis Proctor, 1973)
Dickson, Lovat. *H.G. Wells: His Turbulent Life and Times* (New York 1969)
Dilman, Ilham. *Freud and Human Nature* (Oxford 1983)
Dowling, David. *Bloomsbury Aesthetics and the Novels of Forster and Woolf* (1985)
Dowse, R.E. *Left in the Centre: The ILP 1893–1940* (1966)
Doyle, Brian. *English and Englishness* (1989)
Duncan, Graeme. *Marx and Mill: Two Views of Social Conflict and Social Harmony* (Cambridge 1973)
Duncan, Graeme (ed.). *Democratic Theory and Practice* (Cambridge 1983)
Dunn, John. *Western Political Theory in the Face of the Future* (Cambridge 1979)
Dutt, R. Palme. 'Bertrand Russell 1872–1970', *Labour Monthly* 52 (March 1970) 97–110
Eames, Elizabeth Ramsden. *Bertrand Russell's Theory of Knowledge* (1969)
Edel, Leon. *Bloomsbury: A House of Lions* (1979)
Ehrlich, Stanislaw. *Pluralism On and Off Course* (Oxford 1982)
Eliot, T.S. *The Sacred Wood* (1920)
Collected Poems 1909–19362 (1963)
Notes Towards the Definition of Culture (1948)
Eliot, Valerie (ed.) *The Letters of T.S. Eliot* vol. I: *1898–1922* (1988)
Elliott, W.Y. *The Pragmatic Revolt in Politics* (New York 1928)

Emy, H.V. *Liberals, Radicals and Social Politics 1892–1914* (Cambridge 1973)
Ensor, R.C.K. *England 1870–1914* (Oxford 1936)
Evans, Eric J. (ed.). *Social Policy 1830–1914: Individualism, Collectivism and the Origins of the Welfare State* (1978)
Feinberg, Barry, and Ronald Kasrils. *Bertrand Russell's America: His Transatlantic Travels and Writings* vol I: *1896–1945* (1973)
Feinberg, Joel. *Social Philosophy* (Englewood Cliffs, NJ 1973)
Figgis, J.N. *Churches in the Modern State* (1914)
Fitzgibbons, Athol. *Keynes' Vision: A New Political Economy* (Oxford 1988)
Flanagan, Owen J. *The Science of the Mind* (Cambridge, Mass., 1984)
Flew, A.G.N. *Evolutionary Ethics* (1967)
Flugel, J.C. *A Hundred Years of Psychology* (1964)
Forbes, Ian, and Steve Smith. *Politics and Human Nature* (1983)
Forster, E.M. *Aspects of the Novel* (1927; Harmondsworth 1962)
Freeden, Michael. 'J.A. Hobson as a New Liberal Theorist: Some Aspects of his Social Thought until 1914', *Journal of the History of Ideas* 34 (1973) 421–43
'Biological and Evolutionary Roots of the New Liberalism in England', *Political Theory* 4 (1976) 471–90
The New Liberalism: An Ideology of Social Reform (Oxford 1978)
Liberalism Divided: A Study of British Political Thought 1914–1939 (Oxford 1986)
Freeman, John. *Face to Face with John Freeman* (1989)
Fremantle, Anne. *This Little Band of Prophets* (1960)
Three-Cornered Heart (1971)
Freud, Sigmund. *The Interpretation of Dreams* (1900; English trans. 1954)
Introductory Lectures on Psychoanalysis (English trans. 1922; 1961 edn)
The Complete Psychological Works (ed. James Strachey, vols. XIV (1914–1916) and XXI (1927–1931) incl. 'The Future of an Illusion' and 'Civilization and its Discontents')
Froebel, Friedrich. *The Education of Man* (New York 1894)
Fulford, Roger. *Votes for Women* (1957)
Fussell, Paul. *The Great War and Modern Memory* (Oxford 1975)
Gadd, David. *The Loving Friends: A Portrait of Bloomsbury* (1974)
Galton, Francis. *Hereditary Genius: An Inquiry into its Laws and Consequences* (1869; 1965 edn)
Essays in Eugenics (1909)
Galton, Ray, and Alan Simpson. *Hancock's Half Hour* (1974)
Garland, Martha McMackin. *Cambridge Before Darwin: The Ideal of a Liberal Education 1800–1860* (Cambridge 1980)
Garnett, David. *The Golden Echo* (1954)
The Flowers of the Forest (1955)
Gasset, Ortega y. *The Revolt of the Masses* (1930)
Gaus, Gerald F. *The Modern Liberal Theory of Man* (1983)
Gay, Peter. *The Dilemma of Democratic Socialism: Edouard Bernstein's Challenge to Marx* (New York 1952)

Freud, Jews and Other Germans: Masters and Victims in Modernist Culture (1978)
Freud for Historians (Oxford 1984)
Gellner, Ernest. *Reason and Culture: The Historic Role of Rationality and Rationalism* (Oxford 1992)
Gerhardi, William. *Memoirs of a Polyglot* (1931)
Gervais, David. *Literary Englands: Versions of 'Englishness' in Modern Writing* (Cambridge 1993)
Giddens, Anthony. *Politics and Sociology in the Thought of Max Weber* (1972)
Gide, André. *Back from the USSR* (1936)
Gloversmith, Frank (ed.). *Class Culture and Social Change: A New View of the 1930s* (Brighton 1980)
Goldman, Lawrence (ed.). *The Blind Victorian: Henry Fawcett and British Liberalism* (Cambridge 1989)
Goodheart, Eugene. *Culture and the Radical Conscience* (Cambridge, Mass. 1973)
Gordon, Lyndall. *Eliot's Early Years* (Oxford 1977)
Gordon, Peter, and John White. *Philosophers as Educational Reformers: The Influence of Idealism on British Educational Thought and Practice* (1979)
Gouldner, Alvin W. *The Future of the Intellectuals and the Rise of the New Class* (1979)
Graves, Robert. *Goodbye to All That* (1929)
Gray, Alexander. *The Socialist Tradition* (1946)
Gray, John, and G.W. Smith (eds.). *J.S. Mill 'On Liberty' in Focus* (1991)
Green, Martin. *The Von Richthofen Sisters: The Triumphant and the Tragic Modes of Love* (1974)
Children of the Sun (1977)
Green, Thomas Hill. *Prolegomena to Ethics* (1883; 1906 edn)
Lectures on the Principles of Political Obligation (1895; 1927 edn)
Greenleaf, W.H. *The British Political Tradition: The Rise of Collectivism* (1983)
Greenspan, Louis. *The Incompatible Prophecies: Bertrand Russell on Science and Liberty* (Oakville, Ont. 1978)
Griffin, Nicholas. *Russell's Idealist Apprenticeship* (Oxford 1991)
Grisewood, H. (ed.). *The Ideas and Beliefs of Victorians* (1949)
Gross, John. *The Rise and Fall of the Man of Letters: Aspects of English Literary Life since 1800* (1969)
Guerin, Daniel. *Anarchism* (1970)
Gunn, Giles. *The Culture of Criticism and the Criticism of Culture* (Oxford 1987)
Guttmann, Amy. *Liberal Equality* (Cambridge 1980)
Guttsman, W.L. *The British Political Elite* (1963)
Guy, Josephine. *The British Avant-Garde: The Theory and Politics of Tradition* (1991)
Haldane, J.B.S. *The Inequality of Man* (1932; pbk edn Harmondsworth 1937)
Halevy, Elie. *The Growth of Philosophic Radicalism* (1st English edn 1928)
The Era of Tyrannies: Essays on Socialism and War (1938; 1st English edn 1967)
Hall, Ruth. *Marie Stopes: A Biography* (1977)
Halliday, R.J. *John Stuart Mill* (1976)

Hamburger, Joseph. *Intellectuals in Politics: John Stuart Mill and the Philosophic Radicals* (New Haven, Conn. 1965)
Hamer, D.A. *Liberal Politics in the Age of Gladstone and Rosebery* (Oxford 1972)
Hamilton, Alistair. *The Appeal of Fascism* (1971)
Hamilton, Mary Agnes. *Remembering My Good Friends* (1944)
Hampshire, Stuart. *Modern Writers and Other Essays* (1969)
Hannah, Barbara. *Jung: His Life and Work* (1976)
Hansot, Elizabeth. *Perfection and Progress: Two Modes of Utopian Thought* (Mass. 1974)
Hardman, Malcolm. *Six Victorian Thinkers* (Manchester 1991)
Hardy, G.H. *Bertrand Russell and Trinity: A Facsimile Reproduction with Introduction by C.D. Broad* (Cambridge 1970)
Harris, Jose. *Unemployment and Politics: A Study in English Social Policy 1886–1914* (Oxford 1972)
Private Lives, Public Spirit: Britain 1870–1914 (Oxford 1993)
Harris, Kenneth. *Talking To ...* (1971)
Harrison, Brian. *Separate Spheres: The Opposition to Women's Suffrage in Britain* (1978)
Harrison, John. *The Reactionaries: W.B. Yeats, Wyndham Lewis, Ezra Pound, T.S. Eliot, D.H. Lawrence* (1966)
Harrison, Ross. *Bentham* (1983)
Harrod, R.F. *The Life of John Maynard Keynes* (1951)
Hart, Bernard. *The Psychology of Insanity* (Cambridge 1912)
Harvie, Christopher. *The Lights of Liberalism: University Liberals and the Challenge of Democracy 1860–1886* (1976)
Havighurst, Alfred F. *Radical Journalist: H.W. Massingham (1860–1924)* (Cambridge 1974)
Hawthorn, Geoffrey. *Enlightenment and Despair: A History of Sociology* (Cambridge 1976)
Hayek, F.A. *The Road to Serfdom* (1944)
John Stuart Mill and Harriet Taylor: Their Friendship and Subsequent Marriage (1951)
Hazlehurst, Cameron. *Politicians at War: July 1914 to May 1915* (1971)
Hearnshaw, L.S. *A Short History of British Psychology 1840–1940* (1964)
Hewins, W.A.S. *The Apologia of an Imperialist* 2 vols. (1929)
Hewison, Robert. *In Anger: Culture in the Cold War 1945–60* (1981)
Too Much: Art and Society in the Sixties 1960–75 (1986)
Heyck, T.W. *The Transformation of Intellectual Life in Victorian England* (1982)
Himmelfarb, Gertrude. *Victorian Minds* (1968)
On Liberty and Liberalism: The Case of John Stuart Mill (New York 1974)
Hirst, Paul, and Woolley, Penny. *Social Relations and Human Attributes* (1982)
Hobhouse, L.T. *The Labour Movement* (1896)
Democracy and Reaction (1904)
Morals in Evolution: A Study of Comparative Ethics 2 vols. (1907)
Liberalism (1911)

The Metaphysical Theory of the State: A Criticism (1918)
Hobsbawm, E.J. *Labouring Men: Studies in the History of Labour* (1964)
Hobsbawm, E.J., and Terence Ranger (eds.) *The Invention of Tradition* (Cambridge 1983)
Hobson, J.A. *The Psychology of Jingoism* (1901)
Imperialism (1902)
The Social Problem: Life and Work (1902)
The Crisis of Liberalism (1909)
Free Thought in the Social Sciences (1926)
The Confessions of an Economic Heretic (1938; repr. with an introduction by Michael Freeden, Brighton 1976)
Hobson, S.G. *National Guilds and the State* (1920)
Hollis, Martin, and Steven Lukes (eds.). *Rationality and Relativism* (Oxford 1982)
Holroyd, Michael. *Lytton Strachey: The Unknown Years 1880–1910* (1967)
Lytton Strachey: The Years of Achievement 1910–1932 (1968)
Unreceived Opinions (1973)
Holton, Bob. *British Syndicalism 1900–1914: Myths and Realities* (1976)
Horden, Peregrine. *Freud and the Humanities* (1985)
Horsley, Lee. *Political Fiction and the Historical Imagination* (1990)
Howard, Michael. *War and the Liberal Conscience* (Oxford 1981)
Hsiao, K.C. *Political Pluralism* (1927)
Hughes, H. Stuart. *Consciousness and Society: The Reorientation of European Social Thought 1890–1930* (1959)
Hunt, Lynn (ed.). *The New Cultural History* (Calif. 1989)
Huxley, Aldous. *Crome Yellow* (1921)
Brave New World (1932)
Letters (ed. Grover Smith, 1969)
Huxley, Julian. *Essays in Popular Science* (1926; pbk edn Harmondsworth 1937)
Hyams, Edward. *The New Statesman: The History of the First Fifty Years 1913–1963* (1963)
Hylton, Peter. *Russell, Idealism and the Emergence of Analytic Philosophy* (Oxford 1990)
Hynes, Samuel. *The Edwardian Turn of Mind* (Princeton 1968)
Edwardian Occasions (1972)
The Auden Generation: Literature and Politics in England in the 1930s (1976)
Inglis, Fred. *Radical Earnestness: English Social Theory 1880–1980* (Oxford 1982)
Popular Culture and Political Power (1988)
Cultural Studies (Oxford 1993)
Jager, Ronald. *The Development of Bertrand Russell's Philosophy* (1972)
James, William. *The Will to Believe and other Essays in Popular Philosophy* (1897)
Pragmatism: A new name for some old ways of thinking (1907)
A Pluralistic Universe (1909)
Memories and Studies (1911)
Jardin, André. *Tocqueville: A Biography* (1988)
Jenkins, Roy. *Asquith* (1967)

Jennings, Jeremy (ed.). *Intellectuals in Twentieth-Century France: Mandarins and Samurais* (1993)
Joad, C.E.M. *Introduction to Modern Political Theory* (Oxford 1924)
Johnson, Lesley. *The Cultural Critics: From Matthew Arnold to Raymond Williams* (1979)
Johnstone, J.K. *The Bloomsbury Group* (1954)
Joll, James. *The Second International 1889–1914* (1955)
The Anarchists (1964)
Jones, Ernest. *Essays in Applied Psycho-Analysis* (1923)
Jones, Gareth Stedman. *Outcast London: A Study in the Relationship between Classes in Victorian Society* (Oxford 1971)
Jones, Greta. *Social Darwinism and English Thought: The Interaction Between Biological and Social Theory* (Brighton 1980)
Jung, C.G. *Modern Man in Search of his Soul* (1933; repr. 1976)
'The Development of Personality' in *Collected Works* vol. XVII (1934)
'The Archetypes and the Collective Unconscious' in *Collected Works* vol. IX Pt I (1959)
Memories, Dreams, Reflections (1963)
Kahan, Alan S. *Aristocratic Liberalism: The Social and Political Thought of Jacob Burckhardt, John Stuart Mill, and Alexis de Tocqueville* (Oxford 1992)
Kalin, Martin G. *The Utopian Flight from Unhappiness: Freud against Marx on Social Progress* (1975)
Kaufmann, Walter. *The Portable Nietzsche* (New York 1954)
Nietzsche: Philosopher, Psychologist, Antichrist (Princeton 1968)
Kennedy, Thomas C. *The Hound of Conscience: A History of the No-Conscription Fellowship 1914–1949* (Fayetteville 1981)
Kenner, Hugh. *The Invisible Poet: T.S. Eliot* (1959)
Kermode, Frank. *History and Value* (Oxford 1988)
Keynes, J.M. *The Economic Consequences of the Peace* (New York 1920)
Two Memoirs: Dr Melchior – A Defeated Enemy and My Early Beliefs (1949)
Kidd, Benjamin. *The Principles of Western Civilisation* (1902)
Kirkup, Thomas. *History of Socialism* (1892)
Knights, Ben. *The Idea of the Clerisy in the Nineteenth Century* (Cambridge 1978)
Kojecky, Roger. *T.S. Eliot's Social Criticism* (1971)
Kolakowski, Leszek. *Bergson* (1985)
Koss, Stephen. *Asquith* (1976)
Kropotkin, Peter. *Mutual Aid: A Factor of Evolution* (1902; 1914 edn)
The Conquest of Bread (1906; repr. with an introduction by Paul Avrich, 1972)
The Essential Kropotkin (eds. Emile Capouya and Keitha Tompkins, 1975)
Kumar, Krishan, *Utopia and Anti-Utopia in Modern Times* (Oxford 1987)
Kumar, Krishan, and Stephen Bann (eds.). *Utopias and the Millennium* (1993)
Lachs, John. *George Santayana* (Boston 1988)
Laski, Harold J. *Studies in the Problems of Sovereignty* (New Haven, Conn. 1917)
Authority in the Modern State (New Haven, Conn. 1919)
A Grammar of Politics (1925)

Holmes–Laski Letters 1919–1935 2 vols. (Oxford 1953)
Lawrence, D.H. *Women in Love* (1920)
England my England (1922)
Letters of D.H. Lawrence (ed. Aldous Huxley, 1932)
Phoenix vol. I (ed. E.D. McDonald, 1936); vol. II (eds. W. Roberts and H.T. Moore, 1968)
Letters to Bertrand Russell (ed. Harry T. Moore, New York 1948)
Leavis, F.R. *Mass Civilization and Minority Culture* (Cambridge 1930)
The Great Tradition (1948; repr. Harmondsworth 1967)
The Common Pursuit (1952)
Introduction to Mill on Bentham and Coleridge (Cambridge 1980)
Leavis, F.R., and Denys Thompson. *Culture and Environment* (1933)
Leavis, Q.D. *Fiction and the Reading Public* (1932; repr. Harmondsworth 1979)
'Henry Sidgwick's Cambridge', *Scrutiny* (September 1949) 3–11
Le Bon, Gustave. *The Crowd: A Study of the Popular Mind* (1893)
Lee, Alan J. *The Origins of the Popular Press 1855–1914* (1976)
LeMahieu, D.L. *A Culture for Democracy: Mass Communication and the Cultivated Mind in Britain Between the Wars* (Oxford 1988)
Lepenies, Wolf. *Between Literature and Science: The Rise of Sociology* (Cambridge 1988)
Letwin, Shirley Robin. *The Pursuit of Certainty: David Hume, Jeremy Bentham, J.S. Mill, Beatrice Webb* (Cambridge 1965)
Levenson, Michael H. *A Genealogy of Modernism: A Study of English Literary Doctrine 1908–1922* (1984)
Leventhal, F.M. *The Last Dissenter: H.N. Brailsford and His World* (Oxford 1985)
Levine, George, and William Madden. *The Art of Victorian Prose* (Oxford 1968)
Levitas, Ruth. *The Concept of Utopia* (1990)
Levy, Paul. *Moore: G.E. Moore and the Cambridge Apostles* (New York 1979)
Lewis, John. *Bertrand Russell: Philosopher and Humanist* (1968)
Lichtheim, George. *Marxism: An Historical and Critical Study* (1961)
The Origins of Socialism (1969)
A Short History of Socialism (1970)
Collected Essays (New York 1974)
Lindsay, A.D. 'The State in Recent Political Theory', *Political Quarterly* I (February 1914)
Lively, Jack. *The Social and Political Thought of Alexis de Tocqueville* (Oxford 1962)
Lorrain, Jorge. *The Concept of Ideology* (1979)
Marxism and Ideology (1983)
Lucas, John. *The 1930s: A Challenge to Orthodoxy* (Brighton 1978)
Lukes, Steven. *Individualism* (Oxford 1973)
Power: A Radical View (1974)
McBriar, A.M. *Fabian Socialism and English Politics 1884–1918* (Cambridge 1966)
An Edwardian Mixed Doubles: The Bosanquets versus the Webbs (Oxford 1987)
MacCallum, G.C. 'Negative and Positive Freedom', *Philosophical Review* 76 (1967) 312–34

McCloskey, H.J. 'Liberalism', *Philosophy* 49 (1974) 13–32
McDougall, William. *An Introduction to Social Psychology* (1908)
Psychology: The Study of Behaviour (1912)
McGuinness, Brian. *Wittgenstein A Life: Young Ludwig (1889–1921)* (1988)
Macintyre, Alasdair. *Secularisation and Moral Change* (1967)
A Short History of Ethics (1967)
After Virtue: A Study in Moral Theory (1981)
Macintyre, Stuart. *A Proletarian Science: Marxism in Britain 1917–1933* (Cambridge 1980)
Mack, Mary P. *Jeremy Bentham: An Odyssey of Ideas 1748–1792* (1962)
MacKenzie, Norman and Jeanne. *The Time Traveller: The Life of H.G. Wells* (1973)
The First Fabians (1977)
McLellan, David. *Karl Marx: His Life and Thought* (1973)
Macpherson, C.B. *The Life and Times of Liberal Democracy* (Oxford 1977)
MacRae, Donald G. *Weber* (Glasgow 1974)
Magid, H.M. *English Political Pluralism* (New York 1941)
Magnus, Philip. *Gladstone* (1954)
Mairet, Philip. *A.R. Orage: A Memoir* (1936)
Maitland, Frederick William. Introduction to Otto Gierke, *Political Theories of the Middle Age* (Cambridge 1900)
Malcolm, Norman. *Ludwig Wittgenstein: A Memoir* (1967)
Malleson, Constance. *After Ten Years: A Personal Record* (1936)
Mandelbaum, Maurice. *History, Man and Reason* (Baltimore 1971)
Mangan., J.A., and James Walvin (eds.). *Manliness and Morality: Middle Class Masculinity in Britain and America, 1800–1940* (Manchester 1987)
Mannheim, Karl. *Ideology and Utopia: An Introduction to the Sociology of Knowledge* (1936)
Manning, D.J. *Liberalism* (1976)
Martin, David A. *Pacifism: An Historical and Sociological Study* (1965)
Martin, David E., and David Rubinstein (eds.). *Ideology and the Labour Movement* (1979)
Martin, Kingsley. *Harold Laski: A Biography* (1953)
New Statesman Profiles (1957)
Father Figures: A First Volume of Autobiography 1897–1931 (1966)
Editor: A Volume of Autobiography 1931–1945 (1968)
Martin, Wallace. *The New Age under Orage: Chapters in English Cultural History* (Manchester 1967)
Martin, Werner. *Bertrand Russell: A Bibliography of His Writings 1895–1976* (1981)
Marwick, Arthur. *Clifford Allen: The Open Conspirator* (1964)
The Deluge: British Society and The First World War (Harmondsworth 1967)
Britain in Century of Total War (1978)
Class, Image and Reality in Britain, France and the USA Since 1930 (1980)
Marx, Karl. *Economic and Philosophic Manuscripts of 1844* (1973 edn)
Marx, Karl, and Friedrich Engels. *Selected Works* 2 vols. (Moscow 1958)

The German Ideology (Moscow 1964)
Masterman, C.F.G. *The Condition of England* (1909; edited with an introduction and notes by J.T. Boulton, 1960)
Matthew, H.C.G. *The Liberal Imperialists: The Ideas and Politics of a Post-Gladstonian Elite* (Oxford 1973)
May, Keith M. *Nietzsche and Modern Literature* (1988)
Meacham, Standish. *A Life Apart: The English Working Class 1890–1914* (1977)
Meisel, Perry, and Walter Kendrick (eds.). *Bloomsbury / Freud: The Letters of James and Alix Strachey 1924–1925* (1986)
Meyers, Jeffrey. *Homosexuality and Literature 1890–1930* (1977)
Mill, John Stuart. 'Bentham' (1838) in *Collected Works* vol. x (ed. John M. Robson, intro. F.E.L. Priestley, Toronto 1969)
'Coleridge' (1840) in *Collected Works* vol. x
On Liberty (1859) in *Collected Works* vol. xviii (ed. John M. Robson, intro. Alexander Brady, Toronto 1977)
Utilitarianism (1861) in *Collected Works* vol. x
Considerations on Representative Government (1861) in *Collected Works* vol. xix (ed. John M. Robson, intro. Alexander Brady, Toronto 1977)
'The Subjection of Women' (1869) in *Collected Works* vol. xxi (ed. John M. Robson, intro. Stefan Collini, Toronto 1984)
Autobiography (1873) in *Collected Works* vol. i (ed. John M. Robson and Jack Stillinger, Toronto 1981)
Miller, David. *Anarchism* (1984)
Miller, Karl. *Doubles: Studies in Literary History* (Oxford 1985)
Miller, Martin A. *Kropotkin* (Chicago 1976)
Milliband, Ralph. *Parliamentary Socialism: A Study in the Politics of Labour* (1961; 2nd edn 1973)
Milne, A.J.M. *The Social Philosophy of English Idealism* (1962)
Milton, Colin. *Lawrence and Nietzsche: A Study in Influence* (Aberdeen 1987)
Mirsky, Dmitri. *The Intelligentsia of Great Britain* (1935)
Mitzman, Arthur. *The Iron Cage: An Historical Interpretation of Max Weber* (New York 1970)
Monk, Ray. *Ludwig Wittgenstein: The Duty of Genius* (1990)
Moore, G.E. *Principia Ethica* (1903; Cambridge 1959 edn)
Moore, Harry T. *The Priest of Love* (1976)
Moran, Margaret, and Karl Spadoni (eds.). *Intellect and Social Conscience: Essays on Bertrand Russell's Early Work* (Hamilton, Ont. 1984)
Morgan, David. *Suffragists and Liberals: The Politics of Woman Suffrage in Britain* (Oxford 1975)
Morrell, Ottoline. *Ottoline: The Early Memoirs* (ed. Robert Gathorne-Hardy, 1963)
Ottoline at Garsington: Memoirs 1915–1918 (ed. Robert Gathorne-Hardy, 1974)
Morris, A.J.A. *Radicalism Against War 1906–1914: The Advocacy of Peace and Retrenchment* (1972)
Morris, A.J.A. (ed.). *Edwardian Radicalism 1900–1914* (1974)

Morris, William. *Selected Writings* (ed. G.D.H. Cole, 1944)

Moscovici, Serge. *The Age of the Crowd: A Historical Treatise on Mass Psychology* (Cambridge 1985)

Mowat, C.L. *Britain Between the Wars 1918–1940* (1955)

The Charity Organisation Society 1869–1913: Its Ideas and Work (1961)

Muggeridge, Kitty, and Ruth Adam. *Beatrice Webb: A Life 1858–1943* (1967)

Mulhern, Francis. *The Moment of 'Scrutiny'* (1979)

Murray, Gilbert. *An Unfinished Autobiography* (1960)

Murray, Penelope (ed). *Genius: The History of an Idea* (Oxford 1989)

Nairn, Tom. 'The English Literary Intelligentsia' in Emma Tennant (ed.) *Bananas* (1977)

Nakhnikian, George (ed.). *Bertrand Russell's Philosophy* (1974)

Newberry, Jo. 'Russell as Ghost-Writer', *Russell* 15 (Autumn 1974)

Nicholls, David. 'Positive Liberty 1880–1914', *American Political Science Review* 56 (1962) 114–28

The Pluralist State (1975)

Nisbet, Robert A. *The Sociological Tradition* (1966)

Social Change and History (Oxford 1969)

The Social Philosophers (1976)

Nowell-Smith, Simon (ed.). *Edwardian England 1901–1914* (Oxford 1964)

Ochse, R. *Before the Gates of Excellence: The Determinants of Creative Genius* (Cambridge 1990)

Orwell, George. *Collected Essays, Journalism, and Letters*, 4 vols. (eds. Sonia Orwell and Ian Angus, 1968; pbk edn Harmondsworth 1970)

Packe, M. St. J. *The Life of John Stuart Mill* (1954)

Park, Joe. *Bertrand Russell on Education* (1964)

Parris, Henry. 'The Political Thought of Bertrand Russell', *Durham University Journal* 58 (1965–6) 86–94

Passmore, John. *A Hundred Years of Philosophy* (Harmondsworth 1966)

The Perfectibility of Man (1970)

Pateman, Carole. *The Problem of Political Obligation: A Critique of Liberal Theory* (1979)

Paterson, R.W.K. *The Nihilistic Hedonist: Max Stirner* (Oxford 1971)

Pearson, Karl. *The Groundwork of Eugenics* (1909)

Pearson, Robert, and Geraint Williams. *Political Thought and Public Policy in the Nineteenth Century* (1984)

Pedersen, Susan, and Peter Mandler (eds.). *After the Victorians: Private Conscience and Public Duty in Modern Britain* (1994)

Peel, J.D.Y. *Herbert Spencer: The Evolution of a Sociologist* (1971)

Pelczynski, Zbigniew, and John Gray (eds.). *Conceptions of Liberty in Political Philosophy* (1984)

Pelling, Henry. *Modern Britain 1885–1955* (1960)

A Short History of the Labour Party (1965)

Origins of the Labour Party (1965)

Pierson, Stanley. *Marxism and the Origins of British Socialism* (New York 1973)

British Socialists: The Journey from Fantasy to Politics (Cambridge, Mass. 1979)
Pike, E. Royston. *Human Documents of the Lloyd George Era* (1972)
Pimlott, Ben. *Labour and the Left in the 1930s* (Cambridge 1977)
Plamenatz, John. *Karl Marx's Philosophy of Man* (Oxford 1975)
Plumb, J.H. (ed.). *Studies in Social History: A Tribute to G.M. Trevelyan* (1955)
Pocock, J.G.A. *Virtue, Commerce, and History* (Cambridge 1985)
Poirier, Richard. *The Renewal of Literature: Emersonian Reflections* (1987)
Powell, Anthony. *Afternoon Men* (1931; 1979 edn)
Qualter, Terence J. *Graham Wallas and the Great Society* (1980)
Quinton, Anthony. *Political Philosophy* (Oxford 1967)
'Absolute Idealism', *Proceedings of the British Academy* 57 (1971) 303–29
Thoughts and Thinkers (1982)
Radice, Lisanne. *Sidney and Beatrice Webb: Fabian Socialists* (1984)
Rae, John. *Conscience and Politics: The British Government and the Conscientious Objectors to Military Service 1916–1919* (Oxford 1970)
Raison, Timothy. *The Founding Fathers of Social Sciences* (Harmondsworth 1969)
Randall, John Herman, Jr. *Philosophy After Darwin* (New York 1971)
Raymond, John. *The Baldwin Age* (1960)
Read, Herbert. *The Cult of Sincerity* (1968)
Remmling, Gunter W. *The Sociology of Karl Mannheim* (1975)
Rempel, Richard A. *Unionists Divided: Arthur Balfour, Joseph Chamberlain and the Unionist Free Traders* (1972)
'From Imperialism to Free Trade: Couturat, Halevy and Russell's First Crusade', *Journal of the History of Ideas* 40 (1979) 423–44
Richards, I.A. *Principles of Literary Criticism* (1924; 1967 edn)
Richter, Melvin. *The Politics of Conscience: T.H. Green and His Age* (1964)
Ridley, F.F. *Revolutionary Syndicalism in France: The Direct Action of Its Time* (Cambridge 1970)
Rieff, Philip. *The Triumph of the Therapeutic* (Harmondsworth 1966)
Ritter, Alan. *Anarchism: A Theoretical Analysis* (Cambridge 1980)
Roach, John. 'Liberalism and the Victorian Intelligentsia', *Cambridge Historical Journal* 13 (1957) 58–81
Robbins, Keith. *The First World War* (Oxford 1984)
Roberts, George W. (ed.). *Bertrand Russell Memorial Volume* (1979)
Roberts, Robert. *The Classic Slum* (Manchester 1971)
Robson, John M. *The Improvement of Mankind: The Social and Political Thought of John Stuart Mill* (1968)
Robson, John M., and Michael Laine (eds.). *James and John Stuart Mill: Papers of the Centenary Conference* (Toronto 1976)
Rogers, J.A. 'Darwinism and Social Darwinism', *Journal of the History of Ideas* 33 (1972) 265–80
Rorty, Richard. *Philosophy and the Mirror of Nature* (Oxford 1981)
Rorty, Richard, J.B. Schneewind, and Quentin Skinner (eds.). *Philosophy in History: Essays on the Historiography of Philosophy* (Cambridge 1984)
Rose, Jonathan. *The Edwardian Temperament 1895–1919* (Ohio 1986)

Rosenbaum, S.P. *Victorian Bloomsbury* (1987)
'Keynes, Lawrence and Cambridge Revisited', *Cambridge Quarterly* 11 (1982) 252–64
Rosenbaum, S.P. (ed.). *The Bloomsbury Group: A Collection of Memoirs, Commentary and Criticism* (Toronto 1975)
Russell, Dora. *The Tamarisk Tree* vol. 1: *My Quest for Liberty and Love* (1975)
Ryan, Alan. *The Philosophy of John Stuart Mill* (1970)
J.S. Mill (1974)
Property and Political Theory (Oxford 1984)
Bertrand Russell: A Political Life (1988)
Ryan, Alan (ed.). *The Idea of Freedom* (Oxford 1979)
Sabine, George. *A History of Political Theory* (1937)
St John Stevas, Norman. *Walter Bagehot* (1959)
Saleeby, C.W. *Parenthood and Race Culture: An Outline of Eugenics* (1909)
Salvadori, Massimo. *Karl Kautsky and the Socialist Revolution 1880–1938* (1979)
Santayana, George. *Winds of Doctrine* (1913; 1940 edn)
My Host the World (1953)
Sassoon, Siegfried. *Memoirs of an Infantry Officer* (1930)
Schilpp, Paul A. (ed.). *The Philosophy of Bertrand Russell* (Chicago 1944)
Schneewind, J.B. (ed.). *Mill* (1968)
Schoenman, Ralph (ed.). *Bertrand Russell: Philosopher of the Century* (1967)
Schultz, Bart (ed.). *Essays on Henry Sidgwick* (Cambridge 1992)
Searle, G.R. *The Quest for National Efficiency* (Oxford 1971)
Eugenics and Politics in Britain, 1900–1914 (Noordhoff 1976)
Shaw, G.B. (ed.). *Fabian Essays in Socialism* (1889; repr. with introduction by Asa Briggs, 1962)
Essays in Fabian Socialism (1932)
Collected Letters vol. 1 (ed. Dan H. Laurence, 1965)
Showalter, Elaine. *Sexual Anarchy: Gender and Culture at the Fin de Siècle* (1991)
Sinfield, Alan. *Literature, Politics and Culture in Post-War Britain* (Oxford 1989)
Skidelsky, Robert. *John Maynard Keynes: Hopes Betrayed 1883–1920* (1983)
Skinner, B.F. *Walden Two* (New York 1948; repr. 1962)
Beyond Freedom and Dignity (Harmondsworth 1973)
Small, Christopher. *The Road to Miniluv: George Orwell, the State, and God* (1975)
Smart, J.J.C., and Bernard Williams. *Utilitarianism For and Against* (Cambridge 1973)
Soffer, Reba N. 'New Elitism: Social Psychology in Prewar England', *Journal of British Studies* 8 (1969) 111–40
'The Revolution in English Social Thought 1880–1914', *American Historical Review* 75 (1970) 1938–64
Ethics and Society in England: The Revolution in the Social Sciences 1870–1914 (Calif. 1978)
Sorel, Georges. *Reflections on Violence* (1915; repr. New York 1941)
From Georges Sorel: Essays in Socialism and Philosophy (ed. John L. Stanley, Oxford 1976)

Spencer, Herbert. *Principles of Sociology* (1876)
The Man versus the State (1884; repr. with an introduction by G.B. Macrae, Harmondsworth 1969)
Spragens, Thomas A., Jr. *The Irony of Liberal Reason* (Chicago 1981)
Stanley, John L. *The Sociology of Virtue: The Political and Social Theories of Georges Sorel* (Berkeley 1981)
Stansky, Peter. *Gladstone: A Progress in Politics* (1979)
Stansky, Peter, and William Abrahams. *The Unknown Orwell* (1974)
Orwell: The Transformation (1981)
Stark, W. *The Sociology of Knowledge* (1958)
Staude, John-Raphael. *The Adult Development of C.G. Jung* (1981)
Steintrager, James. *Bentham* (Oxford 1977)
Stern, J.P. *Nietzsche: His Life, Work, Writing and Ideas* (Brighton 1978)
A Study of Nietzsche (Cambridge 1979)
Stevenson, John, and Chris Cook. *The Slump: Society and Politics During the Depression* (1977)
Stevenson, Leslie. *Seven Theories of the Human Nature* (Oxford 1974)
Storr, Anthony. *Jung* (1973)
Strachey, John. *The Coming Struggle for Power* (1931)
Swartz, Marvin. *The Union of Democratic Control in British Politics During the First World War* (Oxford 1971)
Swingewood, Alan. *The Myth of Mass Culture* (1977)
A Short History of Sociological Thought (1984)
Symons, Julian. *The Thirties: A Dream Revolved* (1960; pbk 1975)
Tait, Katharine. *My Father Bertrand Russell* (1976)
Tawney, R.H. *The Acquisitive Society* (1921)
Equality (1931)
Taylor, A.J.P. *The Troublemakers: Dissent over Foreign Policy 1792–1939* (1957)
English History 1914–1945 (Oxford 1965)
Taylor, Michael. *Community, Anarchy and Liberty* (Cambridge 1982)
Ten, C.L. *Mill On Liberty* (Oxford 1980)
Terrill, Ross. *R.H. Tawney and His Times: Socialism as Fellowship* (Cambridge, Mass. 1973)
Thatcher, David S. *Nietzsche in England 1890–1914: The Growth of a Reputation* (Toronto 1970)
Therborn, Goran. *Science, Class and Society* (1976)
Thody, Philip. *Aldous Huxley: A Biographical Introduction* (1973)
Thomas, Hugh. *John Strachey* (1973)
Thomas, J.E., and Kenneth Blackwell (eds.). *Russell in Review: The McMaster Centenary Celebrations 1972* (Toronto 1975)
Thomas, William. *The Philosophical Radicals: Nine Studies in Theory and Practice 1817–1841* (Oxford 1979)
Thompson, Dennis F. *John Stuart Mill and Representative Government* (Princeton 1976)
Thompson, E.P. *William Morris: Romantic to Revolutionary* (1955; rev. edn 1977)

The Poverty of Theory and Other Essays (1978)
Thompson, John B. *Ideology and Modern Culture: Critical Social Theory in the Era of Mass Communication* (Oxford 1990)
Thompson, Paul. *The Edwardians: The Remaking of British Society* (1977)
Tonnies, Ferdinand. *Community and Association* (1887; 1955 edn)
Treadgold, Donald W. *The West in Russia and China: Religious and Secular Thought in Modern Times* 2 vols. (Cambridge 1973)
Trigg, Roger. *The Shaping of Man: Philosophical Aspects of Sociobiology* (Oxford 1982)
Trilling, Lionel. *Matthew Arnold* (1939)
Trotter, William. *Instincts of the Herd in Peace and War* (1916)
Tsuzuki, D.F.B. *Marxism and Individualism* (Oxford 1980)
Ulam, A.B. *The Philosophical Foundation of English Socialism* (Cambridge, Mass. 1951)
Vance, Norman. *The Sinews of the Spirit* (Cambridge 1985)
Veblen, Thorstein. *The Theory of the Leisure Class* (1925)
Vellacott, Jo. *Bertrand Russell and the Pacifists in the First World War* (Brighton 1980)
Vincent, Andrew, and Raymond Plant. *Philosophy, Politics and Citizenship: The Life and Thought of the British Idealists* (Oxford 1984)
Vogeler, Martha. *Frederic Harrison: The Vocations of a Positivist* (Oxford 1984)
Wallas, Graham. *Human Nature in Politics* (1908)
The Great Society (1914)
Our Social Heritage (1921)
The Art of Thought (1926)
Social Judgement (1934)
Men and Ideas (1940)
Wallimann, Isidor. *Estrangement: Marx's Conception of Human Nature and the Division of Labour* (Conn. 1981)
Warnock, Geoffrey. *English Philosophy since 1900* (1969)
Warnock, Mary. *Ethics since 1900* (Oxford 1960)
Watling, John. *Bertrand Russell* (1970)
Watson, George. *The English Ideology: Studies in the Language of Victorian Politics* (1973)
Watson, John B. *Behaviourism* (1911)
Webb, Beatrice. *My Apprenticeship* (1926; repr. with an introduction by Norman MacKenzie, Cambridge 1979)
Our Partnership (eds. Barbara Drake and Margaret Cole, 1948)
The Diaries (eds. Norman and Jeanne MacKenzie, 4 vols., 1982–5)
Webb, L.C. (ed.). *Legal Personality and Political Pluralism* (Melbourne 1958)
Webb, Sidney and Beatrice. *A Constitution for the Socialist Commonwealth of Great Britain* (1920; repr. with an introduction by Samuel H. Beer, Cambridge 1975)
The Decay of Capitalist Civilization (1923; repr. New York 1970)
The Letters (ed. Norman MacKenzie, 3 vols., 1978)

Weber, Max. *The Methodology of the Social Sciences* (eds. Edward A. Shils and H.A. Finch, Ill. 1949)

Webster, Charles (ed.). *Biology, Medicine and Society 1840–1940* (Cambridge 1981)

Weiler, Peter. 'The New Liberalism of L.T. Hobhouse', *Victorian Studies* 15 (1972) 141–61

Wells, H.G. *Anticipations of the Reaction of Mechanical and Scientific Progress upon Human Life and Thought* (1901)

A Modern Utopia (1905)

First and Last Things: A Confession of Faith and Rule of Life (1908)

The New Machiavelli (1911)

An Englishman Looks at the World (1914)

War and the Future (1917)

The Outline of History (1920)

Russia in the Shadows (1920)

The Open Conspiracy: Blue Prints for a World Revolution (1928)

The Work, Wealth and Happiness of Mankind (1932)

Experiment in Autobiography: Discoveries and Conclusions of a Very Ordinary Brain (Since 1866) 2 vols. (1934)

Werskey, Gary. *The Visible College: The Collective Biography of British Scientific Socialists of the 1930s* (1978)

White, Stephen. *Britain and the Bolshevik Revolution* (1979)

Wiener, Martin J. *Between Two Worlds: The Political Thought of Graham Wallas* (Oxford 1971)

English Culture and the Decline of the Industrial Spirit 1850–1980 (Cambridge 1980)

Williams, Raymond. *Culture and Society 1780–1950* (Harmondsworth 1958)

Keywords (1976)

Culture (1981)

Towards 2000 (1983)

Wilson, Duncan. *Leonard Woolf: A Political Biography* (1978)

Wiltshire, David. *The Social and Political Thought of Herbert Spencer* (Oxford 1978)

Winter, Jay (ed.). *The Working Class in Modern British History: Essays in Honour of Henry Pelling* (Cambridge 1983)

Winter, J.M. *Socialism and the Challenge of War: Ideas and Politics in Britain 1912–1918* (1974)

'The Webbs and the Non-White World: A Case of Socialist Racialism', *Journal of Contemporary History* 9 no. 1 (January 1974) 181–92

Wohl, Robert. *The Generation of 1914* (1980)

Wolfe, Willard. *From Radicalism to Socialism: Men and Ideas in the Formation of Fabian Socialist Doctrines 1881–1889* (New Haven, Conn. 1975)

Wolff, R.P. *The Poverty of Liberalism* (Boston 1968)

In Defence of Anarchism (New York 1970)

Wolin, Sheldon S. *Politics and Vision: Continuity and Innovation in Western Political Thought* (Boston 1960)

Wollheim, Richard. *Freud* (1971)

Wood, Alan. *Bertrand Russell the Passionate Sceptic* (1957)

Wood, Allen. *Karl Marx* (1981)
Woolf, Leonard. *Sowing: An Autobiography of the Years 1880–1904* (1960)
Woolf, Virginia. *Collected Essays* (ed. Leonard Woolf, 4 vols., 1966–7)
The Letters (ed. Nigel Nicolson, 6 vols., 1975–80)
The Diary (ed. Anne Olivier Bell, 5 vols., 1977–84)
Wright, A.W. *G.D.H. Cole and Socialist Democracy* (Oxford 1979)
Zylstra, B. *From Pluralism to Collectivism* (Assen, Netherlands 1968)

Index

IDEAS IN CONTEXT

Edited by QUENTIN SKINNER (*General Editor*),
LORRAINE DASTON, WOLF LEPENIES, RICHARD RORTY
and J.B. SCHNEEWIND

1 RICHARD RORTY, J.B. SCHNEEWIND and QUENTIN SKINNER (eds.)
Philosophy in History
*Essays on the historiography of philosophy**

2 J.G.A. POCOCK
Virtue, Commerce and History
*Essays on political thought and history, chiefly in the eighteenth century**

3 M.M. GOLDSMITH
Private Vices, Public Benefits
Bernard Mandeville's social and political thought

4 ANTHONY PAGDEN (ed.)
The Languages of Political Theory in Early Modern Europe*

5 DAVID SUMMERS
The Judgment of Sense
*Renaissance nationalism and the rise of aesthetics**

6 LAURENCE DICKEY
Hegel: Religion, Economics and the Politics of Spirit, 1770–1807*

7 MARGO TODD
Christian Humanism and the Puritan Social Order

8 LYNN SUMIDA JOY
Gassendi the Atomist
Advocate of history in an age of science

9 EDMUND LEITES (ed.)
Conscience and Casuistry in Early Modern Europe

10 WOLF LEPENIES
Between Literature and Science: The Rise of Sociology*

11 TERENCE BALL, JAMES FARR and RUSSELL L. HANSON (eds.)
Political Innovation and Conceptual Change*

12 GERD GIGERENZER *et al.*
The Empire of Chance
*How probability changed science and everyday life**

13 PETER NOVICK
That Noble Dream
*The 'objectivity question' and the American historical profession**

14 DAVID LIEBERMAN
The Province of Legislation Determined
Legal theory in eighteenth-century Britain

15 DANIEL PICK
Faces of Degeneration
A European disorder, c.1848–c.1918

16 KEITH BAKER
Approaching the French Revolution
*Essays on French political culture in the eighteenth century**

17 IAN HACKING
The Taming of Chance*

18 GISELA BOCK, QUENTIN SKINNER and MAURIZIO VIROLI (eds.)
Machiavelli and Republicanism*

19 DOROTHY ROSS
The Origins of American Social Science*

20 KLAUS CHRISTIAN KOHNKE
The Rise of Neo-Kantianism
German academic philosophy between idealism and positivism

21 IAN MACLEAN
Interpretation and Meaning in the Renaissance
The case of law

22 MAURIZIO VIROLI
From Politics to Reason of State
The acquisition and transformation of the language of politics 1250–1600

23 MARTIN VAN GELDEREN
The Political Thought of the Dutch Revolt 1555–1590

24 NICHOLAS PHILLIPSON and QUENTIN SKINNER (eds.)
Political Discourse in Early Modern Britain

25 JAMES TULLY
An Approach to Political Philosophy: Locke in Contexts*

26 RICHARD TUCK
Philosophy and Government 1572–1651*

27 RICHARD R. YEO
Defining Science
William Whewell, natural knowledge and public debate in early Victorian Britain

28 MARTIN WARNKE
The Court Artist
The ancestry of the modern artist

29 PETER N. MILLER
Defining the Common Good
Empire, religion and philosophy in eighteenth-century Britain

30 CHRISTOPHER J. BERRY
The Idea of Luxury
*A conceptual and historical investigation**

31 E. J. HUNDERT
The Enlightenment's 'Fable'
Bernard Mandeville and the discovery of society

32 JULIA STAPLETON
Englishness and the Study of Politics
The social and political thought of Ernest Barker

33 KEITH TRIBE
German Economic Thought from the Enlightenment to the Social Market

34 SACHIKO KUSUKAWA
The Transformation of Natural Philosophy
The case of Philip Melanchthon

35 DAVID ARMITAGE, JACQUES HIMY and QUENTIN SKINNER (eds.)
Milton and Republicanism

36 MARKKU PELTONEN
Classical Humanism and Republicanism in English Political Thought 1570–1640

37 PHILIP IRONSIDE
The Social and Political Thought of Bertrand Russell
The development of an aristocratic liberalism

Titles marked with an asterisk are also available in paperback

Lightning Source UK Ltd.
Milton Keynes UK
UKHW01f0157040618
323679UK00001B/18/P

9 780521 024761